Also by Gustavo Arellano

¡Ask a Mexican!
Orange County: A Personal History

TACO USA

How Mexican Food Conquered America

GUSTAVO ARELLANO

Scribner

New York   London   Toronto   Sydney   New Delhi

Scribner
A Division of Simon & Schuster, Inc.
1230 Avenue of the Americas
New York, NY 10020

First Scribner hardcover edition April 2012

SCRIBNER and design are registered trademarks of The Gale Group, Inc. used
under license by Simon & Schuster, Inc., the publisher of this work.

For information about special discounts for bulk purchases,
please contact Simon & Schuster Special Sales at
1-866-506-1949 or business@simonandschuster.com.

The Simon & Schuster Speakers Bureau can bring authors to your live event.
For more information or to book an event contact the Simon & Schuster Speakers
Bureau at 1-866-248-3049 or visit our website at www.simonspeakers.com.

Designed by Carla Jayne Jones

Manufactured in the United States of America

3   5   7   9   10   8   6   4

ISBN 978-1-4391-4861-7
ISBN 978-1-4391-5765-7 (ebook)

To all the Mexican workers—busboys and waitresses, line cooks and sous chefs, janitors and crop pickers, and so many more—who toil anonymously in our food industry, making American cuisine even more Mexican than we can ever realize.

Contents

Contents

TACO USA

Introduction

What's So Cosmic About a Burrito?

Two hundred and thirteen miles up in space, the Earth below cerulean blue, the universe around them infinite and awesome, José Hernández and Danny Olivas wanted Mexican food.

The two had come prepared. They were astronauts on STS-128, a NASA mission that flew the *Discovery* space shuttle to rendezvous with the International Space Station on August 30, 2009. *Discovery*'s seven-member crew spent ten days at the research station, primarily to resupply the people already up there and to rotate members. Olivas—raised in El Paso, Texas—went on a space walk to repair an ammonia tank, among other tasks; Hernández—who picked crops in California's Central Valley alongside family members as a child—sent his thoughts to our planet *en español*. "*Espero la cosecha de mi sueño sirva como inspiracion a todos!*" he enthused via Twitter. "I hope the harvest of my dream serves as inspiration to all!"

On September 8, the *Discovery* crew undocked from the Space Station. It was morning. It was time for breakfast burritos. The rest of the crew had earlier asked Hernández and Olivas if they might cook the meal, because Olivas was the NASA member who knew how to make

1

them best. Of course. A video camera transmitted footage of the duo floating toward the galley of the middeck to open a shelf containing the ingredients needed to construct the cylindrical god in zero gravity: flour tortillas sealed in a vacuum pack, clumps of ready-to-eat scrambled eggs, and fat sausage patties.

Olivas pulled out a tortilla, letting it float in front of him while tearing open a thumb-sized salsa packet. He smeared a smiley face on the tortilla and tried to roll it up; since it wasn't cooked, the flour flatbread bent into a U-shape but wobbled back into its outstretched natural state. Hernández, meanwhile, opened a pouch that contained the patty. Olivas placed the tortilla near the meat, expecting the sausage to plop down on it, as it would on terra firma. Instead, the brownish, glistening mass popped out of the bag, away from the tortilla below it, and would've presumably continued on an endless trajectory if the fast-thinking Olivas didn't snatch the sausage with the tortilla. The salsa acted as a binding agent and secured the incipient Icarus.

The eggs proved more manageable. Hernández cut them out of a packet; Olivas used a spoon to guide each minimound onto the tortilla, then promptly chopped them up into smaller pieces, the better to smush and smear—if the tortilla might only bend. The moment of truth arrived: Olivas folded the vessel in half, wrapping one flap over the other, and rolled it tight. Success; a breakfast burrito was born, and more were on the way.

This wasn't the first time burritos orbited Earth—Olivas had made a batch on his previous visit to the Space Station two years earlier. In fact, NASA had used tortillas for astronaut sustenance as early as 1985, when Mexican scientist Rodolfo Neri Vela requested a pack as part of his food provisions, to make tacos. The media treated Neri's food choices at the time with bemusement, but astronauts quickly took to flour tortillas—and not just because of the flavor, redolent of flour and slightly sweet, better than most of the sterilized slop astronauts ate. Tortillas didn't spoil easily. Astronauts could wrap one around anything and make a quick meal. They also weren't dangerous, like bread, whose crumbs crippled air vents and sensitive equipment.

NASA took tortillas so seriously that they tinkered with the recipe—which hadn't substantially changed in millennia save for the introduction of flour—to keep stacks fresh for up to six months. Scientists created a nitrogen-filled packet that removed almost all the oxygen present in the pouch, to prevent mold from growing. One major problem arose: astronauts discovered that six-month-old space tortillas became bitter—and *no one* deserves a bitter tortilla. Finally, NASA found a manufacturer who made an extended-shelf-life tortilla that lasted up to a year and retained its allure, a maker that also sold their product to fast-food titan Taco Bell. Hundreds of thousands of dollars well spent.

"I cannot think of anything that cannot be put on a tortilla, or has not been put on a tortilla," wrote Sandra Magnus, a veteran astronaut, in a blog post while up in the International Space Station in 2008. "When a Shuttle shows up you are in tortilla heaven because they show up with tons of them and graciously donate all of the extras to the ISS crews. You really want to be swimming in tortillas your whole increment."[1]

And for short missions of five to seven days? Astronauts often bring their flour tortillas fresh from a Houston *tortillería*—a tortilla factory. No customizing, no chemicals—just unadulterated rapture. The perfect food.

"Danny is an expert in zero-g burrito making," Hernández radioed to Mission Control after their burrito party. It was a mission of celebration: never had two Mexican-Americans flown up in space on the same mission, and never did burritos shine so brightly. Sure, Hernández and Olivas offered a service to their crewmates that hundreds of thousands of their fellow Mexican provided daily back on Earth—prepping Mexican food for Americans more than happy to gobble it up. Their feast made the news; a video soon went viral across the Internet, the astronauts' beaming, proud smiles as they hoisted their fast food for humanity to see. So high in the heavens, up above the world, the burrito not only had become universal—it was now, finally, truly, cosmic.

Mexican food is at our state dinners, in elegant presentations. Mexican food is in our school cafeterias, packaged as chimichangas or in bags of Fritos, in convenience stores heating on rolling racks, waiting for the hands of hurried customers. Mexican food sponsors college bowl games such as the Tostitos Fiesta Bowl and buys naming rights for sporting venues such as the Taco Bell Arena at Boise State in Idaho. Mexican food commercials blanket television airwaves hawking salsa and hard-shelled taco packets and high-priced tequilas and imported beers promising a day at the beach. Mexican food fills our grocery aisles, feeds underclassmen, sits in our freezers and pantries, is the focus of festivals, becomes tween trends or front-page news—and if you don't know what I'm talking about, ask your kid about spaghetti tacos.

That wonderful culinary metaphor the melting pot has absorbed Mexican in this country just like so many immigrant cuisines of the past—but in a demanding way, unique from other traditions that have penetrated the American palate. While there are more Chinese restaurants than Mexican in this country, Mexican food is the easier sell—you don't see hundreds of different soy sauce brands sold at supermarkets like you do hot sauce, or General Tso's chicken cook-offs at your local community fair like you do with bowls of chili. While pizza is the best-selling and farthest-reaching item of Italian-American cuisine, its rise and that of pasta and subs is only relatively recent; the United States, on the other hand, has loved Mexican food for more than 125 years—bought it, sold it, made it, spread it, supplied it, cooked it, savored it, loved it.

Comida mexicana in the United States is like M. C. Escher's *Relativity*, each staircase helping the climber reach a particular plateau but only to whisper promises of higher, better planes, in an endless hat dance of discovery. Americans have defined Mexican food as combo platters and enchiladas, margaritas and guacamole, tortilla chips and actual tortillas, frozen burritos and burritos made to order. Mom-and-pop shops and multinationals. Taco carts and tamale men. Taco trucks operating under cover of night and luxe-*loncheras* that tweet their latest specials. Beans, rice, carne asada, soyrizo. All of it absorbed by Americans, enjoyed, demanded—and all of it whetting appetites for more. And with this country's latest Great Migration stretching brown folks beyond the American Southwest and to all fifty states, in virtually all metropolitan areas, from the prairies and flatlands of the Midwest to Maine's rocky shores, Alaska's tundra to the Florida Keys, we're experiencing a renaissance of Mexican food—a perpetual foreigner perfectly at home.

We've had generations of Americans who scarf down tacos and burritos like previous generations forked through chicken pot pies and ate pastrami on rye. And that's just the United States: as globalization sets in, so does Mexican food. Mexican restaurants operate across Europe, in Turkey, in Nepal and Addis Ababa. Down under, Taco Bill's has sold Australians fish tacos for nearly twenty-five years. Sometimes it's Mexicans who run these restaurants; many times it's American expats. Sometimes the locals dine there, but it's often American tourists who patronize the places, seeking a taste of home. It's too easy to say Mexican food is an all-American food: to say as much is to ignore the tortured relationship between Mexicans and their adopted country. But Mexican food is as much of an ambassador for the United States as the hot dog, whether either country wants to admit it or not.

Let me give *ustedes* an example. Tom Tancredo doesn't like Mexicans—no way, no how, no *duh*. The former Colorado Republican congressman and onetime presidential candidate spent most of his political career railing against a supposed invasion of the United States by Mexico—and while intelligent minds can disagree about unchecked migration to this country, Tancredo flat-out feels Mexicans are downright deficient.

In November 2010, we debated in Denver about whether Mexicans ever assimilate. I maintained that we do; Tancredo didn't accept the possibility, yet never explained how someone like myself—who spoke only Spanish when I entered kindergarten; was the child of two Mexican immigrants, one of whom came into this country in the trunk of a Chevy; and who now favors English and Chuck Taylor All-Stars—did it. The back-and-forth squabble happened at Su Teatro, an old movie house now housing one of the most vibrant Chicano theaters in the United States. There is no need to go into the details of our discussion, except for one pertinent point: before lambasting Mexicans and our supposed refusal to join American society, Tancredo joined me for a Mexican dinner.

The restaurant was across the street from Su Teatro: El Noa Noa, a large eatery that advertises itself as the Mile High City's "best and most authentic Mexican restaurant." At night, Art Deco–style neon lights flash the restaurant's name on its marquee, a reference to a legendary nightclub in Ciudad Juárez that was the subject of a famous Mexican song. A party on your plate. The atmosphere isn't aggressively ethnic: no strolling mariachis or women fluttering fans and eyelids. Eaters sit; waiters bring out a plate of chips and salsa and fetch drinks. People of all nationalities come in to eat, though the clientele leans more to American than Mexican.

Tancredo and I sat down near the middle of the restaurant; Patty Calhoun, editor of *Westword* (the city's alternative weekly, which carries my "¡Ask a Mexican!" column), and others joined us. We traded small talk, saving our salvos for the discussion to come—but around us, tables whispered, fingers pointed. Some people approached our table to greet Tancredo, wish him luck for the evening. Another woman offered her appreciation for my upcoming public confrontation of someone she considered a living embodiment of Satan. She wanted to make a scene, but her chile relleno supper was getting cold.

Our plates came. I drank tequila, of course; Tancredo, a dry red wine. He ordered the tamale dinner, hold the rice. Two of them, slathered (or, as more accurately stated in the Denver lexicon, "smothered") in green chile, each as long as a palm, as thick as a copy of this book, sat before him. They shimmered with the dabs of lard needed to make a tamale moist and more than mere cornmeal and shredded pork. I stole bites of the same plate from Calhoun. Soft, spicy, filling. The pork's sweet essence melted on my palate; the green chile piqued toward the end. These weren't the tamales of my youth—they were smaller, but that was okay. The chile—borne from the fertile soil of southern Colorado—seared differently from the Mexican chiles I grew up on and were so flavorful, they needed no extra salsa.

Tancredo thought so as well. He polished off the plate, laughing and talking between each bite, getting fueled for a night to decry the very culture that had just fed him. More than a year later, I can only recall some of the points of our philosophical fisticuffs, but the scene I can't get out of my head is Tancredo's ear-to-ear, tamale-induced smile. Tom Tancredo may not like Mexicans, but he sure loves his Mexican food. *Of course* he does.

It's not just Tom who holds this contradictory position. From the early days of Mexico's birth in 1810, when our young country longingly looked west toward its newly christened southern neighbor's vast territories, lonely and so full of potential, Mexican food has entranced Americans even while Mexicans have perplexed Americans. In the history of Mexican food in this country you'll find the twisted, fascinating history of two peoples, Mexicans and Americans, fighting, arguing, but ultimately accepting each other, if only in the comfort of breakfast, lunch, and dinner. The greatest apostles of Mexican food in this country haven't been Mexicans but rather Americans who, having tasted from the bread of life that is a steaming taco, a pot of menudo, or a foil-wrapped burrito, sought to proclaim its gospel with every new unearthing. While we've long quarreled with Mexico over seemingly everything, we've always embraced the food, wanting to experience the "authenticity" of the other half: enjoying the meals Aztec emperors might have feasted on before meeting their fate, dining before handsome bronze-skinned waiters and pretty señoritas, eating like a Mexican might eat on the street, in poverty back in Mexico, in the cantina, through cookbooks, canned products, classes, trips to the motherland or the local *taquería*—but always within the prism of America. That consumption hasn't always been pretty: caricatures of hot tamales, Montezuma's revenge, questionable ingredients, Frito Banditos, talking Chihuahuas, and sleeping peons litter the landscape and continue to influence American perceptions of Mexican food and of Mexicans. But even negative stereotypes and digestive concerns never stopped our collective yen for the stuff.

Mexican food's American journey is obviously personal to me. I consider tortillas and hot sauce as essential to life as oxygen, walk through the day with a bag of Serrano peppers in my pocket, have served as a food editor for a newspaper for nearly a decade, and have always pushed my paper to treat Mexican food seriously. My fondest childhood memories usually involve smuggled cheese wheels from my parents' ancestral villages; my mom was a tomato canner and got up early in the morning to make us a Mexican breakfast of eggs and beans, went to work, and returned in the evening with the wherewithal to make us a full meal for dinner. Mexican food is a way of life, which isn't a surprise, of course. But that so many Americans, with no blood ties to Mexico, who might not even like the country, revere my cuisine? The reporter in me is fascinated; the Mexican in me, flabbergasted.

This book isn't about me, though: it's about a food that deserves documentation, examination, celebration, and to be hailed as the epic it is. While Mexican culinary culture is an unquestioned part of America's gastronomic essence, the stories behind how we got to this point are largely unknown. The evolution of food in the United States has, until recently, been dismissed as a frivolous subject, but we're now in an age of culinary reminiscing, when scholars and journalists alike examine cuisine as customs. The history of Mexican food in the United States has bubbled up in articles and chapters in books over the years, but never in a full volume that tracks each foodstuff, each craze, each pioneer, each controversy.

What's so cosmic about a burrito? *Everything*. It says something about us that Taco Bell makes billions of dollars in sales each year, that Koreans in this country are making millions by stuffing their barbecue in tortillas and selling them from fancy food trucks—and it's a good thing. Anyone who dismisses this reality as not indicative of something seismic in the American story is more deluded that someone who thinks refried beans are actually fried twice. It's been conquest by a thousand tacos, a million tamales, and a hell of a lot of salsa, which surpassed ketchup as America's top-selling condiment back in the 1990s. Through interviews and archival material, via chronological and thematic chapters, and never, ever losing focus that we are, after all, talking about food, behold the story of the best cuisine on Earth, one now set on taking over the world. The United States is on the losing side of this Mexican-American War—and boy, are we grateful.

One final point: this book is *not* about the history of Mexican food in Mexico. Mexican cookery is as multifaceted, if not more so, than its American cousin, with each state offering unique culinary practices slowly trickling into our country, as I mentioned earlier. But those who dismiss Taco Bell, the taco pizza, even a church enchilada booth as somehow not Mexican because Mexicans aren't the main consumers or creators miss an imperative point. We must consider the infinite varieties of Mexican food in the United States as part of the Mexican family—not a fraud, not a lesser sibling, but an equal. As I've driven and flown around the country and come across a mild salsa, a mutated *muchaco* (a ground-beef taco served in a pita bread by the midwestern Taco Bueno chain), and other items I immediately wanted to decry, I remembered the concept of what the legendary Chicano scholar Américo Paredes deemed Greater Mexico: that the influence of Mexico doesn't cease at the Rio Grande. Wherever there is something even minutely Mexican, whether it's people, food, language, or rituals, even centuries removed from the original mestizo source, it remains Mexican.

Even in outer space.

Chapter One

You Mean Mexico Gave the World More Than Just Tacos?

Before we begin our study of Mexican food in the United States, it's wise to start at the source: Mexico. Trying to figure out who created what dish or harvested what crop first is a silly exercise, but there is an acknowledged Bethlehem, where foreigners first became entranced by the food and then sought to sing its glories ever after: Mexico City.

The mother in this Nativity scene, of course, is the Virgin of Guadalupe, whom the Catholic Church says appeared to the peon Juan Diego in 1531 as a brown-skinned Mother of Christ dressed in the simple shawl of an Aztec maiden pregnant with child. It was this mestizo Mary, this exercise in syncretism, that seared herself on the apron of the Indian Juan Diego so he might show it to disbelieving Spanish priests as proof of Her message: that the newly conquered Aztecs and other tribes were worthy of mercy. Millions of pilgrims visit that *tilma,* kept at the Basilica of Our Lady of Guadalupe, early in the morning of every December 12 in a ceremony broadcast around the world and reenacted at parishes across the United States. Although Roman Catholic in veneration, Guadalupe is uniquely Mexican, embraced by a nation that finds redemption in her swarthy gaze and the promise of salvation by the good works involved in consuming steaming tamales and Mexican hot chocolate customary after Her Mass.

But if *la gudalupana* is the mother, Her son is far less beloved. A statue of Christ sits dejectedly about five miles away from the basilica, inside the St. Joseph Chapel of the Metropolitan Cathedral of the Assumption of Mary of Mexico City. It's near the former location of the Templo Mayor, a towering achievement of Aztec architecture, a shrine to the two saints that best personified their dual outlooks on life: Huitzilpochtli, the god of war, and Tlaloc, the god of water. The Spaniards leveled this Brobdingnagian pyramid shortly after possessing Tenochtitlán, and used its massive stones to erect the cathedral. Syncretism.

Christ of the Cacao, at the Metropolitan Cathedral of the Assumption of Mary in Mexico City. Mexicans have left cacao beans at the statue's feet as alms for centuries, a show of the power Mexican food immediately had on culinary neophytes. *(Photo by Daniel Hernandez)*

During the cathedral's construction in the 1700s, Christ appeared to the Aztecs' descendants in the form of El Señor del Cacao—Christ of the Cacao, a life-sized statue. Whereas Guadalupe offered emancipation from this vale of tears, this was the Christ of defeat. It's this Christ who is alone in the cathedral's St. Joseph Chapel, the God accessible to the touch of the public unlike heavenly Guadalupe, who towers over Her children at the basilica, encased in glass. He sits slumped, head resting on His fist, elbow on knee, ribs poking out of pallid skin. The Nazarene wears a crown of thorns, but that isn't what pains Him the most. In His other hand, Jesus holds the branch of a cacoa tree, the plant whose fruit gives us chocolate. The Catholic Church had noted that the Aztecs paid tribute to their gods at the Templo Mayor with cacao beans, so they replaced the statues of those deities with theirs—but allowed believers to keep leaving their deistic gifts, now calling them alms toward the cathedral's construction.

People continue to venerate the statue, although they now tend to leave pesos and caramel candies between the Christ of the Cacao's grimy feet instead of actual cacao—the beans themselves, which grow in the wild and on plantations just hours away from Mexico City, are far too valuable to waste on penance. But the idea of taking the food of pilgrims is the cross that the statue bears. For while the Spanish Empire subjugated the land, its explorers also discovered foodstuffs that they shipped back to Europe and across the world, items the world soon turned into global products, items whose origins and journey to our tables we take for granted today. Some, such as amaranth and turkey, had only minimal impact on the world's eating customs; others, such as tomatoes, corn, and chile peppers, found lives outside the Mexican diet and came to define other cuisines. And then there's the two filched foods: vanilla and chocolate, indisputably Mexican, beloved by almost all, creators of fortunes for nearly everyone but their motherland.

The Christ of the Cacao weeps. The world feasts. Yum.

Accurate accounts of the first encounters between the Spaniards and the various natives they met upon landing in what's now Mexico are notoriously difficult to ascertain: readers must take contemporary accounts such as Hernán Cortés's letters to King Charles V, and his soldier Bernal Díaz del Castillo's *The Discovery and Conquest of Mexico,* as biased apologias for their actions, while Aztec dialogues and codices written years after the Conquest under the careful eyes of Spanish priests serve better as anthropological curiosities than truthful dialogues. Nevertheless, one of the consistent themes that emerge from the various tellings of the tale is that the Spaniards fast became enamored with the various, never-before-seen foods that appeared before them nearly daily during their expeditions, a template that prefigured and predicted the American devotion to Mexican food by centuries.

We do know the first time Europeans enjoyed a Mexican lunch, however. In early 1517, a group of Spaniards stationed in Cuba convinced the governor of the territory to let them sail to the lands west of the island. Led by Francisco Hernández de Córdoba, the expedition brought with them for the journey bacon, salted beef, and bread made from cassava, a New World tuber that the Spanish explorers had already incorporated into their diet. Upon reaching what's now the tourist hideaway of Cozumel (just off the coast of the Yucatán), according to Bartolomé de las Casas's *Historia de las Indias (History of the Indies),* a group of Maya on ten canoes approached the strangers, boarded their boat, and offered water and snacks. They were made from corn, an item the Spaniards had already tasted, but the Maya produced their food in a way unfamiliar to the explorers: in a type of gruel made from maize that was probably a form of masa, the cornmeal that has served as the linchpin of the Meso-American diet for millennia. Córdoba's men reciprocated by giving the Indians beads and a cotton shirt.

The Maya asked the Spaniards to allow a Cuban Indian who accompanied the expedition to travel with them to the mainland, to transport food back for the ship; the Spaniards agreed, and some even joined the Maya. That night, though, two natives approached the sleeping Spaniards with bows and arrows; the frightened Spaniards slew them. In the standoff, as a peace offering, the Indians brought the Spaniards gold and bread and what was most likely two roasted *guajolotes*: turkeys.[1]

It was all a ruse: the Maya ambushed the Spaniards, and the battered Córdoba expedition returned to Cuba. They returned the following spring under the command of Juan de Grijalva, armed with more men and a taste for the new food. In a break during fighting, the troops hunted and ate rabbits and deer; upon approaching a friendly village, according to Castillo, they offered beads in return so that villagers "might bring us some food and poultry." On the return home, Grijalva's ship needed repairs; locals fed them "with great goodwill."[2]

Cortés was the next Spaniard to take on Mexico, leaving Cuba with eleven ships and about five hundred men early in 1519. News of the Spaniards' arrival in Mexico reached Moctezuma II, the emperor of the Aztecs. He had lived a life of gluttony up to that point, a daily cycle of feasts and banquets that his advisers warned was insulting to the spartan ways of their ancestors and was leaving His Highness susceptible to softness, a quality unbecoming of the emperor of such a vast, volatile kingdom. Something world-changing was on its way to Tenochtitlán—the Aztecs knew it, but not what or who. Maybe gods, per the claim by the Spanish chroniclers, who pointed out that Cortés arrived the year Aztec chroniclers had pegged as the reappearance of Quetzalcoatl, a light-skinned, bearded god who had left his faithful centuries ago but had promised to return. Maybe worse.

Food became one of the primary tests the Spaniards and the Aztecs used on each other to determine if the other side was amigo or foe. Moctezuma had emissaries greet Cortés along the way with meals that his advisers insisted revealed upon their eating whether the coming swarm were deities or demons: turkey, turkey eggs, tortillas, and comestibles covered in human blood, the latter of which left Cortés and his men retching and fearful of what lies ahead in their long march. Another account maintains that a commoner made his way from the coast of the Gulf of Mexico to Tenochtitlán to alert the emperor of these strange white men who had landed on the coast. The messenger brought with him biscuits, bacon, and dried beef given to him by the Spaniards; he had eaten some, but left most of it for the emperor. The awestruck Moctezuma refused to eat "under the pretext they were exquisite foods of the gods," instead having a coterie of hunchbacks taste the gifts; they reported the biscuit was "sweet and soft."[3] Afterward, Moctezuma placed the exotic meals in pots and had the food burned.

Along the way, the Spaniards found allies among tribes who had long paid tribute to the Aztecs with their unique crops: chiles, squash, fruits, cocoa beans, and other delights the Spanish also learned to enjoy. Together the alliance reached Tenochtitlán, the Aztec capital, and the site of modern-day Mexico City. It was one of the world's great metropolises at the time, famously compared to Venice by royal chroniclers, and its carnival of food wowed the Spaniards almost as much as Tenochtitlán's architecture or geography. The city's main market in the Tlateloco district saw daily crowds upward of sixty thousand walking around stalls stocked with so much variety—fish from the Gulf of Mexico and the Pacific, vegetables from Guatemala and points north, insects and game from the desert, from the jungles, from the mountains, and seemingly all points of the known world—that Bernal Díaz del Castillo remarked, "I could never finish naming them, and so will leave them."[4]

The Aztecs, like the Spaniards, were conquistadors themselves, coming from the northern regions of modern-day Mexico and settling into the Valley of Mexico in the 1300s. As the Aztecs battled their way to the top, food became part of the spoils of war. As newcomers to the region, they originally foraged from the swamps—fish, tadpoles, grub. Maize and chilies would have been the only foodstuffs with which they had any familiarity; chocolate and vanilla were aspirations, items reserved only for the wealthier tribes—and even then, limited to the upper classes of their societies. Regardless of provenance or position in the Valley of Mexico's hierarchy, almost all foodstuffs made it into one of two primary vessels: the tortilla, a flat disk made from masa, or the tamale, a more substantial bulk of cornmeal stuffed with an ingredient, then steamed and wrapped in a corn husk. The tortilla never went beyond Mexico and parts of Central America, but the tamale found a home from northern Mexico to Chile and Argentina. Its simple status belies its remarkable nature: they keep for days. They're nutritious. They can get carried, distributed, and eaten easily—the ultimate movable feast.

Together, tortillas and tamales transfixed the Spaniards. Díaz's prose turned purple at the descriptions of the feasts Moctezuma held in honor of Cortés's arrival, with the ruler's cooks preparing a banquet that played to their master's gourmand tendencies, the tendencies his advisers had warned were leaving him weak. The chronicler described "more than thirty styles of dishes made according to their fashion and usage," and more than a thousand meals for just one sitting.[5] But the soldiers' amazement at the gastronomic bounties of their hosts faded as they realized this fountain of wealth was in disarray, and the Spaniards took Moctezuma captive. A full accounting of the conquest of Mexico isn't germane to this discussion, except for one final anecdote: as part of Moctezuma's peaceful surrender, Cortés demanded that his court supply the conquistadors with native food, which they had grown to enjoy. Moctezuma complied, and his supporters "were angry with the king and no longer revered or respected him." But they did as they were told.[6]

The appropriation of Mexican food had begun.

Mexico underwent the convulsions that occur when one people supplant another, mixing yet keeping distinct identities. The Spaniards incorporated tamales, tortillas, and other ingredients into their daily lives; in return, they introduced bread along with beef, lamb, pork, and chickens, and other flora and fauna that profoundly changed the Mexican diet. The Spaniards also brought along distillation, which allowed the creation of new alcoholic drinks based on the maguey, the slow-growing plant the Aztecs used to intoxicate themselves. Cows introduced milk and cheese.

Instead of fully embracing two-way fusion, however, Mexico's new rulers tried to wean the indigenous off the tortilla and tamale diet and hook them on wheat. Bernardino de Sahagún, the Franciscan friar whose ethnographies of the Aztecs remain one of the most thorough resources on them, urged his readers to eat wheat, "that which the Castilian people eat because it is good food, that with which they are raised, they are strong and pure and wise . . . you will become the same way if you eat their food."[7] The natives, however, wouldn't have it, complaining that it tasted like famine food. What the Spaniards hadn't yet realized was the marvel the natives enacted each day when creating masa, the corn dough made by women after treating freshly picked kernels through one of the more serendipitous culinary innovations in human history: nixtamalization. It's one of those food-chemistry wonders that, like fish sauce or sauerkraut, is a testament to the human capacity to let food rot in the quest to create a tastier product—and in this case, unleashing a modest food's full potential.

Although maize traces its genetic roots to Mexico, natives had already cultivated the crop across the Caribbean and North America by the time Columbus reached Hispaniola. It was the centerpiece of the diet for most of Mexico's indigenous, one filled with mystery and ceremony—but consistently eating it raw is potentially deadly due to corn's lack of niacin, which leads to pellagra, a wasting disease. Somewhere in the past, some genius tinkered around with corn and discovered the process that removed the danger of pellagra by introducing niacin. The method, then as now, is as follows: after harvest, dried maize kernels are soaked in an alkaline solution made of lime and ash, poisonous on its own yet amazingly not contaminous to the maize. The kernels steep in the liquid for the day; that step loosens the kernel's husk and absorbs the many minerals (calcium, potassium, zinc, niacin, and others) created in the alkaline solution unavailable by eating raw corn. The kernels become easier to grind, but the chemical reaction also adds a component to the eventual masa that allows it to keep a firmness necessary for the plying and flipping and stretching to come. The technique improves the flavor and aroma of the meal as well, and reduces the toxins in corn that induce pellagra.

Nixtamalization allowed its practitioners to subsist on an almost all-corn diet since time immemorial. The Spaniards tried their darndest to eradicate the old ways, but no threats of punishment, no promises of evolution ever decimated the tortilla and tamale's hold on Mexicans. Nixtamalization was never exported to the world like nearly all the rest of Mexico's bounty. No, there'd be other things to get rich off of.

If you can't travel to Papantla, a gorgeous municipality on the Gulf of Mexico, a land of jungles, white-sand beaches, and architecture featuring a clash of colonial and indigenous, then go on YouTube. Typing in the city's name will bring up numerous videos of *voladores*—fliers.

Here's one. Five men sweat under the humid heat of Papantla. Clothing covers everything but their faces and hands; stockings stretch over bright-red pants; a festooned tunic covers their chest; from it peeks a long-sleeved, chalk-white shirt. Topping each hombre is a skullcap decorated with flowers, crowned with a miniature, multicolored crest that, in a flash, looks like a midget rainbow Mohawk.

They are Totonacs, an ethnic group that predates the Aztecs and Maya, long ridiculed across Mexico for their backward ways except for one trait: they are the last practitioners of *la danza de los voladores,* the dance of the fliers, crowned an intangible cultural heritage by UNESCO to save the pageant from extinction. It's a dance as splendid as the costumed men: they first find a tree about a hundred feet tall, which they chop down and form into a smooth pole, thanking the tree for honoring them with its utility. The pole is raised in a public square and secured to the ground—this is where the *danza* will occur. But before any acrobatics, the men perform a ceremony: the quintet circles the wooden beam while each dancer twirls in an individual trance. One plays a high-pitched plea on a flute while keeping time with a tiny drum.

The five men ascend the pole, climbing up planks nailed from the base to the summit, and sit on four longer planks connected together so they form a rickety square that rotates; the flute player stands on top of the pole. Each ties a rope around his waist to his section of the square. After a bit of meditation, the *danzantes* hang off the square, give themselves a quick spin, and fling into the air. The square rotates; the centrifugal force that is four men throwing themselves simultaneously into the sky keeps each dancer upside down at a tight forty-five-degree angle instead of dropping like dead weight. The crowd gasps. The flute player continues his piercing song, sitting on the tiny top of the pole without any rigging to keep him from falling, as the dancers slowly descend, twisting and twirling. Flying. It's studied for years before its practitioners attempt the dance, traditionally practiced only by men.

The *voladores* finally returned to earth, flipping themselves onto their feet just as their heads are about to slam into the ground, and emerge unscathed. The crowd applauds. The color, the spectacle, the beauty: it's the diametrical opposite of the adjectival tense of the Totonacs' greatest contribution to the world: vanilla.

From the verdant valleys of Papantla and its surrounding regions in what's now the Mexican state of Veracruz, the Totonacs have harvested the orchid that produces the vanilla bean for generations. Upon subjugating the Totonacs, the Aztecs demanded the group pay tribute to them via the beans, which found their fragrant way into their drinks—but the secret of domesticating the orchids by manual pollination stayed with the Totonacs. The relationship was exploitative enough that the tribe gladly aligned with the Spaniards to take down the Aztecs—the Totonacs were the first to pledge allegiance to Cortés, the first to treat them to a steady supply of Mexican food.

Vanilla arrived in Europe shortly after the Conquest, specifically as a flavoring agent for the chocolate that the Spaniards were already imbibing, as a drink, in large quantities. Through the royal courts, the vine took hold in France, where the House of Bourbon prized vanilla for its scent. The demand increased enough that small vanilla plantations existed by the eighteenth century from Veracruz to northern Guatemala—but how to pollinate the plants and thus make a profitable industry out of harvesting vanilla remained with the Totonacs, who worked the fields. Scientists, investors, traders, and others vainly attempted to decipher the pollination puzzle, going as far as to bribe the Totonacs and even spy on their methods. But still, the secret remained intact, and the Veracruz area continued as the center for the vanilla trade, Papantla its main port of commerce.

The Totonacs didn't get rich off of their homegrown industry, of course: they were Indians. It was fitting, in a karmic way, that another slave finally discovered how to manually pollinate the vanilla orchard: Edmond Albius, a native of the tiny island of Réunion, east of Madagascar, in 1841. Belgian professor Charles Morren had actually discovered his own way to hand-pollinate vanilla and even published a paper on his findings in 1838, but his version was too complicated. Albius, while tending the garden of his master, decided to try to pollinate the vanilla flower the same way he pollinated the other orchids in the garden. He grabbed—depending on which retelling you trust—a blade of grass, a toothpick, or a bamboo splinter, to separate a flap on the flower. With his other hand, Albius dabbed pollen from the vanilla flower on his finger, then smeared it on the stigma of the plant. This step, so fiendishly simple, remains the most common way to manually pollinate the plant.

By that point, vanilla bloomed around the tropical colonies of Europe, but growers had to rely on natural pollination to have the orchids produce the mystical beans, which didn't always result in reliable harvests. The procedure revolutionized vanilla production, and the French soon introduced plantations to Madagascar, Tahiti, and its other territorial holdings. Albius gained his freedom only after France outlawed slavery in its colonial holdings, and died poor; nearly a century after his death, Albius's hometown of Sainte-Suzanne finally erected a monument in his honor. Meanwhile, Frenchmen cornered the world vanilla market.

Back in the United States at about the same time as Albius's breakthrough, Boston chemist Joseph Burnett took on a challenge issued by a customer: was there any way to make vanilla flavoring like what was sold in France? Burnett, so his company's history states, bought some beans and tinkered with a recipe for a couple of years before finally inventing vanilla extract in 1850. The synthesized results introduced vanilla's flavor on a mass scale to American home cooking, and the secret of the Totonacs was breached again. "The world-famous ruby mines of Burmah [*sic*] have scarcely been more jealously guarded, more surrounded by mystery and commercial interest, than has the Valley of Mazantla, classical home of the remarkable orchid known as Vanilla," began the introduction to *About Vanilla,* the fiftieth-anniversary book of the Joseph Burnett Company published in 1900. Its cover featured the Pico de Orizaba, the eighteen-thousand-foot mountaintop considered sacred by the Totonacs that towers over most of Veracruz's vanilla-growing region.[8]

Totonacs still harvest vanilla in their native lands, but the bean's cultivation is in some ways more endangered than the dance of the fliers. Madagascar is now the premier grower of the crop, while Mexico contributes only a couple of tons to the world's harvest each year. The vanilla of Veracruz no longer has the mystical cachet it once possessed; now the world desires vanilla from Tahiti, from Madagascar, from anywhere but Mexico. Deforestation of its native region has contributed to the plant's native collapse, along with immigration to the United States of Veracruzans who can no longer subsist on the orchid that once brought them meaning and life.

There's a chocolate museum in Canada, nearly a dozen in France, and even one in Estonia. Hershey's keeps a public repository of its history, as does Cadbury in England, Germany's Ritter Sport, and the Perugina brand of Italy. Nestlé keeps two, in Switzerland and Mexico City. But the world's premier exhibition on chocolate is Choco-Story: The Chocolate Museum, in a fifteenth-century-era four-story building in Brussels, Belgium. The Belgian confectionary concern Belcolade underwrites the project, but it's impressively objective in recounting chocolate's past, present, and future via exhibits that range from computer screens and artifacts to mannequins dressed as conquistadors standing on a minigalleon and appearing ready to pounce off and rush onward toward empire. They have a second museum, in Prague, and organize chocolate festivals across Europe, but Brussels is the place to visit: four floors of chocolate madness—and it's expanding.

Choco-Story is hardly a pretentious place, but it's far removed in presentation and monetary investment from the drinkable museum offered by the people behind the Academia Semillas del Pueblo Xinaxcalmecac (Seeds of the People Academy), a charter school in the working-class El Sereno neighborhood of Los Angeles. Pupils learn English and Spanish, but also Mandarin Chinese and Nahuatl, along with Mayan concepts of mathematics in addition to the reading, writing, and arithmetic of public education. It's a brave experiment in self-sustainability, and one that's working—a high school is in the works to continue Semillas del Pueblo's work, and they operate Xocolatl Café, a coffee shop where they're trying to return mankind to the original chocolate, the elixir of Moctezuma's court, to save the sweet treat from what its popularity has wrought upon itself.

It's almost too quixotic a venture, given modern-day chocolate's multibillion-dollar, worldwide stranglehold on the cocoa industry. But you haven't tried chocolate until you try Xocolatl's version—and if you're a guest of Semillas principal Marcos Aguilar, a tall, slender man with jet-black hair slicked back and tied into a ponytail that hangs down to his back, you will.

Even if he's in a pinstriped suit, BlackBerry constantly pinging new alerts, Aguilar will whip up the old-school drink. He'll grab cocoa paste, untreated and without sugar, and place it in a metal container, pouring boiling water spiked with chile on top of it. In goes a jigger of aguamiel, the sap of the maguey plant that, in another incarnation, serves as the base for the ancient alcoholic beverage pulque. Then comes the whisking: immediately furious, yet increasing in intensity as every second adds up into two minutes. Aguilar pours the chocolate into a clay mug and places it on the table. His eyes are penetrating but kind as he waits for you to sip.

The first feature of Aguilar's hot chocolate that tweaks the senses is the foam: unadulterated cocoa butter, velvety and invigorating. Candy-makers discard most of the cocoa butter when producing their chocolate bars, so to taste gobs of the stuff is akin to capturing the mythical angel's share of distilled alcohol, the portion of every barrel that naturally evaporates. Next comes the watery sweetness of the aguamiel, followed by the chile water's subtle kick. Chocolate seems almost an afterthought in this drink, but only because the modern human palate is accustomed to Snickers and Kisses and virtually every cocoa concoction except its rawest, purest, most intoxicating form. The postprandial buzz makes a double-shot espresso seem as jolting as a droplet of water.

"The world needs to remember this drink," Aguilar says, with the conviction of a bodhisattva who has just experienced nirvana but won't be content until everyone has. "The world *will* know this drink."

How chocolate became a global sweet is oft told, and is perhaps the most chronicled segment of Mexican culinary history, one too broad to properly cover in this volume. What does need recounting for our purposes, however, are those early years of exposure, to document again the power Mexican food has to turn skeptical, outright hostile foreigners into zombies to the taste.

Botanists place cacao's genesis somewhere in South America, and it migrated northward to find its most fruitful roots around Guatemala, El Salvador, and the sylvan highlands of southern Mexico. The Mayans first elevated cacao as something holy and revelatory; ruins show how they roasted, cracked, and deshelled cocoa beans until what was left of the bean was a smoky, bitter part called the nib. These nibs were ground into a paste, then placed into a pot upon which preparers slushed boiling water. They poured the cocoa water from one pot to another until the liquid foamed, and finished the drink with chilies, aguamiel, vanilla, and other aromatics. Only the upper classes enjoyed this beverage, and only on special occasions, a ceremony that migrated into Tenochtitlán. The Aztecs imported the cocoa beans and their exalted role from those Mayan regions, expanding those eligible to taste it to warriors who distinguished themselves in battle. The drink became so valued that cocoa beans became a type of currency, a way for commoners and the conquered to pay tribute.

The Spaniards were in awe of the power cacao held for the Aztecs. Díaz observed a banquet where Moctezuma's servants brought him more than fifty jars of the drink, but the chronicler mostly focused on the women who served those jars, for he claimed the drink "was for success with women." Cortés, ever a vigilant warrior, found cacao fascinating for another reason: in a letter to King Charles V of Spain, he described it as "the divine drink, which builds up resistance and fights fatigue. A cup of this precious drink permits man to walk for a whole day without food," alluding to chocolate's naturally occurring caffeine kick. The Spanish priests who came after the Conquest were of mixed opinion: Sahagún thought it "deranges one" in excess but in moderation "it gladdens one, refreshes one, consoles one, invigorates one." Bartolomé de las Casas was more succinct but no less celebratory: "It is very substantial, very cooling, tasty, and agreeable, and does not intoxicate."

Galleons loaded with cacao sailed to Spain's colonial holdings east and west for growing on plantations, introducing the world to an addiction that's never really ceased. "Chocolate on its own, as the ancients used to prepare it, is incredible and healthy," Aguilar says. "But the Spaniards changed it—they added milk and sugar. And then Nestlé and Hershey changed it even more—it's now basically all sugar, and, of course, that's all unhealthy."

He looks at a tray of chocolate nibs—roasted and deshelled but otherwise unprocessed—that an assistant laid out before him; they're small and dark. The nibs smell more like caffeine than anything Western nostrils know as chocolate, and the flavor is somewhere between charcoal and caramelized onions. They're not soft at all—harder than biting through a sunflower seed, and grainy like coffee grounds once they break down on the tongue. But the zip they possess—nearly electric. Chocolate's essence seeps into each taste bud; anyone who grabs a couple snack on them until they're gone.

"I didn't know what chocolate was until tasting these," Aguilar said. "And these are just the nibs. When I learned the proper ways, chocolate became incredible."

Aguilar first encountered the archaic ways of chocolate making while a student at the University of California at Los Angeles in the 1990s. At a party he attended, guests from the Zapotec tribe of southern Mexico brought balls of chocolate paste to prepare for their hosts on a chilly night. The clean tastes and effortless yet intricate preparation, one that hadn't changed substantially from the Mayas, stunned Aguilar. He was used to Mexican hot chocolate, specifically the Abuelita brand owned by Nestlé that dominates the Mexican hot chocolate market.

"Tasting" the Zapotecs' chocolate, Aguilar says, speaking in a soft voice that's nevertheless authoritative, "was like a part of my ancestors suddenly came back from the dead and demanded I not only acknowledge them, but bring them back from obscurity."

Over the following years, Aguilar tinkered with his own chocolate recipes. Shortly after helping to open Semillas in 2002, Aguilar and his board decided that merely educating children wasn't enough; they also needed life skills after graduating, and better if it involved their heritage. Xocolatl Café (now closed to the public, unfortunately, but still operating for students and community fund-raisers) tapped into a growing network of Chicano-themed coffee shops in Southern California—Antigua Coffee House in nearby Cypress Park, Tia Chucha's Café (run by author Luis Rodriguez), and Café Calacas in Santa Ana, nearly all run by first- and second-generation Latinos who were longtime community activists and who wanted the societal trappings of café culture but with a marked political bent.

"Small Latino-Chicano coffeehouses provide the alternative settings versus conglomerates," says Yancey Quiñones, one of the people behind Antigua and an adviser to Xocolatl in its early days. "A space to showcase our culture and to involve community interaction. I also believe it's an opportunity to have a sustainable business in our neighborhoods and the pathway to Latino entrepreneurial and cultural advantages."

Part of that commitment for Aguilar, Quiñones, and others also meant going down to southern Mexico and working directly with farmers to source organic chocolate—costlier but necessary. He traveled to Chiapas, to heirloom chocolate farms that development had yet to swallow, farmed by people whose families tilled the land uninterrupted since the heyday of the Maya. But before debuting Xocolatl to the public in December 2009, Aguilar had one constituency he needed to please: Semillas's students. He had them taste his chocolate, then took them to IHOP to try their hot chocolate. Aguilar still chuckles when remembering the field trip. "One boy said, 'It tastes like you're biting into a spoonful of sugar,'" the principal says, of IHOP's limp effort.

Aguilar also is working with incorporating heirloom vanilla from the Totonacs and plans other culinary projects, all to reacquaint Mexicans with the foods of their ancestors. "The concept of Mexican food is you don't think of Mexican food as healthy or organic," he says. "Yet this is the birthplace of chocolate. Chocolate in its purest form *is* healthy. You see the stereotype of Mexicans getting too drunk for parties? It wasn't like that. Before, our ancestors used chocolate as the beverage of choice during festivities. It was a wonderful thing, and we need to remind people about this."

Yet such lofty goals face a race against time, economics, and development. Two thirds of the world's cocoa production is in Africa, with Mexico accounting for less than 2 percent of the industry. Organic cocoa production like what Aguilar favors represents less than half of 1 percent of the world's total product.[9] In Mexico's chocolate-growing regions, the government encourages cacao farmers to chop down their trees and grow soybeans and bananas for the international market, developments that sadden Aguilar.

"As in any trauma, the only thing that will help you survive is resilience," Aguilar says. "And it's a testament to the resilience of Mexican food and the culture that it survives. When you look at the chemical properties, chocolate offers resilience. Antioxidants. Theobromine. That's symbolic. There's a recovery from that exhaustion. And to do it on our terms is important. Liberation comes through the stomach, it comes through what we eat and how we eat it."

The principal stops, realizing he's now sounding much more dogmatic than someone trying to get people to enjoy food needs to sound. Aguilar smiles.

"And on top of that, our Xocolatl is *really* good."

Mainstream America isn't ready for Aguilar's chocolate, truthfully. We're still too focused on gargantuan meals, belly-stuffers, to care about leaving the chocolate cartel for a boutique variety, even if it's the original. But there is hope for Aguilar, hope from history: Americans have scoffed at food from Mexico before, only to turn it wholly their own.

Chapter Two

Whatever Happened to the Chili Queens and Tamale Kings?

Beaten down, battered, and bruised but still standing and defiant—this is the story of Chicago in general, its South Side in particular, the Marquette Park neighborhood specifically, and the description fits Fat Johnnies Red Hots to the proverbial T.

That's a hot dog stand near the corner of 72nd Street and Western Avenue, a tired-looking wood shack once painted white but now tinted the discolored hue of a cigarette tip due to weathering decades of the Windy City's brutal summers and unforgiving winters. About a block away is the community's most notorious claim to fame: Marquette Park, where the Reverend Martin Luther King Jr. tried to lead a march protesting housing discrimination in 1966, only to be met by thousands of angry white residents who pelted him with epithets and rocks, leading the secular saint to remark, "I have never seen anything so hostile and so hateful as I've seen here today."

That summer spurred an emptying of the area's houses and apartments, and the Lithuanians, Poles, Germans, and Irish of a previous generation left for whiter pastures; in their place arrived blacks, Mexicans, Palestinians, and other immigrants. But the neighborhood's essence abides: working class, skeptical and uneasy of new ways, a place for lower-class families to move on up in the strata of Chicagoland.

Each group keeps their mores, their festivals, and their restaurants, but communion comes at Fat Johnnies. "Dinners on a Bun Fit for a King," reads a sign standing as tall as the sagging restaurant, and that's truth in advertising. They sell more than a dozen different hot dogs here, fast and sloppy, all odes to the zesty essence of the great Chicago dog: the poppy seed bun that lingers after every bite, simultaneously mushy and toasty; the David Berg links, juicy and spicy and all-beef with a hell of a snap; sport peppers and diced onions on top, and a fresh cucumber slice snuggling next to the wiener acting as a palate cleanser. Have it topped with chili, have it topped with a smear of mustard, or have it plain: this is a dog worthy of a cable channel.

Fat Johnnies's red hots aren't limited to sausages. Also on the menu are tamales. In a bowl of chili, christened a Tamale Sundae. Plain. Or, most gloriously, as a Mother-in-Law: a tamale inside a hot dog bun, slathered in chili. The tamale, related to its Aztec progenitor only by name, disintegrates in the warmth of your mouth into fatty crumbs. This rendition is small, thin, made from a cornmeal shell as airy as polenta filled with a mixture of ground beef and spices. Look at it lengthwise, and it looks like an unsheathed lipstick. But this Chicago tamale possesses an earthiness, a sweetness its Mexican cousin can't reach. Fat Johnnies's chili, flecked with beans and meat, as pasty as a jar of Gerber's, is similarly subtle, not too spicy and more on the sugary side. The tamale absorbs the chili, transforms into a ruddy-yellow vessel that spills out of the hot dog bun, which labors to keep its innards inside and fails, like a Dixie cup trying to hold back Lake Michigan.

On a hot summer day, with some chairs and tables out, Fat Johnnies is a shrine. The Mother-in-Law is a South Side specialty, one not found anywhere else in the United States, and it's an entirely appropriate anomaly. For here in the Second City, more than a century ago, legend has it that Mexican food made its national debut at the 1893 World's Columbian Exposition, better remembered as the Chicago World's Fair. It's the same grand soiree that gave America its first ride on the Ferris wheel, its first bite of a hamburger, and where Frederick Jackson Turner lectured on the closing of the American West, signifying a new era for the still-young republic. It's here, so the history books read, that tamales and chili—the latter on display by the Texas delegation at their palatial exhibit headquarters—became such a sensation that the country soon demanded them in restaurants, giving the country its first taste of Mexican food and becoming as much a part of American cuisine as pizza and frankfurters.

Oh, but if legends were true, then Paul Bunyan would've been our Zeus. The two foodstuffs were already traveling across the United States, peddled by Mexicans and immigrants to the working class and piquing the interest of the upper crust. Chicago *was* a crossroads for chili and tamales, the place where they emerged as worthy enough for a hungry nation—but each took a loopy path involving exiled queens, strikes, and the coming of the Tamale King. Nothing as simple as a mere World's Fair.

While the tamale dates to the foundation of civilizations in Meso-America, food historians will forever debate the origins of chili. Only two points are undisputed: it was created somewhere in the vast expanse north of the Rio Grande when the area wasn't the state of Texas but rather *Tejas,* and the dish first received significant American attention in San Antonio in about the late 1870s under the label *chile con carne* (pepper with meat, which has it backward, as it was the pepper that was the condiment, not the main ingredient), when the city was undergoing a tourism boom, full of Americans eager to seek out the conquered territories of a previous generation.

The Alamo had fallen just forty years earlier; the wounds of the

Mexican-American War of 1848 festered raw for many residents. The Galveston, Harrisburg, and San Antonio Railway Company was just about to enter the city, then a frontier town where cattlemen ruled and beef was as common as water. Coming to a town that was essentially Mexican, curious tourists happened upon makeshift markets across San Antonio, vendors huddling in plazas from morning to the late hours. Baskets, blankets, and other merchandise were exchanged between peddlers and visitors, but what struck the national fancy was chile con carne hawked by a specific gender: women.

Dozens of these *mujeres* arrived to the plazas—Milam, Military, Alamo, the scenes changed with the tolerance of city fathers over the years—at dusk, with precooked meals in sturdy cauldrons placed over roaring fires. Each brought tables, stools, lanterns to light the booth, and their fetching selves. Accompanying the ladies were musicians to play for customers. It wasn't just Mexican food on sale, but rather the romance of a vanquished people, a slice of Old Mexico in a state that hadn't yet fully joined the Republic.

In a *Scribner's* 1874 write-up, one writer described a visit to San Antonio's Mexican quarter, known as Laredito (after Laredo, a Texas border city), where "the life of the Seventeenth Century still prevails, without any taint of modernism." Although urging a visit to the Alamo, "that shrine to which every pilgrim to this strange corner of America must do utmost reverence," the writer also noted "many Americans" flocking to San Antonio, specifically for Mexican food. Already, he wrote, Mexicans had "learned to turn American curiosity about his cookery to account.

"The fat, tawny Mexican mater-familias will place before you various savory compounds, swimming in fiery pepper, which biteth like a serpent," the *Scribner's* story described. "This meal, with bitterest of coffee to wash it down, and liquid dulcet Spanish talked by your neighbors for dessert, will be an event in your gastronomic experience."[1]

The *Scribner's* report lured other writers into San Antonio, and city boosters took note. The 1882 *Alamo City Guide* pointed readers to

Military Plaza, where they could "delight in the Mexican luxuries of tamales, chile con carne and enchiladas" prepared "in the open air in the rear of the tables and served by lineal descendants of the ancient Aztecs"—never mind that a good portion of the vendors traced their ancestry to Spain and the Canary Islands.[2]

A chili con carne stand in San Antonio's Haymarket Plaza during the 1930s. "Chili queens" were the first superstars of Mexican cooking in this country, starting in the 1880s, but San Antonio officials eventually legislated them out of existence
Chili stands, Haymarket Plaza, San Antonio, Texas, 1933, San Antonio Light Photograph Collection, University of Texas at San Antonio Libraries Special Collections

Not all the dispatches were kind. A *Harper's* correspondent joked that the women lording over the pots "look[ed] like one of the witches in Macbeth."[3] Meanwhile, author Stephen Crane described chile con carne as "pounded fire-brick from Hades" and said of its vendors, "Many of the young girls are pretty, and all the old ones are ugly." But even Crane acknowledged their attraction: "The first question asked by [visitors] is, 'Where are those chile stands I have heard so much about?'" A local scribe lost to history labeled the women "chili queens" to further embellish the dish's exotic quality, and they became as associated with the city in its early days as the Alamo, a bit of colonized yin to the conquerer's yang.

And so we return to the fabulous origin story of chili con carne's exodus out of San Antonio and across the United States. Scholars have long recycled the claim that the 1893 World's Columbian Exposition featured a re-creation of the chili queens by Texas's official delegation with a sign reading "The San Antonio Chili Stand," and that the simulacra of the phenomenon sparked a demand for chili that went nationwide. However, no contemporary account of the scene exists. No clippings in the Chicago and San Antonio newspapers of the era mention the exhibit, even though the *San Antonio Express* and the *San Antonio Light* meticulously reported the many updates involving Texas leading up to the exposition, and even though there was a sizable San Antonio contingent in Chicago at the time.

In his thousand-page-plus account of the exposition, *The Book of the Fair,* historian Hubert Howe Bancroft mentions that the main structure that housed the official Texas delegation at the exposition was "patterned after the old Catholic missions of San Antonio" and designed by a San Antonio architect, and that a formal ball concluded the all-day celebration Texas held for itself on September 16, Mexican Independence Day. Bancroft—a prodigious historian who was one of the earliest chroniclers of the American West—made no mention of any chili. In the official cookbook of the exposition, a collection of recipes gathered by the Board of Lady Managers, which represented the states that participated, the recipe that Bernadette B. Tobin (the head of the Texas state board) provided to represent Texas wasn't for chile con carne but rather almond blanc mange. Meanwhile, the lady manager for New Mexico contributed a recipe for "Mexican Enchiladas," while the recipe that Vicenta Chaves of New Mexico contributed was for "tamales de chile," which called for the use of "carne con chile"[4] and also included a recipe for dessert tamales.

The earliest mention of Chicago's supposed San Antonio Chili Stand didn't appear until 1927, when San Antonio's then commissioner of taxation, Frank H. Bushick, wrote a remembrance for the *Frontier Times*. "They were the raven-haired, flashing-eyed senoritas [*sic*] of more or less pulchritude who served the customers and presided with easy grace," he wrote.[5] The author, however, had a vested interest to embellish San Antonio's past: Bushick was one of the heads of the Fiesta San Jacinto Association, a coalition of merchants and the gentry that held the city's annual Fiesta celebration, which remembered the city's past by imagining it as a Spanish wonderland.

Chili con carne had appeared on American menus long before the World's Columbian Exposition. Newspapers in Washington, D.C., and Hawaii were already advertising the dish in the 1880s.[6] At the 1889 Paris World's Fair, Australian George Brougham—an adviser for Libby, McNeil, and Libby, a Chicago canning company—showed off a canned version.[7] Even at the Columbian Exposition, many of the canning companies proudly displayed their chili, already described in trade journals as "a popular article of food, chiefly exported to the markets of Mexico and California."[8] The 1890s was a time of great innovation for canning products, with Chicago the epicenter of the industry, given its proximity to stockyards and railroads, and chili con carne was just another food for the industry to stuff in a can and sell.

Regardless, chili con carne took firmer hold across the country during the 1890s and beyond, dropping the Spanish portion of its name for easier digestion. A cheap mixture of meat, beans, and spice of varying heat, affordable and canned, became an easy meal for a burgeoning, starved nation. Native Texans didn't let national attention for their dish bloom without snide remarks, though. San Antonio booster Charles Ramsdell mocked the degradations of the "brimstone bowl" as it proliferated, talking of the "perversion practiced Up North, where the Yankee tosspot who lurches from his unsteady couch after a fluid evening and cries out for 'chillee cahn corny' is resuscitated with a bland goo tasting of tomatoes and sugar."⁹ But even as chili became popular, the city that brought it fame legislated against its queens.

In 1889, San Antonio mayor Bryan Callaghan initiated a building boom that beautified the city but also drove the chili queens out of the plazas near the Alamo. The vendors returned with no license, thus beginning a cat-and-mouse game that lasted decades in a city trying to promote itself nationally as a garden city but one needing its bowl of red. During the last decades of the chili queens' reign, O. Henry, in his 1919 tale "The Enchanted Kiss," lamented their slow extinction. "A few years before, their nightly encampments upon the historic Alamo Plaza, in the heart of the city, had been a carnival, a saturnalia that was renowned throughout the land," he wrote. "Then the caterers numbered hundreds; the patrons thousands. Drawn by the coquettish *señoritas,* the music of the weird Spanish minstrels, and the strange piquant Mexican dishes served at a hundred competing tables, crowds thronged the Alamo Plaza all night.

"But the earthy air and pungent odor of the plaza are gone," O. Henry continued. "The singers still gather around your car and serenade you. But without the chili queens to exchange anatomical insults with them in sonorous Spanish, they seem a bit lackadaisical and depressed."¹⁰

The death knell came, strangely enough, when the city fathers decided to embrace the queens in the 1930s—first as cultural artifacts to attract tourists looking for a bit of Old San Antone, then via the efforts of Mayor Maury Maverick. He successfully campaigned for Mexican-American votes by promising to leave the queens alone, a move reported nationally. Instead of letting them set up pots as during their heyday, Maverick forced them into screened tents to allay any hygienic fears and required them to register with the health department, insisting that crowds desired to see such a seal of approval before returning. Those regulations, however, had the opposite effect—the crowds didn't materialize because the allure of the original queens, shadowy and fierce, had been domesticated to a sad imitation. After World War II, the queens just disappeared.

Chili con carne, now plain ol' chili, was a harbinger of things to come for Mexican food. It was a Mexican dish, made by Mexicans for Mexicans, but it was whites who made the dish a national sensation, who pushed it far beyond its ancestral lands, who adapted it to their tastes, who created companies for large-scale production, and who ultimately became its largest consumer to the point that the only thing Mexican about it was the mongrelized Spanish in its name. The Mexicans, meanwhile, shrugged their shoulders and continued cooking and eating their own foods, all the while ostracized by Anglos who nevertheless tore through whatever Mexicans put in front of them.

Meanwhile, the memory of the chili queens persists. For decades, San Antonio has held the Return of the Chili Queens in Market Square, a procession of young lasses who put on the airs of the legend that the Alamo City can never quite get over.

In 1896, Sigmund Krausz published *Street Types of Great American Cities,* a collection of photographs and vignettes that sought to capture the feel and denizens of America's rapidly expanding, rapidly changing urban centers. The country teemed with immigrants who tapped the entrepreneurial vein of capitalism and created jobs that genteel Americans viewed with bemusement when they weren't claiming they were promoting vice.

Photojournalism was in its infancy—at the beginning of the decade, Jacob Riis's *How the Other Half Lives* had shocked the country with its unsparing exposé of New York City's tenement slums. But Krausz had no such muckraking desire for his project. In 1891, he had published *Street Types of Chicago* with the express purpose of showing the great unwashed that made his "fire-tried" home great, the men and women "who are not of the order of those who control the destinies of the city by the vastness of the enterprises they direct, but all of them in their modest sphere contribute their mite [*sic*] to the active rush which ebbs and flows along our busy thoroughfares."[11] It was a success, and Krausz expanded the collection on a national scale with his sequel five years later.

In between portraits of organ grinders, heavily accented newspaper boys, rag pickers, banana sellers, and, um, a "niggah," is a "new and interesting type on our thoroughfares," one the public should "welcome his advent": the tamale man, or *tamalero*. An accompanying photo shows a tamalero posing in his natural state of selling. Unlike the chili queens' smoldering ethnicity, he wears all-white: coat with black buttons, white apron that hangs down to just above his ankles, white pants—the picture of sterility. A paper tied around the pot blares CALIFORNIA CHICKEN TAMALES and features a drawing of a standing tamale man. The in-the-flesh tamalero holds the cover from a metal steam pot in his left hand; his right hand reaches into the pail, ready to grab one of what Krausz describes as the "toothsome mysteries of this steaming bundle of cornhusks.

"It is the Ambrosia of our Mexican friend," Krausz writes, so "delicious" that "the angels in heaven could enjoy." But he understood why "to the average American at first trial a tamale seems more like a foretaste of that tropic climate, a graphic description which has been given to us by immortal Dante," instead of a fine meal.[12]

The tamalero looks Mexican, but maybe he was a Greek, Italian, Pole, or any of the many other immigrant groups flowing into the Windy City in those years. His pencil-thin mustache is sharp, his eyes wide open and nearly shining in the black-and-white shot, his mouth agape. A big hat tops his head, but it isn't a sombrero: instead, he wears a stovepipe hat emblazoned with the name of his company.

The United States in the 1890s was in the midst of a tamale man invasion that strolled hand in hand with the chili con carne craze. Their nearly universal singsong call—"Hot ta-ma-leeees! Hot ta-ma-leeees!"—rang from Montana to Tacoma.[13] They hit the streets with such popularity that one newspaper opined that the tamale had "supplanted the wienerwurst in the hearts of the people."[14] The rise of the tamale was such that the hoity magazine the *Epicure* felt the need in 1901 to declare that "the once ridiculed bunch of corn husks with exceedingly warm contents now figures at 'swell' eating-houses, while illuminated advertisements, bearing the name of firms claiming their excellence of make, are everywhere in evidence."[15]

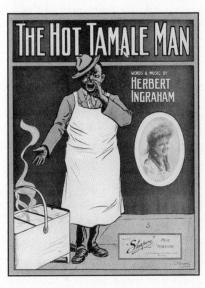

Tamale men spread across the United States from the 1890s well into the 1940s, embedding themselves into popular culture ranging from plays to films to songs like 1909's "The Hot Tamale Man." Mexicans, African-Americans, and European immigrants dominated the trade.
Image: "The Hot Tamale Man," Historic American Sheet Music, David M. Rubenstein Rare Book & Manuscript Library, Duke University Libraries

Tamaleros infiltrated popular culture. They became bit players in dramas: a review of *On the Bowery,* a play about the rough Manhattan neighborhood, noted that the tamale man "gets such a big reception when he appears upon the stage."[16] Songs celebrating the "Hot Tamale Man" were composed and sung in different genres, from Dixieland to jazz to the blues. "Hot tamaleeees! Hot tamaleeeees. If you're growing old / hot tamales will save your soul," sang minstrel singer Arthur Collins in 1909. There was a children's game called Hot Tamales, a variant of Hot Potato: children formed a circle around someone designated as the tamale man. The tamalero shouted his siren song and threw a knotted piece of fabric at a child, who tossed it at another one and so on. It was the objective of the tamalero to get back his livelihood.[17]

The tamale man even became the subject of national jokes. A 1900 political cartoon imagined Mexico as a tamale vendor with a basket that read "Central American possessions"; across the street stood men with hats that read TRUSTS along with John Hay, the ambitious secretary of state under presidents William McKinley and Theodore Roosevelt who had successfully negotiated the treaty with Spain that annexed Cuba, Puerto Rico, and the Philippines. "The Tamale Man: I hope they won't try to Annex my Basket," the caption read.[18]

In New York, Chicago, and other major metropolitan areas, tamale men ruled the streets, hundreds of them taking to corners and alleys, bars and businesses, with their trademark pails, almost all dressed in the same baptismal white coat and apron as Krausz's muse. But by the beginning of the twentieth century, the tamale man had already been relegated to history, remembered as one of the "Odd Characters of Bygone Days."[19]

"Some 10 or 12 years ago, the tamale . . . business was far different from what it is to-day," a 1904 mock obituary read. "Industrial conditions have contrived to relegate 'the old guard'" to "vanish." The story featured an illustration of a dejected man holding a pail and a box. He's now dressed in black, bowler hat bent out of shape, looking down and walking down the street at night, crowds long gone.[20]

The tamale man lingered on in small towns for decades to follow, and lived on in popular media. "Here Comes the Hot Tamale Man" is a staple of Charleston-style jazz, the trumpet, sax, and clarinet mimicking the rollicking strut of the vendor. Immortal bluesman Robert Johnson's "They're Red Hot" is a classic of ragtime guitar, double entendres, and good tamales. In 1931, a film short titled *The Tamale Vendor* came and went, directed by a William Goodrich, a pseudonym for Fatty Arbuckle, the former Hollywood star whose career was ruined in a sex scandal for which he ultimately was acquitted. And a tamale man makes a cameo in *A Streetcar Named Desire,* his call for "red hots" making Blanche Dubois scream. But he's now relegated to the rag pickers and street urchins of the past—yet even they're remembered more often.

How did the tamale man disappear from the nation's streets, instead of embedding himself like chili? It's a familiar story of food: cult status, rapid expansion, and death by your own success as competitors swooped in. Get them while they're hot.

Early 1890s San Francisco. Babylon by the Bay is slowly civilizing. The decadence of the Gold Rush years has dimmed, and city fathers are trying to turn the city into the Paris of the West. Cable cars climb the city's steep hills. Americans are flocking to the town. And all around, Mexicans sell tamales on the street.

It was a cacophony of street vendors, and the tamale men were the kings of them all. Their meals had become the culinary binder of the city, originally introduced to the region by the Californios, the original Spanish settlers of California who glumly watched as rapacious Americans took their lands and businesses after the Mexican-American War. Unlike the classical Mexican tamale, stuffed with meat steeped in salsa, these also came with olives, a legacy of Franciscan fathers who brought the tamale from Mexico and the olive tree from Spain. Though the people who made the tamales were Mexicans, their sale was a wholly immigrant affair—Chileans, Mexicans, Brazilians, even Arabs walked the San Francisco streets peddling the food.

Most of the tamale factories and workers centered around the city's Barbary Coast district, and spilled up to Russian and Telegraph Hills. Mentions of the tamale men are found in San Francisco newspapers as early as the 1880s, and the *Boston Journal* in 1884 even made mention of "A queer article of food, known as 'tamales' . . . sold in the streets of San Francisco at night by picturesquely clad Spaniards."

Tamales weren't unique to San Francisco, of course. Most of the chili queen articles from San Antonio made cursory mentions of the masa meal, and the city even went by the nickname Tamale Town or Tamaleville for decades after its initial fame.[21] But America streamlined the San Francisco tamale—bigger than its Mexican ancestor, engorged within a husk, then coming to a dramatic taper at ends tied with strings or strips of corn husk—in earnest in the early 1890s thanks to the efforts of a San Francisco businessman named Robert H. Putnam. He created the California Chicken Tamale Co. in 1892 with the desire to send San Francisco–style tamale vendors nationwide. But instead of allowing his employees to dress in the stereotypical style of Mexicans—a poncho, sombrero, and pantaloons—Putnam created a uniform for his workers: a white linen coat, overalls, and hat that brought, if not class, at least an assurance to the public that these vendors cared about appearance and sanitation. He equipped them with steam pails—fire on the bottom, boiling water in the middle, and the hot tamales on top—to ensure that the ten-cent treasures within always kept warm.

Putnam's first target was Chicago in February 1892, which was preparing for the following year's Columbian Exposition. Chicagoans, a scribe for the *San Francisco Chronicle* asserted, "had all heard of Frisco's celebrated tamale men, but he had dropped into their midst so quietly and without so much ceremony as a brass band that they did not know him when they saw him."[22] The first Windy City night for Putnam's tamale men was disappointing. The temperature was below zero; the tamale men stood at their stations, pail in hand but silent. Putnam was unfazed; after that first disastrous night, he rallied his workers and ordered them to yell loudly to customers what they sold: "Hot chik'n tamales, tensentsapiece."[23]

Putnam created a smash; within five months, he was hiring two to three men a week until he amassed a force of more than five hundred working Chicago's streets. He also found partners who helped incorporate the California Chicken Tamale Company in Illinois with a capital stock campaign of ten thousand dollars. But imitators immediately clawed into Putnam's business. A former California Chicken Tamale worker named Newman, full name lost to history, broke off and sold a tamale called the San Antonio that undercut his boss by selling the bigger tamale for five cents. Putnam was so angered that he reported Newman to the police for trying to ruin him. He also accused

Newman of encouraging California Chicken Tamale workers to form a union, and inspiring them to strike. Putnam armed his employees with guns because "we expect trouble any night" from Newman's crew, but no reports of bloodshed were ever lodged.[24] Newman's scheming worked: just a couple of months into Putnam's reign, four hundred of his tamale men organized themselves into a union, demanding an increase in wages.[25]

The California Chicken Tamale Company nevertheless pushed forward. In the spring of 1893, they penetrated Gotham. A newspaper account of a tamale vendor with a "brogue" noted "if New Yorkers . . . get the taste for them, tamale sellers will be as common here as they are in the far South and in San Francisco and Southern California." That fall, a restaurant simply called The Tamale opened in New York's Tenderloin slum; the restaurant sold tamales, chili con carne, "enchelladas," and Spanish dishes such as gazpacho.[26] Back in Chicago, Putnam's tamale men roamed the World's Columbian Exposition, finding eager eaters who had never had a bite of one. The frenzy amused visiting Californians, one of whom remarked, "None of these effete towns can hope to rival California. We ate some tamales at the World's Fair in Chicago, and they would have made a . . . dog sick."[27]

The tamale man was ascendant. The tamale man's days were numbered.

Back in San Francisco, city fathers seethed at the Chicago exposition's success. *Chronicle* publisher Michael H. de Young had been the commissioner of the California Exhibits and vice president of the fair's national commission, and was looking for a way to promote his city and push it out of its wild days. Even before the fair ended, de Young and other San Francisco businessmen concocted plans for their own version to top it: a Midwinter Fair, a welcome respite from the season to bring America to the balm and promise of California. "When the gates open," de Young's paper promised, "California will be seen not only as one of the greatest States in the Union, but as one of the greatest countries in the world."[28]

In just seven months, de Young and other businessmen set up their own extravaganza, held at Golden Gate Park over hundreds of acres. It mimicked many of the World's Columbian Exposition exhibits—the Ferris wheel, as well as state buildings and various "natives" from across the globe—but also included snippets of life in California. In that spirit, someone proposed a "Tamale Village" to highlight the city's industry, and two men assumed the responsibility of creating it: Carroll Cook and Ned Foster.

Foster was one of the city's many colorful characters, the proprietor of the ill-famed Bella Union burlesque house and a consummate showman who found wealth in the mines of Nevada but was on his way down. The theater was in ruins. Cook was his lawyer, and had helped him earn a deadlocked jury on the charge that Foster illegally sold alcohol to patrons. Their Tamale Village for the Midwinter Fair was to be a wholesome, get-rich-quick scheme. The plan was simple: an adobe-style building, stuccoed and adorned with shards of colored glass to evoke California's days of Spanish dons and doñas. San Francisco–style tamales were the item of attraction. Women dressed in period outfits, manning all the jobs, from the metate from where women ground corn into masa, to the stoves where the tamale got cooked, to the waitresses who served the tamales to ravenous tourists. The *Chronicle* celebrated Foster's decision to assume responsibility over the exhibit and felt that "everybody said the climax had been reached" with the inclusion of the village into the fair.[29]

The California Midwinter International Exposition opened in January 1894, and Foster had his serving señoritas partake in the inaugural parade, pulled on carriages. The final Tamale Village structure, however, looked more like an Alpine hut than anything southwestern. It didn't matter—the village (also known as Tamale Cottage or the Tamale Palace) opened as a phenomenon from the beginning.

"The Eastern visitor to the Midwinter Fair is usually bent upon solving the mystery of a Mexican tamale," a reporter wrote. "The veranda and garden of the 'Tamale Cottage' are generally crowded with people sitting at small tables, on which the smoking delicacy is served by gaily appareled Spanish girls"[30] (a misnomer, of course, given those waitresses were Mexican, and a misnomer we'll study later in this book). Accompanying the article was a smiling girl in her Victorian best, sitting underneath an umbrella, emptied husks on the table.

Tamales became an American fad, and the tamale men, whether sponsored by Putnam or not, invaded towns looking for the success earned in Chicago and San Francisco. *Good Housekeeping* offered its first tamale recipe in 1894, noting that "the dish is sold in the streets of San Francisco the same as hot corn and hot roasted chestnuts are sold with us."[31] In Montana, Salvador Truzzolino and his brother made tamales and sold them around Butte in 1896; to this day, his family carries on the family business. But while the tamale man introduced himself to the United States, he was disappearing in San Francisco. Just a year after the Midwinter International Exposition, a shortage of husks forced many independent tamale vendors out of business—that year, early rains had destroyed the corn crop in Mexico, and the shortage raised prices astronomically. Foster tried to open a tamale restaurant, but having sold all his tamale husks (he had bought fifty tons for the exposition and sold off those that he didn't use) and having purchased peppers and chickens, he went into financial ruin; Foster died broke five years later. Restaurants muscled into the business, and newspapers noted that "these places are very careful in the preparation of their wares and many of them make them in view of their customers," as opposed to the tamale men, who had to deal with the pesky urban legend that their chicken was in reality seagull meat.

In Chicago, Putnam and Newman's rivalry ended with both sides losing. "The 'tamale' men's return is as quiet as their going three years ago was tempestuous," the *Tribune* reported in 1896. "They went away after an internecine war that was hotter than the peppery food they served" that led to "a scattering of forces so thoroughly that reorganization was never attempted." The new tamale men were now "colored," the paper moaned, and "he cannot hold a candle to the venders who howled and screeched at each other in Chicago when the war was on."[32]

But a funny thing happened: the California tamale stuck around and became the Chicago tamale. The olives disappeared from the tamale, and it became more cylindrical, smaller. Cornmeal replaced the masa, perhaps an influence of the many African Americans from Mississippi who migrated North during the mid-1930s and brought over *their* tamales, also relics of the early days of the tamale men. To this day, the tamales of Chicago and the Mississippi Delta are the only American-born, non-Mexican-dominated tamale traditions that date back to that era, enjoyed only in their regions, accepted long ago as uniquely theirs—even if those tamales originally came from California.

New York tired completely of the tamale men. The height of their penetration was in 1894, with Putnam having forty tamale men; within a couple of years, almost all had disappeared. And in San Francisco, they gamely carried on. By 1910, Sikh immigrants sold tamales in San Francisco, dropping their trademark turban to appear Mexican.[33] Seven years later, the Board of Supervisors passed a statute barring the sale of street tamales.[34] The tamale man, rejected and ostracized after decades of feeding a city, was gone "into oblivion with the dodo."[35]

The *San Francisco Chronicle* had a love-hate relationship with the tamale man. As early as 1895, in an article under the subtitle "The Swarthy Mexican with His Bucket and Lantern Gives Way to the Factory," the *Chronicle* cheered on the demise of the sellers by trying to paint them as dirty and dangerous. The paper dismissed the tamale men as "dead," replaced by "enterprising Americans" who were building canning factories to seal San Francisco's tamales and transport them via railcar to households across America.[36] California businessmen figured Americans wanted tamales in a can, a guarantee that the product inside was hygienic, unlike their streetside sellers.

Those businessmen were right; by the 1900s, canned tamales sold briskly across the United States. And no one did more to revolutionize the industry and the spread of tamales than Charles H. Workman. The North Carolina native was so poor that by seven, he had to work as a mule driver in a mine to earn fifty cents a day—at least according to Workman's account. He moved to San Francisco in 1885 at age eighteen, initially working as a cable car conductor until realizing there was ore to strike in "the familiar cry of the tamale huckster."[37] Using his savings, Workman opened the W. G. M. Canning company in 1900, with the goal of canning clams and making tamales and enchiladas to sell fresh to restaurants. He was entering a fierce business, with competitors trying to outsell each other via innovations, and the two main competitors were the Kapp & Street Canning Company—which ran one of the first tamale parlors in the city geared to attract upper-class eaters in the wake of the Midwinter Fair—and IXL Canning.

IXL (remember your Roman numerals, and a surprise awaits you. Forgot them? Fine. It's 49. Get it? San Francisco? 49ers? I'll be here all week) had already established itself as a popular brand since its inception in 1896, sponsoring a baseball team of the same name and advertising in national papers as early as 1899.[38] Founder Julius Bunzl filed in 1897 for the country's first patent on canned tamales, and IXL was one of the American exhibitors at the 1900 Paris World's Fair, along with Kapp & Street,[39] winning an award at the exposition for "the surpassing excellence of their product awarded to any competitor of their class."[40]

Workman, befitting of his surname, outmaneuvered the competition. When he opened in 1900, his factory made only three hundred tamales a day; the following year, Workman had upped the output to eighteen hundred in a new plant. In 1902, he bought out Kapp & Street and moved his factory to their location; two years later, IXL was his. By 1911, the Workman Packing Company had opened bigger and more modern factories but it kept the IXL brand.[41]

There was a problem, though: canning tamales at the time was inefficient. Workers had to manually line the masa in the can, then add the meat, limiting output and creating an inconsistent product. Workman tinkered with machinery to automate the stuffing, creating a can-lining machine for which he applied for and obtained a patent in 1915. He had already implemented the machines at his factories, to astounding results: in 1912, IXL sold 48,384 cans of tamales, according to its records; the following year, sales reached nearly 140,000, along with almost 44,000 cans of enchiladas and 11,000 cans of chili, processed in a newly built three-story factory.[42]

Like Putnam and his California Chicken Tamale, former employees opened their own factories to try to mimic Workman's work. Nationwide, others traded their tamale-man routes for factories and shops as well, taking IXL's concepts and branding. "But they can't get away with it," a confident Workman told a reporter. "The competitor who starts out has to undersell me; but the very minute he does so he loses money. I produce the best quality; he may equal it, but not at as low a manufacturing cost. You can't undersell at a loss all the time, and keep your head above water."[43]

In 1915, San Francisco hosted another big fair: the Panama-Pacific International Exposition. Workman had a model plant in his booth and a booklet of tamale recipes that one observer said was "second in value only to the burned library of Alexandria."[44] But the U.S. market wasn't enough for IXL. They sent representatives to Australia to "illustrate how quickly and simply these delicate dishes are prepared for the table."[45]

The advances of Workman devastated the few remaining tamale men around the United States; one report estimated that the sales of husk tamales had decreased from forty thousand per year to four thousand in a decade. Who needed hot tamales sold by immigrant men when they were now canned? "Clean, sanitary kitchens displace the dingy, unsanitary places of manufacture of the old time husk tamale with its doubtful ingredients," the California State Federation of Labor reported in a section called "What Has Become of the 'Tamale Man'?" "White men and women are employed the year around to prepare this delicious condiment for the tables of the world."[46] When Workman died at age fifty-five in 1922; the nickname "Tamale King," which the San Francisco press had already affixed to him, accompanied his obituaries. By then all the major canners sold canned tamales and chili con carne, and the United States was ready for its next Mexican meal.

Chapter Three

How Did the Taco Become Popular Before Mexicans Flooded the United States?

Chili and tamales represented Mexican food to most Americans for nearly sixty years, from their mass introduction during the 1890s through the end of World War II. Sure, the stray Mexican restaurant opened in cities and states with no significant Mexican population, serving mostly . . . chili and tamales (and other Tex-Mex favorites, but we'll address that in a couple of chapters). It wasn't until the 1950s that the next Mexican food rage flooded the United States, and to pay our proper respects to the man and company whom America credits for this innovation, we must travel to my backyard: Orange County, California.

Three flags fly high over a business plaza in the city of Irvine, just off Interstate 5: the United States, California, and Taco Bell. These nations each warrant their own banner for this setting, and each hang at the same height, *especially* the one that hawks Crunchwraps® for a living. Billions of dollars in annual revenue inspire such ego, and why doesn't the company deserve the right to wave as tall as the Stars and Stripes? California and the United States are fading, after all, while the world's largest Mexican fast-food chain continues to spread around the globe like wind currents. Taco Bell's corporate headquarters anchors this plaza, a building once occupied by another past-its-prime dominion, Ford, and the conglomerate has ensured that the reformatted offices are a testament to their might. Naming the road that leads into your offices 1 Glen Bell Way, after the man who founded the business? Sure. Having the handles to the glass doors that open up to the lobby created of cast iron and in the shape of a bell? Of course. Large screens on the first floor showing the latest ads for the company? That's the business, so why not?

But there's a dirty secret about Taco Bell's headquarters: there are no longer any tacos for sale on the premises.

Before their move here a couple of years ago, the multinational comfortably occupied a twenty-seven-story building across town, its distinctive campanile logo visible for miles. In the old headquarters, the Glen Bell Cafeteria sold food on the bottom floor—sandwiches, salads, hot foods, and other healthier options from the Bell Bistro, but mostly offerings from Taco Bell and its sister companies, Pizza Hut and KFC. The cafeteria seated three hundred, and the eaters weren't all corporate drones: from its opening in 1987, wide-eyed tourists who wanted to see the cheesy center of the restaurant that introduced them to Mexican food rubbed elbows with name-badge-wearing employees and suits observing said yokels to try to find the next big thing. A patio, a fountain, even a gift shop—Taco Bell's temple to itself was knowingly hokey, but the Glen Bell Cafeteria served as a living, breathing reminder of Pa Bell's rootsy beginnings.

That's no longer the case. Taco Bell didn't install a cafeteria in its new digs for the general public. Most of its employees now leave the campus for lunch, since the closest franchise is about three miles away, in the neighboring city of Lake Forest. They actively follow the many top-shelf taco trucks that flood Irvine's corporate parks every day, standing in dozens-long lines, enticed by Twitter feeds and word of mouth to wait for tortillas stuffed with Korean barbecue, with Argentine sausage, with sautéed tofu and even jackfruit—everything but the hard-shelled version. These luxe *loncheras*—the vegan Seabirds, the organic Lime Truck, the Argentine-Mexican Piaggio on Wheels, the Asian-Mexican Dos Chinos, and others—offer more than Mexican, but it's the taco that allows them to sell in the shadow of the Bell.

"Oh, those employees," one owner says with a laugh, as a line stretches out before him. "They're some of my best customers. They act as if they've never seen a taco before."

The taco at Taco Bell is dead. Long live the taco.

Such a simple, brilliant meal: a tortilla wrapped around a stuffing. No utensils needed. The taco. That's it. Oh, modifications are possible: fold the tortilla in half and deep-fry it to create a taco dorado, what Americans know as the hard-shelled taco. Roll it like an enchilada, deep-fry it, and you have taquitos (also called flautas). Eat them at breakfast? Breakfast tacos. Fine for lunch and dinner. As a snack. As a full meal. Serve them with one or two tortillas. From a truck, from a grill, from fine china. Sprinkle some salsa, maybe some cilantro and onions. Grasp and grub. That's it.

Tacos have existed since there was a tortilla, even if they didn't exist by that name (the earliest mention of "taco" as a food dates only to the late nineteenth century; previously the word stood for everything from a pool cue to a hammer to getting drunk.)[1] They now cover the United States the way chili and tamales once did—the world, really. They're huge in Sweden, popular in Japan, big in Peoria, where El Mexicano offers them to city residents with chorizo that shines the shade of orange you want transmission fluid to reflect.

What's so remarkable about the foodstuff's odyssey, however, is its delayed start in this country. Unlike the enchiladas, frijoles, tamales, and beef stews that dominated the travelogues of American visitors to Mexico and the American Southwest, tacos didn't merit a mention in American literature until a Los Angeles socialite traveling in Mexico City came across them, describing the dish as a "fried turnover, filled with chopped, highly seasoned meats."[2] Tacos originally migrated to California and Texas in the 1920s, and only made it into scattered Mexican cookbooks written by Americans in about the 1930s. They didn't become easily available nationwide until Taco Bell and its numerous imitators rushed to colonize the United States during the 1960s, selling tacos that the average Mexican derided as inauthentic but the average American gobbled with gusto.

A Cinco de Mayo Festival at Olvera Street in Los Angeles in 1952. The tourist attraction influenced Mexican restaurants for decades by catering almost exclusively to Americans. Pictured from right are Consuelo de Bonzo, owner of La Golondrina Café, and Los Angeles mayor Fletcher Bowron
Courtesy of UCLA Charles E. Young Research Library Department of Special Collections, Los Angeles Times Photographic Archives. Copyright © Regents of the University of California, UCLA Library

Such a delay is almost counterintuitive. The taco is now the quintessential Mexican meal in the United States, so wedded to Americans' perception of the cuisine that even Irish pubs will sell corned beef tacos during Cinco de Mayo served by lasses wearing T-shirts boasting

"Irish I Were Mexican." But the ballad of tacos in the United States and their subsequent globalization is also the story of modern-day Mexican immigration to this country—and the eternal fascination Americans had with the treats of their southern neighbor.

The American taco can boast of two birthplaces: Los Angeles and San Bernardino, California. But its baptismal font is the pan angrily bubbling with oil at Cielito Lindo, a tiny stand in downtown Los Angeles named after a classic *ranchera* song meaning "Beautiful Little Heaven." From here come taquitos filled with shredded beef, grabbed fresh from that roiling pan, then anointed in a creamy salsa, more pureed avocado than chile. The cooks hand them to waiting customers in a container better suited for a hot dog, two for three dollars. These taquitos last a minute: people grab them with one hand and chomp, shattering their purchase into shiny shards with the faintest of bites; the shredded, fatty beef hangs off the end of the last bite like tendrils.

Cielito Lindo is the first business people see when entering the northern section of Olvera Street, a stretch of Los Angeles that has evolved along with the city's sense of itself. When the business district first opened in 1931, Los Angeles was simultaneously looking forward and backward. The city was booming, exponentially increasing its population nearly every decade as industries sprang up and boosters lured the nation with images of orange groves and movie stars, sun and sand. The Olympics were just a year away, and the eyes of the developed world prepared to focus on the City of Angels—a dramatic coming of age for a city that just fifty years earlier was still predominantly a Mexican-dominated cow town.

With progress came nostalgia, and the lords of L.A. pined for what the progressive historian Carey McWilliams dubbed California's "fantasy heritage," the idea that the Spaniards and Mexicans who had once ruled the state, before the Mexican-American War, truly lived the good life, and that modernity was laying ruin to paradise. One of those women, a northern California transplant named Christine Sterling, became enraged when she discovered city planners wanted to raze the

old adobes and buildings around the Plaza de Los Angeles, the acknowledged birthplace of the city. The socialite gained citywide notoriety by
placing a sign in front of the Avila adobe, the oldest in the city, that read
in part, "Los Angeles will be forever marked a transient, Orphan city if
she allows her roots to rot in a soil of impoverished neglect."

Sterling solicited the help of Harry Chandler, owner and publisher
of the *Los Angeles Times,* the mighty daily whose incessant drumbeat
for the region influenced the city it covered in a way few newspapers
have before or since. Chandler's use of his paper to promote projects
around the city—many in which his family and friends had a financial
interest—had already turned Los Angeles into one of America's rising
cities, and he used the pages of the *Times* to push forth the idea of El
Paseo de Los Angeles, a reimagined Olvera Street for approved vendors
to sell *mexicanidad* via artisan crafts and food for curious Americans.
But to do that, Sterling, Chandler, and other boosters had to try to kill
once and for all the Mexican food scene that had dominated the area
since the 1880s with tamale wagons.

Given Los Angeles's spread-out geography even in those embryonic
days, wandering tamale men didn't take hold in L.A. as they did in the
rest of the United States; a cart or a wagon was necessary, not only to
travel from home to downtown but also the better to procure a spot on
the bustling streets. The origins of the city's tamale sellers are murky,
although newspaper accounts place them as far back as the 1870s, and
by 1880, a *Los Angeles Herald* article commented, "The experience of
our Eastern visitors will be incomplete unless they sample" a Los Angeles street tamale.[3]

As dusk fell, a cavalry of two-by-four pushcarts and eight-foot-long
wagons with walls that opened up to reveal cooks inside wheeled their
way toward the Plaza and its vicinity, setting up shop until last call and
beyond. On the menu was everything from popcorn to pigs' feet, oys-
ter cocktails to sandwiches, but the majority of them carried tamales
prepared elsewhere and kept warm in steam buckets.

By 1901, more than a hundred tamale wagons roamed Los Angeles, each paying a dollar a month for a city business license. "Strangers coming to Los Angeles," reported the *Times* in 1901, "remark at the presence of so many outdoor restaurants, and marvel at the system which permits men . . . to set up places of business in the public streets . . . and competing with businessmen who pay high rents for rooms in which to serve the public with food."[4]

Not everyone appreciated the food scene, however. As early as 1892, officials tried to ban them outright; in 1897, the City Council proposed to not allow tamale wagons to open until nine at night, at the behest of restaurant owners who didn't like the crowds the tamaleros attracted. Four years later, Police Chief Charles Elton recommended tamale wagons close at one in the morning because they offered "a refuge for drunks who seek the streets when the saloons are closed for the night."[5] And in 1910, a hundred downtown businessmen signed a letter asking the council to prohibit tamale wagons because they didn't reflect well on the district.

The constant attempts at legislating the tamale wagons out of existence didn't succeed initially, however, because they were just too popular. And the tamaleros—knowing what they meant to their fans—pushed back against even the smallest slight against them. In 1903, when the council tried to outlaw them altogether, tamale wagons formed a mutual-aid society and presented the council a petition with the signatures of more than five hundred customers that read in part, "We claim that the lunch wagons are catering to an appreciative public and to deprive the people of these convenient eating places would prove a great loss to the many local merchants who sell the wagon proprietors various supplies."[6]

The time of the tamale wagons was waning, though. "They belong not to the new order of things," the *Times* editorialized in 1924. "They were born of the pueblo—they perish in the metropolis."[7] By then the wagons sold more than mere tamales—the biblical wave of migrants from Central Mexico due to the Mexican Revolution and other problems over the previous twenty years had introduced other Mexican delicacies to the city largely unfamiliar to the region: *birria* (goat stew), menudo (soup made from cow tripe), and different preparations of pork, chicken, and beef, best eaten snuggled in a tortilla: the taco.

That experience with mobile food had long-lasting repercussions for the region. The idea of a movable feast prefigured the drive-throughs that dominated the 1950s. And though Olvera Street developed and pushed out unsanctioned street vending from the area to make way for sit-down eateries such as La Golondrina Cafe, where Chandler and the city's power structure finally found a place to eat Mexican food in a refined atmosphere to their liking, it was simple meals such as tacos that resonated with the public. When Chandler enlisted a Latino writer to pen a piece extolling the authenticity of Olvera Street, even the shill had to plug the tacos.

"I see Mexico in every 'botellon' and 'serape' on the Paseo," the author wrote, "I taste it in the 'tacos,'" which he went on to describe as a "tortilla, folded over meat and vegetables and toasted a little."[8]

Their portability and easy preparation made tacos favorites of workers, who took them everywhere, from the factories to the fields. Tacos made their way onto the menus of the Mexican restaurants in town to become a hit for the working classes and blue bloods alike. Entrepreneurial immigrants as well as Americans saw opportunity in tacos. One of those was Aurora Guerrero, who left her village in Zacatecas during the 1920s to look for her husband, who had earlier settled in Los Angeles. She found poverty instead, and survived by cleaning houses and working the fields until finding an opportunity on Olvera Street selling taquitos from a stall out of a restaurant before renting a spot. Guerrero had to ask for Sterling's blessings to start a business; the matron of Olvera Street agreed with the condition that they sell "something different." And thus arose Cielito Lindo's taquitos.

Guerrero turned them into a living; a daughter, Ana Natalia, branched out with her mother's approval and opened a chain of Anitas restaurants across Los Angeles, taking with her the family's taquitos recipes and opening Las Anitas on Olvera Street, not far from Cielito

Lindo. Competitors copied those taquitos, along with Mexican restaurants across the region, and the modern-day taco took its infant steps toward supremacy.

The efforts of Chandler and Sterling worked; Olvera Street became a sensation. But it came at a cost. Sterling forced all the vendors to dress in "native" costume and affect the pomposity of Spanish dons and señoritas; those who refused faced eviction. Los Angeles's authentic Mexican street food scene had been replaced by Mexicans who played the role assigned to them by white patrons, who looked on in approval while chowing down tacos.

The style of taco varied outside of Olvera Street in those early years; in the workplace and at home, Mexican laborers ate them from soft tortillas, fresh from a grill; in restaurants, Americans enjoyed tacos as tortillas dunked in the fryer, then stuffed. So-called taco houses popped up across Southern California, casual restaurants where patrons enjoyed them freshly made; everywhere else, the taco was just another dish on an increasing number of menus. But preparing the tacos was an arduous task. In the days before fast food, restaurateurs fried each taco shell to order, throwing them into hot oil in a U-shaped form held together by a toothpick. To properly fry them, cooks had to poke around the cooking oil with their fingers or clumsily use utensils to ensure that each side achieved an ideal crispiness, then take out the finished product without scalding themselves. Because of this, taco making wasn't a popular duty, and inventive owners manipulated machines to try to ensure a speedy delivery to ravenous customers.

One of those pioneers was Juvencio Maldonado, a Mexican immigrant who opened his Mexican restaurant, Xochitl, in New York City in 1938. He had immigrated to the United States in 1929, an electrician by trade with hopes of getting to Chicago. But fate called him for a different purpose, and his midtown Manhattan Xochitl served as one of the city's few Mexican restaurant for decades, a point Maldonado made sure to promote in *New York Times* ads. Inside was a mural of the restaurant's namesake: the Aztec goddess of beauty. A previous generation of Manhattanites rejected the tamale men, but demand for Maldonado's meals was such that he opened a tortilla factory a floor above Xochitl.

Tacos were a popular item at Maldonado's restaurant, but the cooks hated them. Their grumblings about oil scaldings inspired Maldonado to create a contraption that allowed cooks to fry tortillas without ever having to touch them. His invention looked like a medieval torture device: Maldonado fashioned seven stainless-steel containers into elongated U's to hold fresh tortillas, then stacked them on top of each other and squeezed them into a box that held the maze together. He applied for a patent on the invention in 1947 and received it in 1950, just beating out Joe Pompa of Glendale, Arizona, who had applied for a patent for a similar device in 1949 but received it in 1951.

On the home front, Ashley's Inc. of El Paso encouraged housewives to make their own tacos. In 1952, George N. Ashley debuted a taco-frying mold, a crude aluminum device in which to place a tortilla and throw into the fryer to achieve a crispy U shape. Each mold came with instructions on how to use it, and a booklet titled *Mr. Taco Comes to America* that explained what a taco was, in pidgin English. "Eet ees my fondest hope, Senora," Mr. Taco concluded, "that we become the fast friends. For, een many ways, I can make your deeners and your fiestas beeg success!"

The *New York Times* celebrated Ashley's and Maldonado's efforts to simplify making fried tacos, which they described as a "savory delicacy, little known to New Yorkers."[9] But Maldonado's invention never caught on in restaurants, and he continued running Xochitl until passing away in anonymity in the Jackson Heights section of Queens, New York, at age eighty-two in 1980. By that point the world credited the prefabricated commercial taco shell to another man: Glen Bell, the founder of Taco Bell.

Glen Bell's maternal grandparents, hardy Minnesotans, moved to

California in 1914. His mother grew up in luxury, as her father had invested wisely in the Southern California real-estate market of the early twentieth century. However, Glen, the second of six children, spent his childhood and teens in unfortunate poverty, with an itinerant father who abandoned the family and a mother too proud to ask her wealthy parents for handouts. In his self-published biography, *Taco Titan: The Glen Bell Story*, the millionaire bitterly recounts the embarrassment he felt as a teen when a girl realized the shirt he wore at school was sewn together from used cement sacks.

World War II finally earned Bell a steady paycheck, and he joined the Marine Corps, assigned to a ship heading toward Guadalcanal. He never saw any action; instead, luck had him work mostly in the mess halls as a waiter and server. Upon returning home, Bell often met his best friend at McDonald's Drive-in in San Bernardino, run by the McDonald brothers. Bell always had an entrepreneurial streak in him—at age five, he supposedly blurted, "When I grow up, I want to be a businessman like my grandpa."[10] And in the parking lot of this restaurant, enjoying the hamburgers that launched the ultimate fast-food behemoth, Bell simmered with jealousy. "You could look in the carport behind the restaurant and see their new Cadillacs," Bell told his biographer in *Taco Titan*.

San Bernardino, about sixty miles east of Los Angeles, was in its initial stages of becoming America's fast-food incubator. Long a center of agriculture, near deserts and mountains, the city was best known nationally as the last major city on Route 66, the famed highway that brought so many people to California, before the Mother Road swung into Los Angeles. After World War II, with veterans looking for an affordable existence away from inner cities, San Bernardino and the towns around it (collectively known in Southern California parlance as the Inland Empire) grew rapidly. Car culture demanded quick meals, and the McDonalds were already mastering the form. Across the Southland, restaurants expanded beyond cafeterias and jacket-only places to keep up with the demand for this new fast dining experience.

Bell wanted in, and opened Bell's Hamburgers and Hot Dogs in San Bernardino in 1948, not far from the original McDonald's; within a year, he sold that stand to his sister's in-laws and opened another. On days off, Bell patronized the Mexican restaurants on San Bernardino's West Side, the city's historic barrio. He noticed how more and more non-Mexicans were eating Mexican food—this in a city that had just desegregated its swimming pools and was about to desegregate housing and schools. Feeling that tacos were the way to beat the McDonald's, Bell passed the idea by his wife, who dismissed it as foolish: whites wouldn't buy the food because it was too spicy, she argued. When Glen suggested toning down the heat, his soon-to-be-ex retorted, "Then even Mexicans won't buy it."

Undeterred, he opened a third Bell's Burgers in 1950 on the West Side, across the street from a Mexican restaurant and down the street from a tortilla factory that enveloped the block with the smell of fresh masa every morning. Bell ate at the neighboring Mexican restaurant frequently, especially favoring the tacos, which he dismissed as "delicious but dripp[ing] melted fat." He'd return to his stand to sell food, but spent late nights after closing time trying to decipher the rival restaurant's tacos, so popular that they opened a walk-up window next to the kitchen so the lines ran faster.

Frying each shell to order wore on Bell's fingers. He fashioned a wire basket that fried six tortillas at a time, and a "taco rail" that allowed him to hold those shells until someone placed an order; at that point all Bell needed to do was dump on the ingredients. "I figured if Mexican food was successful, potential competition would write it off to my location and assume the idea wouldn't sell anywhere else," he's quoted as saying in *Taco Titan*. "No one would copy what I was doing, and that would give me time to perfect it."

Bell's tacos debuted in December 1951. They were simple constructions: prefried shell, ground beef, chopped lettuce, shredded cheese, and a chili sauce Bell modified from the same condiment used on his chili dogs. Tellingly, the Latinos who frequented his stand eschewed the tacos in favor of hot dogs and hamburgers. He racked up sales that opening day, but no one wanted the tacos. Finally, a white man ordered one, mispronouncing it as "take-oh." The shell was already cold, waiting for its fillings; Bell prepared it and handed it to the gentleman. Juice from the ground beef inside dribbled on his pinstriped suit, but the man ordered another. Bell was ecstatic.

"I didn't invent the taco," Bell boasted, "but I believe I improved it."

The pleasure was short-lived: Bell was so driven by success that he neglected his family, prompting his wife to file for divorce; she took the West Side stand as part of the divorce settlement. But the taco bug never left Bell. He opened two other burger stands farther east, in the desert cities of Barstow and Indio. The original intention with the Barstow stand was to sell only tacos, but Bell decided just before opening to sell American fast food as well. The tacos outsold all other items, however, giving Bell the courage to go only Mexican. The following year, 1954, Bell planned for a Mexican restaurant on Baseline Street, one of San Bernardino's main thoroughfares, about a mile from his original West Side restaurant and a mile from the original McDonald's. He leased a former diner with a soaring marquee and neon lights, and hired an art student to conceptualize a look that was Mexican enough to entice eaters but not so Mexican that it reminded them of the nearby West Side. The art student suggested Bell name the new restaurant "La Tapatia," a flowing name that referred to the women of the Mexican city of Guadalajara, long famed for their beauty, and one attractive to Mexican customers. Bell's business partner vetoed the suggestion, arguing it was too ethnic, and suggested the nonsense Taco-Tia ("Taco Aunt"), which he felt was easier to pronounce.

For the opening of Taco-Tia, Bell bought thousands of sombreros made from shredded palm leaves extending off the brim of the hat, standing up, so that it looked like some culinary Medusa; all read "Taco-Tia" on the brim. His brother nailed the hats to a truck and drove around town, hoping to attract people to the restaurant's opening that night. Children stole the hats at every stop sign and proceeded to wear them, providing even more advertising. The opening-night crowd numbered in the hundreds, all looking to try these newfangled tacos. Bell also hired strolling mariachis, women dressed like Spanish maidens snapping castanets, and spotlights highlighting the black desert sky. It was an opening Bell repeated for decades.

Bell became a fast-food Johnny Appleseed. He sold Taco-Tia and opened another chain, El Taco, along with former NFL players Harland Svare and Charley Toogood and Phil Crosby, son of entertainment legend Bing. They opened six before Bell sold his interest in that chain in 1961, opening a hot dog stand in the oil town of Wilmington; he gave that business to John Galardi, a longtime Bell employee who started at Taco-Tia and moved with him to El Taco; that wiener business became Wienerschnitzel, a name suggested by Bell's second wife. Bell's ideas were endless, but he kept the best one to himself: Taco Bell, which he launched in 1962 in the Los Angeles suburb of Downey.

At this point, Bell's taco restaurants were only ostensibly Mexican—a Spanish title, the fiesta-themed grand opening, and a mascot. El Taco's mascot was a sombrero emblazoned with "El Taco" worn by a Mexican man with a drooping mustache, face clenched as if constipated. For his newest venture, Bell went the full enchilada. His template for all future Taco Bell buildings used the Spanish Revival architecture style popular in Southern California so that each outpost looked like a mini-mission, archways looping around the mock adobe exterior, tiled roof, and even a mock bell tower topping each restaurant. At each restaurant would be a statue of a little Mexican boy, wearing the sandals, white pajamas, and sombrero outfit seared into the American psyche by the Speedy Gonzalez cartoons of the 1950s. It was a slice of fantasy Mexican California plopped into suburbia, and a motif that has influenced the aesthetic designs of Mexican restaurants ever since.

Taco Bell sold only five items at its opening—tacos, tostadas, burritos, a side order of pinto beans, and chiliburgers—but America didn't mind. Bell launched a franchising platform in 1964; by 1967, a hundred Taco Bells existed in California. By the end of the decade, Bell was opening two new spots a week. He ventured away from the Southwest, to places where Mexican food was a rumor. In St. Petersburg, Florida, he took out ads with pictures of his menu and a pronunciation guide, taking that idea from competitors. The eateries succeeded in Texas, the Midwest—everywhere. By the time Bell approved a merger with PepsiCo in 1978, the number of Taco Bells numbered more than eight hundred. Today there are more than fifty-eight hundred Taco Bells, spanning the globe, with annual revenue reaching into the billions.

"We changed the eating habits of an entire nation," Bell states near the end of *Taco Titan,* and for once he isn't merely self-mythologizing. Bell showed other Americans that their countrymen hungered for Mexican grub sold to them fast, cheap, and with only a smattering of ethnicity. Tacos the way Mexicans ate them were out of the question: tortilla factories were still concentrated in the Southwest, and tortillas didn't last long. Preformed shells, on the other hand, lasted weeks and just needed reheating before getting filled.

The day Bell's merger with PepsiCo was announced, Phil Crosby admitted to Bell's biographer, "I choked on my drink," apoplectic at missing out on the business opportunity of a generation. But Crosby was wrong—there was room for more than just Taco Bell. Even as Bell expanded to Florida and the rest of the Southwest, other men established taco fiefdoms outside the American Southwest over the next two decades. World War II navy veteran Ron Fraedrick opened TacoTime in Eugene, near the University of Oregon, in 1960, after having tried Mexican food for the first time a year earlier while visiting Southern California on business. The chain eschewed the American Southwest, concentrating instead on the Pacific Northwest and the Midwest and even across the Pacific: Fraedrick became the first American to ever attempt opening a Mexican restaurant in Japan, during the 1980s. TacoTime's quick success convinced Frank Tonkin in 1962 to turn his drive-in restaurant in the Seattle suburb of Renton into a TacoTime franchise. He and his family went on to open seventy-five locations, all of them in Washington, dominating that state's fast-food taco industry so completely that the family entered into an agreement with the TacoTime company in 1979 that allowed them complete control over all TacoTimes in western Washington. Together they count more than three hundred locations worldwide.

In Wichita, Dan Foley opened Taco Tico in 1962, expanding to more than a hundred locations. In the Panhandle town of Abilene, Bill Waugh created Taco Bueno in 1967 after the El Chico brand of sit-down Tex-Mex restaurants rejected his application for a franchise, feeling no Mexican restaurant stood a chance in that area.[11] Bueno's outposts now number nearly two hundred, almost all of them in the mid-Midwest. And Taco Bueno's success spurred James and Susan Garner to open Taco Mayo in Norman, Oklahoma, in 1978—like TacoTime, in a college town wanting cheap food; there are now more than a hundred locations, almost all in Oklahoma. By this time even smaller taco chains opened everywhere, from New England to Alaska, creating a nation awash in hard-shell heaven.

Taco Bell's main rival, however, came from a former employee of Glen's. Ed Hackbarth had worked at the first Bell's Hamburgers that sold tacos, until Bell's ex-wife fired him after she assumed ownership following the couple's divorce. Bell rehired Hackbarth to operate his burger stand in Barstow, a hellhole in the Mojave desert best known as a resting place between Los Angeles and Las Vegas, with the promise of half of the store if he endured Barstow's brutal weather. A decade later, Hackbarth opened his own taco stand in Yermo, a town fifteen miles east of Barstow and even more forsaken than Barstow. Called Casa del Taco (House of the Taco), its fast success convinced Hackbarth to open three other Casa del Tacos, changing the name of his incipient chain to Del Taco. His employee Dick Naugles then spun off to open another taco chain: Naugles, which grew to more than two hundred locations before merging with Del Taco in the 1980. Hackbarth sold his ownership in Del Taco in 1976 but retained the rights to franchise, and he continues to run locations into his august years; the chain he started now has more than five hundred branches throughout the United States, lagging far behind Taco Bell but still growing.

Exit 132 off Interstate 29 in Brookings, South Dakota, offers two possibilities. A right takes drivers through miles of farms, flatlands that stretch to the horizon, cut up into grids by country roads and picturesque barns, a scenic route that leads nowhere. But a left at the light winds through the town of nineteen thousand, most famous regionally for being the home of South Dakota State University, the state's premier college. The town is more than 95 percent white, and most of the fewer than 1 percent of Latinos in the city are either instructors or students—and yet there are four Mexican restaurants to serve the hungry.

Guadalajara is the town's sole sit-down restaurant, a South Dakota chain with locations in Pierre and something called Spearfish. The food is fine, a mishmash of tacos, burritos, and combo plates with Mexican flourishes—talk to the waiters in Spanish, and their faces brighten; they'll trot out the secret salsa they make for themselves but don't dare share with most customers for fear of torching their tongues. A Qdoba Mexican Grill is also in town, gleaming and vibrant, and attracting a largely student population; the Taco Express sells out of a gas station.

The most popular Mexican restaurant in Brookings is right next to South Dakota State, in a low-slung building of white and orange and yellow tones, evoking the Southwest but looking from the outside like a fabric store. It's Taco John's, the third-largest taco chain in the United States, and one hell of an anomaly. On a brisk morning—and what morning in South Dakota isn't brisk?—the wait in the drive-through already stretches for minutes as coed and businessman alike wait for a fresh batch of Potato Olés. Tater Tots. Found inside flour-tortilla tacos, snuggling against rivulets of sausage and eggs. They're also inside a burrito, the nacho cheese sauce slowly oozing out, each bite into the golden-brown Potato Olés unleashing spurts of sweet grease. Or as part of a scramble, mixed up with green peppers, onions, and shredded cheese, adding body. And most popularly served in small buckets, the better to make them last for a couple of minutes.

There is nothing Mexican about Potato Olés. But they have spurred more than 425 Taco John's across the United States. Only one location exists in Arizona and New Mexico, respectively, three operate in Texas, and none in California. Instead, the chain focuses on the upper Midwest, from Idaho through Wisconsin, and no farther south than the nook connecting Kentucky, Indiana, Illinois, Tennessee, and Missouri. Not exactly where Mexicans roam—but what else to expect from a chain that started in Wyoming?

Air force veteran John Turner opened a restaurant called Taco House in Cheyenne, Wyoming, in 1968. The restaurant offered a menu nearly identical to Taco Bell's—hard-shelled ground beef tacos, beans, tostadas, and burritos—but Taco Bell wasn't anywhere around, ensuring a fast-food Mexican monopoly across Wyoming. James Woodson, owner of the building that Taco House occupied, and another local businessman, Harold Holmes, bought the franchising rights to the restaurant from Turner and his recipes; using their real-estate know-how, they expanded. Like the other regional chains, Taco John's focused on the small towns across the upper Midwest that the larger fast-food franchises, Mexican and not, ignored in favor of urban and suburban America. This is no bumpkin chain, however. In 1989, they applied for and received the trademark for Taco Tuesday, the nearly universal term for specials on that day of the week. They also are the official carriers of Choco Taco, a waffle stuffed with vanilla and covered in chocolate, a product more Mexican than Breyers might ever know. And they conduct business under a self-created moniker: West-Mex.

"People have always said, 'You taste different,'" says Renee Middleton, vice president of marketing and with Taco John's since 1985. "We started with just a man making tacos, and everything goes. Who would've ever thought of putting Tater Tots in a burrito? That's the classic Western mentality. We take that permission of being slightly different and classify ourselves as West-Mex. Our quality service, our small-town focus is West-Mex."

Far removed from areas that historically received Mexican immigration, Taco John's was able to capitalize on that isolation in their efforts to succeed with their Potato Olé's, a "Mexican" snack Middleton admits is bizarre for the average fan of Mexican. "Putting them inside a burrito has had people ask me, 'What are you smoking?'" she say with a laugh. "But it's our flavor—it's our trademark."

Other tacos emerged in the 1980s once America accustomed itself to the hard-shell taco. Restaurants began serving *tacos al carbón*—tacos featuring grilled meats on soft corn tortillas, what Mexicans had eaten at home for decades. Somewhere in the passing on, someone decided to rename them "soft tacos," then "street tacos."

Fish tacos came by way of Ralph Rubio, who opened a Rubio's in the San Diego neighborhood of Mission Bay in 1983. For years, surfers such as Rubio had enjoyed fish tacos in Baja California from seaside posts that grilled freshly caught catches. The success of Rubio's convinced other California companies to also specialize in fish tacos— Wahoo's (operated by the Lams, a trio of brothers born to Chinese parents in São Paulo, Brazil, but raised in Orange County) opened in 1988, while Baja Fresh Mexican Grill started in 1990 and now operates more than 250 locations. The fast-food taco chains incorporated fish and soft tacos into their menus, testament to the taco's mutability and Americans' ceaseless hunger for them.

The Mexicans who unwittingly sparked the taco torrent? Funny you ask. . . .

The corner of Mount Vernon Avenue and Sixth Street in San Bernardino isn't the prettiest intersection in the city. One corner is an empty lot; the other has two abandoned businesses. Graffiti sullies fences, light posts, even the sidewalks. This is the Garden of Gethsemane for the American taco industry.

On one side is Mitla Cafe, the oldest continually operating Mexican restaurant in the Inland Empire, since 1937. It's a roadside classic befitting Route 66, of which Mount Vernon is a part. One part of the restaurant is a counter, where patrons eat and gab while watching television; the other side is a cavernous room with few decorations, as homely as it is classic save for the big picture of the restaurant's founder.

The menu has been almost unchanged since its opening, a snapshot of a previous time—chile rellenos, enchiladas, chile verde and pork, and a dish called the Gloria, after a longtime server: two tortillas wrapped around juicy chicken chunks, bathed in a light salsa, then placed on top of baked cheese, a sort of backward enchilada. But the best sellers at Mitla are their hard-shelled tacos, fried upon order, bursting with ground meat, hiding under a blizzard of shredded cheese. It's a refreshing take on the meal, light-years away from the prefabricated mess America has worshipped for nearly two generations—and it's the taco Glen Bell "adopted." It's the taco Bell ate again and again, trying to decipher its mystery before returning to his Bell's Burgers across the street to replicate.

"He used to come over here all the time," says Irma Montaño, whose in-laws opened the restaurant. She's in her seventies, feisty and commanding waitresses. "My father-in-law would say Mr. Bell kept asking about the tacos, how he made them, and so my father-in-law finally invited him into the kitchen to teach him."

Does Montaño feel cheated that Mitla's tacos spawned a worldwide industry? She smiles—she's of a different generation, one that doesn't easily lob insults or engage in jealousy. "Good for him," she says, repeating it. "He was a self-starter, and he did push those tacos." She smiles again, and walks into the kitchen.

The building that housed Bell's Burgers still stands across from Mitla, a tiny building with a menu not far removed from what Bell envisioned—tacos and burgers. Except the menu has now expanded to serve soft tacos, and a banner advertises menudo on Saturday and Sunday. Nearly sixty years after Bell, it's now Mexican immigrants who sell tacos to Mexican immigrants from this place, now called Amapola Rico Taco.

When a customer asks for a hard-shelled taco with ground beef, the order is repeated in Spanish—*taco dorado con carne molida*. A cook grabs a corn tortilla, places it in a canister, and fries it. No prefabricated mess here—it's the real deal, the opposite of what Bell envisioned. The young lady running the counter doesn't know the history of the building and doesn't care. It's a chilly afternoon, the wind blowing and the clouds unleashing the heavy mist that classifies the typical Southern California rainstorm. Across the street, Mitla Cafe's mascot stares directly at the former Bell's Burgers, stares with a smile, just next to the slogan "Real Mexican Food." Mitla might not have the riches, might never have capitalized on its tacos, but it gets the last laugh.

The Taco Bell taco is dead. Long live the taco.

Chapter Four

Who Were the Enchilada Millionaires, and How Did They Change Mexican Food?

The fast-food taco chains were a gateway drug; no, scratch that. They were a bridge, a guide, for the American gut. From chili con carne and tamales to tacos, cooks and customers alike steadily graduated toward a proper Mexican restaurant experience, a place for a family to enjoy a full dinner instead of snacks. If the tamale men were the scouts to gauge American interest in Mexican food and the taco houses the explorers, then what followed were the colonists, the settlers, the tamers of the frontier: the Mexican sit-down restaurant.

One of those Pilgrims is Larry Cano, the founder of El Torito, a chain that's starting to disappear from the country's landscape but that once ruled casual dining across the country. I met him in the winter of 2010 at a since-shuttered El Torito Grill that stood just upstreet from Angels Stadium of Anaheim. We sat in a booth along with a friend, the octogenarian Cano dashing in a leather jacket and tie.

A waiter approached us. "Would the table care for a tableside margarita?" he asked. The table would. He grabbed a cocktail shaker filled with ice, poured in two shots of 1800 Tequila, vigorously shook the gleaming container for about thirty seconds, then placed it on a tray he set up for the rite. He then rubbed the rim of a goblet with a lime wedge, flipped it upside down, and pressed it onto a circular canister packed with salt, so that granules stuck to the rim.

On invisible Bose speakers, legendary *ranchera* singer Miguel Aceves Mejia hit the impossibly high notes of "La Malagueña" ("The Lady from Malaga"), the *huapango* that paints as best a romantic, nostalgic image of Old Mexico as any song ever composed. The waiter poured the margarita into the glass and placed the drink in front of us. Smooth and tart. We smiled in approval. And the Miles Standish of Mexican food beamed.

"We popularized the margarita in America, you know," Cano stated, with the confidence of memory and pride in a lifetime of work that the founder of a restaurant kingdom has every right to exhibit. "Back at my first restaurant, two young women came in and wanted to spend big at the bar—they had just received a bonus. They ordered a frozen daiquiri, which was really popular at the time. I thought that I should do something like that, except with tequila. I served it to them the next time they came in, and they asked for it again. From there, we started making it better."

Larry Cano at an El Torito Grill in Anaheim, California. Cano's El Torito chain blazed through the United States during the 1970s and 1980s, introducing sit-down Mexican eateries outside the American Southwest. *(Photo by John Gilhooley)*

Any conversation with Cano—any conversation with any pioneer of Mexican cuisine in the United States—comes with a side of such boasts. El Torito spread the practice of tableside guacamole, if you believe Cano. Of the sizzling fajitas platter. Flour tortillas with butter. A public tortilla-making station. Taco Tuesday. The history of Mexican food is peppered with such fantastic, impossible-to-prove claims regarding the genesis of any number of foodstuffs.

But in the case of Cano, the claims he utters are almost all true. It was Cano who took El Torito from a tiki bar in the wealthy Los Angeles neighborhood of Encino to one of the largest Mexican restaurant chains in the United States in its heyday. His company customized California-Mexican cuisine—the endless combos of enchiladas, chile rellenos, burritos, tacos, and guacamole that numerous American families order for dinner every night at their local Mexican restaurant—for the mainstream, while maintaining a proud, nondemeaning Mexican identity. El Torito rescued the meals from the mythologizing amnesia of Southern California and introduced them to areas where customers didn't know how to pronounce the meals they waited for in hour-long lines. Cano weathered vicious restaurant wars, personal missteps, and imitators to achieve an exalted position.

Go grab the next bag of tortilla chips and let Cano spin a yarn.

On a Sunday afternoon on Olvera Street, kids dart from stall to stall while their frantic parents try to spot them in the crowds. A health fair has set up booths near the southern edge, around the plaza where a statue of a Spanish king stands.

In this, the second-largest Mexican city in the world, the conquistadors still reign.

Just north of the statue, in the middle of Olvera Street, stands the Old Mexican village commissioned by Los Angeles's civic fathers and mothers, virtually unchanged in structure and outlook since its opening, with one vital exception: the disappeared mural. In 1932, just a year after Olvera Street's debut, its operators asked the great Mexican muralist David Alfaro Siqueiros to paint a crowning diorama of a tropical America, the better to immortalize what they had reinvented. Instead, Siqueiros created a huge, damning statement on U.S. Latin American policy, complete with an indigenous man on a cross, the American eagle menacingly perched on top of him like those that continuously ate the liver of Prometheus. It scandalized Olvera Street's founder, Christine Sterling, and the rest of the city's elite, who ordered the mural whitewashed and Siqueiros deported. *La América Tropical* stayed hidden from public view and history until the 1960s, by which time the elements washed enough white away so that ghostly outlines emerged. The mural is currently undergoing a restoration effort sponsored by a new generation of city fathers, its promise intimidating: you can hide the Mexican, but the Mexican will emerge.

Olvera Street's stands still offer trinkets—marionettes, sombreros, religious icons, and other tourist magnets. But the main business is now restaurants—Cielito Lindo and Las Anitas, yes, but also more-elaborate places that continue to sell Sterling's imagined past with Cadillac margaritas, strolling mariachis, and enchilada platters, nachos, and taquitos. El Paseo Inn and El Rancho Grande, La Golondrina and others, many dating back decades, with La Golondrina topping them all, operating since 1924—since before there was an Olvera Street.

A trio plays "La Malagueña"—that song again! Although played by Mexicans and written by one, it's actually about an unreachable, gorgeous Spanish lady who rejects the singer. "If for poor you scorn me, I understand," he warbles. "I don't offer you riches, I offer you my heart."

She doesn't care.

Until Cano came along, such was the dual nature of Mexican cuisine in California: food that was really Mexican, but masqueraded as Spanish. It's a schizophrenia explained by the settlement and foundation of the state, and its messy assimilation into the United States, an assimilation different from its Texas cousin in the sense that California has never made peace with its Mexican past, present, and future.

The first Europeans to enter what's now California was an expedition led by Gaspar de Portolà in 1769. They marched from San Diego to the San Francisco Bay; accompanying them were Spanish friars of the Franciscan order charged with creating a network of Catholic missions across the state. Twenty-one of them were established, from San Diego to Sonoma, all connected by a six-hundred-mile trail called El Camino Real (The Royal Highway), now roughly covered by Interstate 5 from the U.S.-Mexico border up to Los Angeles, then Highway 101 from the City of Angels to San Francisco Bay.

Those Franciscan fathers introduced to the territory the foodstuffs of their native Spain—olives, cattle, winemaking, ranching, and nonnative plant species. Wine accompanied nearly every meal, as did a bowl of olives. Tamales were present, of course, and beef was the meat of choice, as cattle became a big industry in the region. Other items made their way up north as Mexicans trickled in, but the California-Mexican diet distinguished itself from the rest of the country.

So did the people. Since many of the original European inhabitants didn't have any blood ties to Mexico—or pretended not to, since pure-blooded Spaniards were at the top of colonial Mexico, mixed-raced individuals in the low middle, and Indians the perpetual Other—California's residents didn't consider themselves Mexicans but instead Californios. Even after California became part of Mexico upon the country's independence from Spain, the region's inhabitants thought of themselves differently from their fellow Mexican citizens—they were *gente de razón* (people of reason), a term that distinguished them from the Indians or those of mixed blood, frequently called *cholos*.

The old ways changed forever, though, with the addition of California to the United States following the Mexican-American War. Many of those Californio families suffered financial ruin in the first few decades after annexation, as Americans squatted on their land grants and as unsympathetic judges refused to accept their deeds issued by the Spanish crown and the Mexican government. The flood of migrants from the United States rarely bothered to distinguish between the long-standing Californio and any recently arrived Mexican; to them, they were all greasers. Americans reviled the Californio conventions, especially the grand soirees that the Californios hosted for themselves and the food eaten at them.

Attitudes about Mexicans in California changed dramatically, however, after the publication of *Ramona,* an 1884 book by Helen Hunt Jackson that sought to expose the plight of California's Indians and the discriminated Californios by imagining a tale of doomed romance between a half-Scot, half-Indian woman and an Indian sheepherder. Instead, the novel created a national bout of nostalgia for the days of the Californios, the forgotten race, the race of leisure, romanticism, and feasts. Not being stupid, the Southern California civic fathers who discriminated against Californios created a tourism industry around this reimagined history, and the rapidly expanding middle and upper classes of California strip-mined the lifestyle of those vanquished Californios. Unsurprisingly, the Anglo celebrants of the *Ramona* days didn't celebrate the era as Mexican or Californio, but "Spanish." It was European men such as Portolà, after all, who had tamed the land, Spaniards such as Father Junipero Serra who kept the region from devolving into anarchy like its sister states to the south. Soon Southern California's elites hosted "Spanish" dinners for themselves,[1] or to impress out-of-towners with the region's "native" culture—even though the food was actually Mexican.[2]

To identify as Mexican in California during the first part of the twentieth century was a dangerous proposition. Segregation was enforced in schools, housing, even in swimming pools. By passing as "Spanish," Mexicans plugged into the memory of the Californios, of *Ramona,* and of everything that Americans such as Sterling and Chandler idealized. In Southern California, an acceptable ethnic alternative was Sonoran, since it was a group of immigrants from that northern Mexico state who had originally settled Los Angeles and who provided most of Los Angeles's Mexican immigrants until the Mexican Revolution. The earliest Mexican restaurants in Southern California therefore called themselves Spanish or Sonoran—anything but Mexican.

The first appetizer of the evening arrives: shredded chicken taquitos accompanied by a red pepper sauce that features a splash of guacamole mousse. The table digs in; slivers of fried tortilla snap and fly off mouths. They're done within minutes.

Cano—skinny, with a full head of ivory-white hair, strong eyes, and the simultaneously stentorian yet kind voice of an *abuelito*—nibbles on one. "Delicious," he says. He was born in East Los Angeles in 1924, the son of a Mexican immigrant from Chihuahua and a mother from San Antonio, with a childhood typical for a young Mexican-American man growing up in Southern California during that era—a hardscrabble upbringing of segregation, work at a young age, and a transformation into manhood during World War II after Cano forsook UCLA to do two tours of Europe in a P-51 Mustang fighter aircraft. After the war, Cano and a friend visited Mexico City for Christmas vacation. "We were treated like kings because of our uniforms," Cano remembers. "There was one restaurant where they told us the tables were full and we couldn't get served. We went back to our hotels and put on our uniforms. The service came quickly after that. That was great, but it got me thinking that *all* customers should get that treatment. And it got me thinking about running a restaurant."

He returned to the States, graduating from the University of Southern California with a business degree before his unit was called to serve in Korea. After the war, Cano returned to Southern California and found a job as a bartender at a tiki-style restaurant called Bali Hai. The thirty-year-old became manager, which wasn't much of a promotion. "I cleaned up the puke, the bathrooms, everything," he says, now laughing but still cringing at the memory. He'd stay the night sometimes, looking to start the following day early, while raising a young family.

In 1954, Bali Hai's owner passed away, and the widow asked Cano if he wanted the bar. Cano knew that the tiki craze popular with veterans had a limited life, and tried to think of what the next big restaurant idea might be. "There weren't too many Mexican restaurants in the San Fernando Valley at the time," Cano said. "I needed a business to make my name, and I figured making a nice Mexican restaurant would do it." Part of the Bali Hai purchase included a ceramic bowl with a bull painted on the inside. From there came the idea to call his new restaurant El Torito—"Or at least, that's the story we tell, and we stick by it," Cano says with a laugh, admitting that the true story is lost to history.

El Torito started at a momentous time in the culinary history of Southern California. Out in the Inland Empire, the McDonald brothers and other fast-food pioneers continued to modify their operations, setting the standards that defined fast-food restaurants for generations. Across the Southland, diners who once classified themselves as "Spanish" shook off the label's fantasy heritage and finally advertised themselves as Mexican. More taco houses surfaced in the suburbs, opened by non-Mexicans looking to make money on customers' demands. A few Mexican restaurants in Southern California opened outside the nexus of Olvera Street—El Cholo Café, the second-oldest continually operating Mexican restaurant in the United States (since 1923), became popular with the Hollywood crowd, while El Coyote (opened in 1931 by husband and wife George and Blanche March) set up near the city's ritzy Westside—but that sit-down scene had yet to establish itself, something Cano knew when he got the idea to purchase Bali Hai.

Cano wasn't much of a cook, so he hired Mexican-born chefs and ordered them to cook what they, as *mexicanos,* ate—but with an eye toward the mainstream. "You have to operate in the area where you are in," Cano rationalizes. "You have to do what you have to do. It would be ridiculous to have spicy food for the first time someone tries Mexican food and kill them. We're talking about the masses."

Success wasn't guaranteed. In the first couple of months, Cano and his young family got evicted from their home, forcing Cano to live in the restaurant while putting up his wife and children with relatives; he built bunkers outside El Torito as a temporary dwelling. Luckily, Encino was one of the better-off neighborhoods of Los Angeles, an enclave of veterans and movie executives more adventurous with their dinners than average suburbanites. Knowing his customers thought better of themselves than their neighbors and wanted to spend more, Cano strove to upscale his new restaurant. "If you greet a guest by their first name, they have already had a good time," Cano said. "Anything we could do to gain an advantage, we did. After all, we were just selling Mexican food."

Tables were covered in white cloth; the *mexicanidad* of the restaurant, while present, was kept to a tasteful din. The concept succeeded; within a year, Cano opened a second location, in Toluca Lake; he started a third one a year after that in Hollywood. Cano remembers the stars who frequented those establishments: Gregory Peck, Lana Turner, John Wayne. Anthony Quinn always demanded a bottle of tequila and got incensed whenever one of his dates forgot to order rice. Roy Disney ended his nights there, always in a booth, always alone.

Another celebrity frequented El Torito as well in those early years. One day, while working in the kitchen, Cano noticed a car parked just outside his Encino restaurant, with a man staring at him inside. A week later, Cano saw the same car, the same man sitting in the car for a long time. An infuriated Cano walked toward the car and demanded to know why he was there. The man introduced himself as Glen Bell and told him, "We're starting a restaurant operation and wanted to see what you're doing."

"I should've charged him for spying on me," Cano now says with a laugh. "That's fine—we did better."

A 1959 ad in the *Los Angeles Times* reflects Cano's plan to mainstream Mexican food. It featured a bean on its back, limbs flailing, and read, "This is a 'Has-Bean.' He's gone stale—so he'll never make it to El Torito—where his lucky pals are not only getting fried daily—but even refried." Under the legume read the slogan "The Ultimate in Fine Mexican Food."

El Torito continued to expand over the next decade, always focusing on upscale communities, the better to target disposable incomes and people looking to try the latest in Mexican food. With each new opening, Cano tinkered with his formula. He claims credit for the Mexican Sunday brunch accompanied by mariachis that any self-respecting sit-down restaurant now stages, along with Mexican restaurants inside a mall and the idea of Taco Tuesday. Each new El Torito offered bigger and bigger bars and patios, the better to entice singles in for their margaritas—at one point, according to company records, El Torito was buying more tequila than any other restaurant chain in the United States. "People came to us to eat tacos, sure," Cano says. "They were really popular at the time. But if all you wanted was that, you'd go to other places. We gave people a great time."

Across Southern California, other restaurants mimicked Cano's innovations, and corporate America took notice. Buyout offers poured in—from competitors, from investors, even from businesses that had no previous experience operating restaurants. "The head of Carnation Milk once took me to lunch in New York," Cano says. "He told me, 'Whatever someone offers you, I'll top it by a million.'" He declined that offer, but the money proved too tempting. In 1976, Cano sold El Torito to W. R. Grace & Co., a multinational chemical company trying to diversify its holdings. Cano had opened twenty-two El Toritos, stretching from Denver to Seattle and all across Southern California, and had amassed a sizable personal worth—but the company still carried debt Cano wanted to retire. Upon buying the company from him for about $20 million, W. R. Grace immediately hired him as president of El Torito with a simple directive: expand. And fast.

Shortly after the sale, Cano had his trusted troops rushing to open El Toritos in places where sit-down Mexican food wasn't already established. He put new employees through nine days of training that came complete with glossaries, menus, the history of certain dishes, even phonetic pronunciations to ensure that waiters didn't flub the proper name of a meal. He had to: the Mongols were on the horizon.

Although El Torito had the advantage of already owning the California market, they faced stiff competition elsewhere. In Texas, a state that beat California to the mainstreaming of Mexican food by decades, "we just got killed," Cano admits. Elsewhere they came up against Chi-Chi's, a chain started in Minnesota by Marno McDermott and former Green Bay Packers star Max McGee. McDermott had previously opened a chain of Taco Bell–esque restaurants called Zapata's, after the Mexican revolutionary leader, but once Taco Bell and its competitors set up camp in the Twin Cities, McDermott sold the Zapata's concept to Kentucky Fried Chicken and opened Chi-Chi's Restaurant in a Minneapolis suburb in 1975.

It was a year before Cano sold El Torito, and Chi-Chi's mimicked Cano's concepts, from dressing women as peasant Mexicans to offering a glossary of items and a pronunciation guide while placing an emphasis on the bar. But this was Mexican food for non-Mexicans who only knew it through fast-food tacos. Even the restaurant's name—the nickname for McDermott's wife, but also crude Mexican Spanish slang for breasts—indicated McDermott's strategy. "You think a name like Chi-Chi's would work in Southern California?" Cano says. "He'd be laughed out of the state."

The two chains found themselves opening restaurants in the same cities during the 1970s at the same time, simultaneously fending off copycat competitors such as Ramón Gallardo. He had moved to St.

Louis in 1960, after stints as a dishwasher in Southern California and a chef's assistant in Chicago. The Mexico City native transitioned into managing restaurants before a boss asked him to take over La Sala, one of a handful of Mexican restaurants in St. Louis at the time.

"I didn't know anything about Mexican food," Gallardo told a reporter years later. "I did some research around town, about what people perceive as Mexican food. I called my family in Mexico for recipes. I made up a new menu, made a few changes, hired a new cook. We made money the first month. The place was packed."[3] Emboldened by the success, Gallardo opened Casa Gallardo in 1975. He hadn't even opened a second location before General Mills proposed a buyout, which he accepted. Casa Gallardo expanded to more than thirty locations, and Gallardo moved up in General Mills, becoming their primary adviser on expanding into the Mexican-food market. Once, Gallardo found himself in a Biltmore hotel in Santa Barbara, site of his first job in the United States, addressing General Mills's board of directors. To the audience's delight, Gallardo told them that this was the first time he had ever entered the Biltmore through the front door instead of the back. "I guess the secret to success is knowing how to make a good taco and a good margarita," he cracked. "Is this a great country or what?"[4]

Cano maintains he never considered Chi-Chi's or Casa Gallardo as a serious competitor, mainly because he and his crew were mostly Mexican, while McDermott was not and Gallardo didn't have the same homegrown team as El Torito. "They had no Mexican background," he says. "They had no restaurant background. They didn't care about authenticity—they just cared about the bottom line." But that approach worked for Chi-Chi's and Casa Gallardo. In 1982, when *Time* magazine ran an article on the rising popularity of Mexican dining titled "The Enchilada Millionaires," Cano got his picture in the profile—but Chi-Chi's earned the magazine's praise for having just gone public on Wall Street, and Gallardo's rags-to-riches story nabbed a mention instead of Cano's. The article noted that Mexican restaurants earned $3 billion in revenue the previous year, a 200 percent increase from as recently as 1977, and that "Mexican-food chains are hotter than chili peppers."[5]

Undeterred, Cano enlisted his soldiers for reconnaissance missions. "Larry was never content to rest on his laurels," says Lee Healy, a Newport Beach public-relations agent who worked as Cano's executive assistant for decades. "We would meet every Monday, and Larry would set people on fire to do great things. Instead of spending money on advertising, he emphasized the guest. Larry would say, 'Get on a plane, rent a car, find the lines at Mexican restaurants, and see why they're there.'" It was Healy who traveled to Texas and saw billboards for a restaurant named Ninfa's—credited with popularizing the fajitas platter in Texas as well as tacos al carbón. El Torito took Ninfa's tacos al carbón and fajitas, and presented the latter tableside in a sizzling cast-iron skillet, an idea a Cano associate observed at another restaurant.

"I'd tell workers to get into a restaurant and start learning—spy," Cano says unapologetically. "Stay a couple of weeks, get fired, then come back and tell us what you learned." Such subterfuge created an endless chain of copying; El Torito took a concept from a mom-and-pop; his competitors eyed what El Torito debuted and took it for themselves. And like a mime, the taco empires modified those ideas for their audience.

At El Torito's height, Cano opened fifty-four in one year. Meanwhile, back in Orange County, he opened other restaurants outside of the El Torito brand after a stranger snidely asked when he'd ever open a "real" restaurant. "That got to me, so I decided to buy some buildings and open new places," he said. In 1977, he debuted Cano's in Newport Beach, which predated the gourmet Mexican restaurant scene popularized by Rick Bayless by nearly a decade. Against the advice of his superiors, Cano bought a French eatery on the cliffs of Laguna Beach called the Victor Hugo Inn (immortalized in *Mildred Pierce*) in 1979 and renamed it Las Brisas, switching the menu to an emphasis on fine-dining Mexican seafood to catch eaters accustomed to coastal resort dining.

By 1988, El Torito operated 248 locations across the United States and took in annual sales of $500 million. They had bought out Casa Gallardo's in 1986 and other competitors. Chi-Chi's kept expanding as well, and other businessmen, Mexican and not, filled in the gap with stand-alone sit-downs. "I always had mole and *chile colorado* on my menus," Cano says. "They never sold in the early days, but it was *my* cuisine. We had to have them on because that authenticity distinguished us from everyone else. I couldn't conceive of preformed taco shells. It just wasn't my cultural experience. Sure, the food had to appeal to a larger audience, but not down to the level of others."

Cano figured it was time to retire as the company's president— "I thought I was getting old." He was sixty-four, a fixture on Orange County's society pages, and he wanted to ski. He'd keep Cano's and a couple of other restaurants, but he gave the reins of El Torito to others.

That's when the troubles began. Cano had to file for Chapter 7 bankruptcy in 1994; a judge ordered all his assets liquidated to satisfy creditors, which meant the closing of his beloved Cano's. Meanwhile, El Torito slowly contracted, a victim of the success it created as newer restaurants claiming they were an authentic alternative to El Torito opened, and a new wave of Mexican immigration introduced different flavors to the United States. In 1998, the company lost a lawsuit against Tortilla Flats of Laguna Beach for supposedly violating the restaurant's trademark on "Taco Tuesday"; terms of the settlement were never disclosed, but Tortilla Flats sought relief in the millions.

Chi-Chi's overtook El Torito nationally as the largest casual-dining Mexican chain in the country, but the company and McDermott faced its own problems. McDermott sold Chi-Chi's in the early 1980s to open Two Pesos, another chain that put an even bigger emphasis on the patio-dining concept Cano had revolutionized. He had originally sought to buy into Taco Cabana, a Texas chain similar to El Torito and Chi-Chi's. When the owners refused, McDermott based his Two Pesos on the Taco Cabana model, from menu to layout to even the use of garish colors on the outside, with Two Pesos using turquoise instead of Taco Cabana's pink.

Taco Cabana sued Two Pesos, and after appeal after appeal, the case reached the U.S. Supreme Court. The 1992 case *Two Pesos, Inc., v. Taco Cabana, Inc.,* was a landmark decision affecting trade dress, the legal concept that protects the intellectual rights of companies and individuals' designs and looks. Taco Cabana bought out Two Pesos a year after the decision and remains popular in Texas and the Midwest.

McDermott's former company fell under a succession of corporate owners after he left—at one point Chi-Chi's was even sister companies with El Torito. But Cano's prophecy proved true: instead of developing consistency, they followed only profits. By 1995, they had 210 locations; within a decade, all Chi-Chi's had closed, a product of mismanagement and a devastating outbreak of hepatitis A in its restaurants in 2003 that left hundreds severely ill and four dead. Chi-Chi's had filed for bankruptcy just a few months before the outbreak. By the time it closed its U.S. restaurant operations for good a year later, the former ambassador of Mexican food was reduced to sixty-five restaurants. It was no longer needed.

El Torito won the battle but also lost the war. In October 2011, parent company Real Mex filed for Chapter 11 bankruptcy; execs pointed their fingers at the Great Recession as their executioner, but the public no longer required its guiding hand to navigate the Mexican-food landscape Cano helped to establish. The pioneer, for his part, feels bad about El Torito's demise but doesn't look back. He regularly sets meetings with investors to pitch new restaurant concepts.

"The fusion of Mexican food with others is the next step," he says, bringing up Korean tacos. "I'm amazed that the *tamal* hasn't played a bigger role so far in Mexican food like the taco and burrito and enchiladas. Maybe there." He smiles—the enchilada millionaire is scheming anew.

Chapter Five

How Did Americans Become Experts at Writing Cookbooks on Mexican Food?

In the summer of 2010, I attended a fund-raiser for the CCNMA: Latino Journalists of California, a trade organization for—yep—Latino journalists. I attended for a couple of reasons: CCNMA is a great group that raises money for scholarships for aspiring Latino journalists entering a lily-white field. This also was a meeting organized in honor of Ruben Salazar, a pioneering Chicano journalist for the *Los Angeles Times* who lost his life to a tear-gas canister through the head fired by sheriffs while covering a demonstration in East Los Angeles in 1971.

I also attended to hear the keynote speaker: Jonathan Gold, the food critic for the *LA Weekly* (the mother paper of my home base, *OC Weekly*), and the only food critic ever to win a Pulitzer Prize. We correspond frequently, mostly via Facebook, but I had only met him thrice up to that evening. CCNMA had invited Gold to offer remarks on Salazar, which had some in the audience of professionals, reporters, and activists wondering what a gourmand knew about a martyr in their field.

Gold felt the same way, confessing his own incredulity about the idea of a restaurant reviewer offering the keynote address that night. But doubters obviously don't know Gold, who can wax poetic on everything from the complexity of a properly formed block of Chinese-style tofu to the poetics of gangsta rap and, yes, the history and importance of Ruben Salazar. After spending a couple of moments on Salazar's career, noting that the icon enjoyed nothing more than a fine French dinner while conversing with friends, Gold weaved a seamless transition onto the question of "authenticity" and how it pertained to Mexican cuisine.

The gossip in Southern California food circles during that time swirled around the opening of Red O, a restaurant that counted on Rick Bayless as a consultant. Bayless, of course, is one of the most famous chefs in the United States and perhaps the country's best-known booster of Mexican food. From his home base of Chicago, Bayless has created an industry: two restaurants, Frontera Grill and Topolobampo, which class up Mexican food to the realm of high cuisine, and a couple of smaller restaurants; multiple cookbooks, almost all instant best sellers; and the PBS series *Mexico: One Plate at a Time,* where Bayless teaches viewers about some of the rarer dishes in Mexico that he says are truly authentic, as opposed to the stale tacos and runny enchiladas he insists characterize Mexican food in this country. America's most ardent defender of "authentic" Mexican: not a bad gig for a boy from Oklahoma.

Everyone in the CCNMA audience knew of Bayless; some admitted to cooking from his books despite being of Mexican heritage, others had even dined at his restaurants. The question of whether a white man had the skills to cook Mexican food wasn't in question. But Gold took issue with Bayless, describing him as a "good" chef who knew his way around Mexican recipes, but sneering at Bayless's nerve in coming to Los Angeles and presuming to introduce Angelinos to "authentic" Mexican cuisine. In particular, Gold zeroed in on Red O's inclusion of *chilpachole* (a seafood soup from Veracruz) as some rarity; Gold said the soup was easily available in the Southland, alongside dozens of other Mexican regional specialties Bayless assumed didn't exist in the birthplace of Taco Bell and El Torito. Then Gold hit below the belt, describing the decor of Red O as "if it survived a nuclear blast," much to the mirth of the crowd.

The food critic went on to extol Southern California's homegrown Mexican cuisine—the burritos with no real ties to Mexico, yet wholly Mexican; the baked nachos; the tacos. Gold mentioned Lupe's #2, a legendary stand in East Los Angeles. The woman who had run it for decades wasn't Lupe, and there was no first location, but that was okay: their burritos were heroic, as he once wrote, "crackly skinned marvel . . . filled to order while the tortilla is still on the griddle so that it develops both intense toasted-grain flavor and spurting fumaroles of spicy beef stew if you are so bold as to slide it out of its paper wrapper as you eat."[1]

I wrote about Gold's mini-lecture for our *OC Weekly* food blog, "Stick a Fork in It," figuring it might spark a fun debate about the merits of Southern California's Mexican-American favorites. What I didn't expect, however, was for Bayless to not only read about the event but also respond. And bitchily:

> First of all, I'm incredulous that Jonathan Gold didn't check his facts. I know it's all the rage for journalists to go into unsupported hyperbole, but I never said I was going to introduce Southern California to "authentic" Mexican cuisine. I said I was going to bring the flavors of Frontera Grill to Los Angeles. Which is completely true. I guess getting a Pulitzer doesn't mean you're beholden to truth. But I'm sure it made for a "fun" evening for all gathered there. Such is the state of modern journalism.

Yikes! We have many "celebrity" commentators on our *OC Weekly* blogs, luminaries such as Abraham Lincoln, Pope Benedict XVI, and the ghost of Robert E. Lee. But this was the real Rick Bayless: not only did the URL match a Chicagoland IP address, but also Bayless tweeted the article to his fans, and they immediately attacked Gold and me.

Others jumped into the conversation as well. A source directed me to an interview Bayless gave to KNBC-TV, in which he explicitly says he helped open Red O because the expert was intrigued by "how the true flavors of Mexico, from central and southern Mexico, would play in Southern California." I updated the post—all of this on a Sunday afternoon, when few are reading—and it became a national story for a couple of days.

It also cost me my opportunity to interview Bayless for this book. I had contacted him before about my interest in speaking with him about his career; he passed me off to his office, which never returned my multiple calls, all before this incident. After the incident? I didn't really want to talk to him. Oh, he's getting his passage in this chapter, because Bayless is a seminal figure in motivating people to move on beyond fast-food and casual-dining Mexican meals and into the realm of lesser-known Mexican dishes and how to prepare them at home. But such a thin skin! So disappointing . . . anyhoo, on to the rest of this chapter . . . okay, let me play nice. Do over!

At 445 North Clark Street in Chicago, diners can gaze into two luscious fantasies. To your right is Frontera Grill, where "loud" is not a suggestion but an order: colors so vibrant they make you exhale rainbows, artisan crafts gleaming on shelves, the chatter of diners eagerly waiting for the latest Mexican regional dish unearthed by Rick Bayless, the greatest cook of Mexican food in the United States.

The atmosphere is more refined next door, at Topolobampo—and if you don't believe me, listen to her. "If Frontera rocks and claps, Topolo slinks," its website purrs. "She is the quiet, sleek, classy sister. And she invites you into an elegant Mexican fantasy world and to dress up a notch for its incomparable, authentic, regional flavors."

Because of Bayless's popularity, most visitors can only gaze: though walk-ins are accepted, reservations at Frontera Grill and Topolobampo have a weeks-long wait, at least. The two restaurants share a bar, a front door, and a case displaying all things Bayless—cookbooks, T-shirts, other mementos meant to exalt this modern-day Tlaloc, the man who helped make Mexican food more than fast or sit-down, but rather *alta cocina*—high-end.

That smile Bayless always beams from the covers of his books, his promos, framed by a salt-and-pepper beard and goatee: it's not just because the guy's personable, it's also because he and others took the easiest step in Mexican food's American evolution—cutting and pasting and gathering and selling recipes on Mexican dishes to an American public with no care for who wrote the book but wanted to learn how to cook Mexican food on their own.

Try this experiment, just like I'm doing right now as I write this sentence: type in "Mexican cookbooks" into Amazon's search engine. If you sort by "Relevance," you'll see that Hispanic-surname authors wrote only two of the books listed. Set your parameters to "Best-Selling"— how did Paula Deen sneak into the list, especially when *Paula Deen's The Deen Family's Cookbook* has nothing to do with Mexican food?

Okay, extremely unscientific query, but my point remains: the Mexican cookbook industry, a multimillion-dollar operation whose bookshelves expand every year, is an overwhelmingly American-written one. Mexicans write books about Mexican food, for sure—since the beginning of the trade, actually. But a succession of white authors and acolytes have prodded Americans out of their Mexican-food comfort zone, challenging the public to not only taste new dishes but also to prepare them at home themselves. In the process they introduced a fraudulent concept to the question of Mexican cuisine in this country: the idea that the food they documented was "authentic," while the dishes offered at your neighborhood taco stand or sit-down restaurant were pretenders to be shunned.

Americans, arbiters of "authentic" Mexican. That smile Bayless always beams? P. T. Barnum approves.

Recipes for Mexican or "Spanish" food had sneaked into recipe collections of Californian women's groups and other social organizations as early as the 1870s; as shown earlier, recipes for Mexican dishes even entered the official cookbook for the 1893 World's Columbian Exposition. But collecting dozens of Mexican recipes wasn't codified as a new book genre until the *Los Angeles Times* hired the son of a New England Methodist preacher to walk from Ohio to the growing city, write about his travels, and become city editor upon arrival. If the tamale men lit the match that started the fire that was popularizing Mexican food nationwide, that scribe, Charles Fletcher Lummis, threw an ocean of propane onto the inferno. Only historians of the West nowadays are aware of him, but Lummis is one of the most influential people in the realm of Mexican cuisine, even if he insisted on calling it "Spanish."

Lummis was a Harvard dropout, a reporter for a no-name Ohio paper itching for an opportunity to escape the Midwest. It came via a family friend, a treasurer for the *Los Angeles Daily Times* (later just the *Los Angeles Times*) who sent copies of the paper to the young Lummis. The publication so wowed him that he wrote a proposal in 1884 to the *Times*'s publisher, Colonel Harrison Gray Otis: hire me, and I'll walk from Ohio to Los Angeles and keep a diary of my travels. Otis, a Civil War veteran and native Ohioan, had purchased a controlling interest in the paper just a couple of years before with the intention of using it as a bully pulpit to turn Los Angeles into the beacon that drew Americans to visit or migrate to Southern California. To have such an enterprising reporter keep a journal of those travels guaranteed attention to the Southwest in general, so Otis agreed to Lummis's idea.

The journey started in Chillicothe, Ohio, where the editor of the *Chillicothe Leader* agreed to publish a weekly Lummis letter from the road. Lummis reached Colorado and originally meant to continue through Utah before deciding to head south into New Mexico. He knew of the region—as Lummis's biographer noted, two of his idols, the anthropologist Frank Cushing and dimestore novelist Mayne Reid, had written of the area, spreading stereotypes of insolent, feckless Hispanics who needed civilization. To his amazement, Lummis found only warmth and camaraderie among them. "I find the 'Greasers' not half bad people," Lummis wrote in his first letter from New Mexico. "In fact, they rather discount the whites, who are all on the make. A Mexican, on the other hand, will 'divvy' up his only tortilla and his one blanket with any stranger, and never take a cent."[2]

Those entries were some of America's first that didn't involve back-handed compliments or outright degradation of Mexican food. In Alcalde, Lummis ate fried mutton (a northern New Mexico specialty) and downed it with coffee spiked with *aguardiente* (Mexican liquor derived from sugarcane), along with three tortillas. "Perhaps you don't *sabe* [know] what a tortilla is," Lummis wrote, already going native, mixing in Spanglish. "It is a thin sheet of unraised bread, cooked in a frying-pan, indestructible as leather, but very good eating, withal." A couple of days later he ate "a queer preparation of wheat, tasting like the New England 'Indian pudding'" that he called "panacha." In Car-nuel he tried a stew of onions, red peppers, and meat: chile colorado. "This was my first venture [with the dish], and will be my last," Lum-mis wrote. "One not used to eating fire might just exactly as well chew up a ripe red pepper raw and swallow it."[3]

Lummis had to chew up his words as well; he sang the dish's virtues throughout the rest of the journey. By the time he reached Los Ange-les, Lummis respected Mexicans, but he also foresaw and feared their inevitable demise. He entered Sonoratown, the area of the city that now constitutes Olvera Street, where most of the remaining Califor-nios and Mexican immigrants lived, and used the curious metaphor of a dog to describe a city that he felt was "a brilliant sample of a tail that has come to wag the whole dog," the dog being Mexican Los Angeles and the tail the new American migrants. Sonoratown, he felt, was "the original dog—a diminutive, lazy and ill-conditioned pup . . . over 100 years old." The tail, on the other hand, "is as wide-awake and beautiful as the dog is neither, and makes more noise in a day than the dog does in a year. In less than another generation there will be no dog left at all, his whole personality being merged and lost in that greedy tail."

Lummis became an indefatigable reporter for the *Times,* filing stories on the growing city and documenting the decaying vestiges of the Californios as the *Ramona* phenomenon echoed across Southern California and throughout the United States. But he worked only three years for the paper before suffering a mild stroke and relocating to New Mexico. There, he penned a series of books based on his travels and experiences that further portrayed the American Southwest as a quaint Eden ripe for American development. Lummis didn't return full-time to Southern California until the late 1890s, when he assumed the editor's role at *The Land of Sunshine,* a magazine funded mostly by the Los Angeles Chamber of Commerce to promote Southern California. Lummis changed the name to *Out West* in the beginning of 1895, and—like his former boss Otis—used it to pontificate about his interests: the celebration and salvation of the Southwest's "Spanish" heritage.

The easiest project was California's mission system, long abandoned and almost all run-down. The same year he took over the newly named *Out West,* Lummis created the Landmarks Club to fund-raise for the restoration of those missions. After stalling for nearly a decade, the club hit upon a wildly successful fund-raising vehicle in 1903: a cookbook, its main selling point an opening section devoted to Mexican food.

In an introductory essay titled "Spanish-American Cookery," Lummis made an impassioned plea for readers to enjoy the indigenous dishes of the Southwest, in honor of its past but also because of their taste: "In a word, diet must be adapted to climate."[4] *The Landmarks Club Cook Book* devoted only 17 of its 261 pages to Mexican recipes, and there were more included from Peru than the American Southwest, but Lummis's point stood: Americans needed to assimilate into Mexican food, not the other way around. He knew that Southern Californians were demanding instructions on how to cook Mexican food—it was no longer enough to eat solely from street vendors.

Lummis's former employer the *Times* also had discovered its readers' appetite for Mexican recipes. In 1898, it published a group of "Spanish Dainties," explaining that "the interest in early California and Spanish souvenirs has been so great of late years."[5] In 1902, in anticipation of its first-ever collection of reader-submitted recipes, the *Times* published seventy Mexican recipes in the paper: "Taken as a whole, they will doubtless be regarded as the finest and most valuable collection that has yet appeared in the series, and will certainly be prized wherever the paper goes."[6] What was most remarkable about the series, among the many recipes for tortillas, enchiladas, chili con carne, and other Mexican standards, were their authors: nearly all non-Mexican women. The *Times* continued the series for decades, growing nearly every year as Los Angeles did.

The newspaper's efforts, along with Lummis's pioneering collection, proved the nationwide selling potential of Mexican cookbooks. In 1905, Harriet S. Loury published *Fifty Choice Recipes for Spanish and Mexican Dishes* out of Denver. The following year, May Southworth came out with *101 Mexican Dishes,* part of a series of cookbooks she authored involving a theme and 101 recipes; this title was the only ethnic entry in the series. But the true heir to Lummis's torch was a midwestern housewife named Bertha Haffner.

Not much is known about her life; newspaper clippings claim she won a medal for baking at the 1904 St. Louis World's Fair, the Louisiana Purchase Exposition, and that she taught popular classes on homemaking across the country during the 1910s. In 1911, Bertha (now Haffner-Ginger) stopped by Los Angeles to conduct public lectures; the appearances attracted hundreds for each sitting. The *Times* hired her the following year to open their School of Domestic Science, which immediately attracted eager students. The lecturer taught women the basics of cooking and baking in an auditorium in the *Times*'s office building specifically built for such purposes.

The *Times*'s offices were in downtown Los Angeles, not far from Sonoratown. One day, Haffner-Ginger decided to stroll through the neighborhood and take in her new city. She walked into Elías & Guzman, a tortilla factory partly owned by Arturo Elías Calles, a former Mexican consul (and half brother of future Mexican president Plutarco

Elías Calles) who had left his post to open the business, seeing that thousands of his countrymen were arriving in Los Angeles (and many more were following) and needed a taste of home. At Elías & Guzman, Haffner-Ginger watched a dozen women making fresh tortillas, enchiladas, and tamales. The sight so delighted the home economist that she invited the owner of the factory to demo tortilla-making for an American public.

The *Times* advertised the event, as they did all of Haffner-Ginger's classes, but this class drew one of its largest-ever crowds. The unnamed "Spanish" woman spoke no English, but no language was needed: the crowd sat and watched, mesmerized as the *mujer* turned masa into tortillas. Then Haffner-Ginger swooped in. The teacher announced she would "Americanize" the enchiladas so as to not upset any stomachs, but Haffner-Ginger's students didn't care for those; instead, they asked how to obtain the materials to cook the authentic version for themselves.[7]

An idea was planted. In 1914, Haffner-Ginger published *California Mexican-Spanish Cook Book*. It was at once fantastical, patronizing, and influential. The cover featured an improbable pastiche of a Mission Revival mansion on the Pacific coast, palm and pine trees flourishing in the sand. "An announcement that my lesson for the day would be Spanish dishes, invariably brought record-breaking crowds in any city in the United States," Haffner-Ginger revealed in the introduction to her collection, but she had a correction for her devoted readers: "It is not generally known that Spanish dishes as they are known in California are really Mexican Indian dishes."[8]

The pages of *California Mexican-Spanish Cook Book* mixed laughable illustrations (a drawing of decrepit Indians with the caption "The mission of the old padres was to make life brighter for such as these") with pictures of "types" of Spanish—dancers from Cafe Verdugo (one of the last Californio restaurants in Los Angeles), brides, and musicians. There was an advertisement for a "regular" dinner and photos of Ramona's purported marriage site and Mexican women making tortillas. But the book is also remarkable for including the first-ever documented recipe and picture of tacos in the United States, although her creation called for sealing the folded tortilla with egg, then deep-frying it and covering it with chile. Toward the end of the book, a picture displayed an auditorium filled with hundreds of American women watching intently as Haffner-Ginger taught them how to make a "Spanish" omelet.

Haffner-Ginger didn't return to the *Times's* School of Domestic Science after that initial run of classes, but the wild success of the series convinced the paper to continue lectures and demonstrations and to print recipes in the paper. Alas, they stuck to the Californio romanticism that Lummis and others propagated well into the twentieth century—a plug for a class in 1932, for instance, promised singing cooks and dancing señoritas to "revive memories of the old pueblo days."[9] Those classes, under the patronage of "Marian Manners" (the pseudonym for the head of the *Times's* Home Bureau Service, the section of the paper responsible for the classes), produced Mexican recipes syndicated across the country. Not to be outdone, the Hearst newspaper chain also had their own domestic goddess, "Prudence Penny," who offered Mexican recipes as well.

Still, Mexican cookbooks didn't advance much for the next couple of decades after Haffner's publication. The Gebhardt Mexican Foods Company, the country's first mass producers of chili powder, produced almost-yearly editions of *Mexican Cookery for American Homes,* a how-to guide for its customers to use their products (and a company we'll examine in more detail later). Random titles trickled out over the years, none particularly memorable. But no one emerged as a national authority on Mexican cuisine until the 1940s, in one of the country's more remarkable up-by-your-bootstraps chronicles, whether Mexican or American.

Elena Zelayeta was the daughter of Spanish immigrants who settled in Mexico but fled to San Francisco after the Mexican Revolution. They were cooks by trade, so Zelayeta learned the craft but didn't strike out on her own until the Great Depression, when she and her husband lost their home and had their car repossessed. Desperate, they served meals out of their living quarters—chile rellenos and enchiladas and a stray Spanish dish here and there. Customers demanded that the Zelayetas open a proper restaurant, so they found a bigger location, in a luxury hotel in downtown San Francisco. Called Elena's Mexican Village, it wowed the city with murals depicting lazy Mexican life, waitresses in Mexican costumes, and Zelayeta clicking castanets every Sunday and Thursday night to the cheers of the crowd.

"Those were the days when anything Mexican was very popular," Zelayeta relayed years later in her memoir. "The ladies did not have to travel all those miles to the border. They could gain a vicarious thrill by coming to my restaurant, eating my Mexican and Spanish food."[10] The success was short-lived: Zelayeta succumbed to an illness that left her blind just a year after her Mexican Village opened. The restaurant closed, and Zelayeta sunk into a deep, understandable depression. But she bounced back, learning how to cook by scent, hearing, and touch. Zelayeta resumed the fiestas she used to hold for friends, and in 1944, the San Francisco Center for the Blind asked her to teach a cooking class. Zelayeta so impressed students and onlookers that a group of home economists urged her to publish a book of recipes, if only to raise enough funds so she might afford a guide dog.

Elena's Famous Mexican and Spanish Recipes, published in 1944, sold briskly, and she embarked on a decades-long career teaching Mexican cooking classes across the country. Three other cookbooks followed, each increasing her following. By the time Zelayeta's final cookbook appeared, in 1967, no less a culinary authority than James Beard wrote the foreword. "Elena is a traditionalist, but she can also pull an inspired new combination of foods out of the air—and make you feel it is the most authentic dish you ever ate," he wrote. "She knows how to prepare a classic, and she also knows how to give it the Zelayeta flair. In short, she has greatness."[11]

Zelayeta's story made her a national name for decades. "This inspiring woman is one of the most marvelous examples of positive thinking I have ever run across," Norman Vincent Peale wrote in his second book on positive thinking. While dining at her home, he asked her for her secret. "Always act as if it were impossible to fail," she told him, "and God will see you through."[12]

High in the forested hills of Zitacuaro, a picturesque town in the Mexican state of Michoacán, a diminutive Englishwoman with a shock of gray hair and gnarled, nearly brown skin lords over the world of Mexican cooking in the United States. Famous chefs make pilgrimages to her compound, a Xanadu of gardens, drying coffee beans, and peppers strewn about, and centered around a gorgeous, expansive home. But beware the person who shows up unannounced: you're likely to get chewed out, if even allowed to enter. A letter of recommendation from previous guests is recommended, as is an obsequious demeanor. That's how Diana Kennedy likes it.

In some ways, Kennedy faced a harder task than men such as Glen Bell and Larry Cano: not only convince Americans that the cuisine was more than fast food and combo platters, but also that it was regal *and* attempt to motivate amateur cooks to not take any shortcuts while they attempted plates most Americans had never heard of. But she succeeded, and Kennedy is now a dining deity—the Mexican government rewarded her with the Order of the Aztec Eagle, the country's highest honor for foreigners, in 1981, more than twenty years before her birth nation rewarded her with an MBE.

She had no experience with Mexican food of any kind until moving to Mexico City in 1957 to join her future husband, Paul Kennedy, Mexico City bureau chief for the *New York Times*. While Paul covered the region, the dutiful housewife took solace in the kitchen, accompanied by Mexican maids who taught her Spanish and the secrets of regional cooking. Mexico was modernizing, and the middle and upper classes were eschewing Mexican dinners in favor of American, French, and other Continental cuisines. Kennedy's maids, however, turned her on to the specialties of their states, piquing her interest not just because of the fantastic flavors but also because of their endangered status.

The Kennedys frequently feted Mexico City's expat community, with Diana mimicking the cooking styles of her workers. One of their frequent visitors was Craig Claiborne, the influential restaurant critic for the *Times* who had his own history with Mexican food. He grew up in Indianola, Mississippi, where the tamale men sang their song long after their type disappeared from the big cities of America. "The Mexican walked the streets of the town with a pushcart that cradled some of the most tempting, mouth-watering hot tamales you could hope to sample," Claiborne wrote in his memoir. "They consisted of incredibly well-seasoned shredded meat encased in a finely ground and sumptuously rich casing, the whole wrapped in dried corn shucks and steamed." But Claiborne felt "hoodwinked" the day he discovered the Mexican had been banished from town: according to the authorities, the tamalero had used cats for his meat filling and they had the skeletons buried under his cabin to confirm such a grotesque claim.[13]

In the pages of the *Times*, Claiborne championed Mexican cuisine, reporting on Zelayeta's Gotham appearances and breathlessly reporting any hints of Mexican food in his cosmopolitan city. With Kennedy, he realized her potential to transform its status in the States. He urged her to write a cookbook collecting the recipes of her maids; Kennedy demurred, as her husband was suffering from cancer, which forced the couple to relocate to New York City in 1965. After Paul passed away two years later, Claiborne asked Diana to teach Mexican cooking classes to occupy her time, but Kennedy again refused. But the critic's insistence paid off, and she taught her first class in 1969, with Claiborne warning the curious, "Don't go there expecting chili con carne and hot tamales."[14]

One of those early students was Frances McCullough, Sylvia Plath's editor at Harper & Row and a California native who ached for the

Mexican food of her homeland. She suggested that Kennedy pen a cookbook, but Kennedy refused again, now claiming she wasn't a writer. But the two eventually collaborated, and *The Cuisines of Mexico* appeared in 1972, to already self-congratulatory importance. In his preface, Claiborne wrote that he and Kennedy agreed that Mexican food was "peasant food raised to the level of high and sophisticated art . . . if this book is a measure of Diana's talent, it will probably rank as the definitive book in English on that most edible art."[15]

A monarchy arose from those books. Following the first was *The Tortilla Book*, then *The Art of Regional Mexican Cooking*; and she combined those three to create *The Essential Cuisines of Mexico*. Kennedy, on her own, traveled the back roads of Mexico, to places the country's intelligentsia dismissed as backwaters, interviewing and chronicling and then publishing the recipes. It's easy to dismiss Kennedy's cookbooks as using the people she insisted she was rescuing from oblivion by printing their recipes in best-selling books; or for bouts of romanticism as egregious as Lummis's—it seems that every woman in Kennedy's Mexico is a housewife or a maid never far from the kitchen, every male a peasant. But the influence those books exerted was extraordinary. Although the number of Mexican cookbooks in the United States had increased since in the 1950s, nearly all concentrated on Mexican-American meals; few bothered with Kennedy's regional rarities.

The grande dame, for her part, waged war on those Mexican-American foodways. In a 1985 interview with *Texas Monthly* knowingly titled "La Reina Diana" ("Queen Diana"), Kennedy dismissed Tex-Mex food as "over-seasoned, loaded with all those false spices like onion salt, garlic salt, MSG, and chili powder . . . they play havoc with your stomach, with your breath, everything." She also called Ninfa's, a Houston institution credited with introducing fajitas and tacos al carbón to the American mainstream, a "disgrace."[16]

Such pugnacity, however, did nothing to discourage fans. One of them was doctoral candidate Rick Bayless, a native Oklahoman whose family operated a barbecue pit in Oklahoma City. The area had a couple of Mexican restaurants in those years, mostly Tex-Mex parlors, given the state's proximity to the Lone Star State. Bayless had an affection for Mexico from a young age; at fourteen, he asked his parents for them to vacation across the country. By the time he was a doctoral candidate at the University of Michigan, studying Mexico yet again, Bayless decided to drop the academic career and focus on culinary ventures. He consulted for a sit-down chain, El Paso Cantina, and hosted a public television series, *Cooking Mexican*, in the late 1970s, in Bowling Green, Ohio, although he didn't actually cook or offer his own recipes.

Bayless and his wife lived throughout Mexico during the 1980s, tasting and gathering and planning. In 1987, the two scored a double debut: Frontera Grill, and *Authentic Mexican: Regional Cooking from the Heart of Mexico*. The release immediately brought the nation's food reviewers to sit in Bayless's pews and hear the man preach. "American-Mexican food has its own style, but unfortunately it does not have the depth and range of dishes as found in Mexico," he told a reporter. "My goal with this book is to bring that depth into American homes."[17] Claiborne, for his part, gushed that *Authentic Mexican* was the "greatest contribution to the Mexican table imaginable."

Another Kennedy acolyte was Marilyn Tausend. Unlike Kennedy or Bayless, she had an earlier, more intimate relationship with Mexican food. Her father worked in produce, and Tausend accompanied him during her childhood to migrant worker camps and the fields across the West. "Tortilla and beans—they'd make them right there," she remembers. "They didn't have money, they didn't have any of that, but they immediately accepted me in and offered food. It was nice being part of their families."

Tausend didn't eat much Mexican food in her adult life, living the classic mid-twentieth-century American housewife experience, someone who'd "never done any real cooking, and only in quantities" to feed her children. The publication of Kennedy's books, though, inspired her to try out the cuisine again. When her husband, an attorney, had business that took him to Michoacán, Tausend tagged along. According to her, they magically took a wrong road and found Kennedy's estate. "If you know Diana, you don't just call her up," she says now with a laugh, "but if you know my husband, you do."

Instead of inviting them into her home, Kennedy sent them to an inn at the base of her estate. A friendship sprouted from that inauspicious introduction, and Kennedy suggested that Tausend do some culinary work with her. From that sprung Culinary Adventures, Tausend's gastronomic tourism business. People who sign up (chefs and regular people alike) accompany Tausend and Kennedy to different parts of Mexico, shopping at markets and cooking from their finds.

"I want the people going on the trips to have a better understanding not just of the food but of the culture," she says, "because you can't cook the food without understanding the people."

Culinary Adventures's audience is now worldwide, and Tausend wrote her own cookbooks. Bayless is a frequent guest, both as student and coinstructor, and their families have spent every Christmas season in Oaxaca for the past twenty years. But she's wary of the school of purism preached by him and Kennedy. "I hate that word 'authentic,'" she admits. "Anything out of your kitchen is authentic!"

She also has issues with the fact that non-Mexicans get most of the acclaim for Mexican cookery in the United States. Tausend is currently writing a cookbook with Ricardo Muñoz, a Mexico City–based chef who has emerged as one of the country's premier chroniclers and practitioners of regional Mexican recipes.

"Ricardo, he's finally going to get his due," Tausend says. "But there's others—Patricia Quintana is one—there hasn't been enough talking about their food, and I think it's unfortunate. When Diana says, 'My Mexico,' I say, 'Come on, you've lived there a long time, but?'"

Downtown Santa Monica, California, during the weekend is a mix of tourists, beach bums, the wealthy, and the hungry. Those tribes often congregate at Border Grill, beckoned by a cursive arrow-shaped, multibulb marquee, feminine and sassy, swooping down and inviting people in. Inside, the walls and ceiling contain whimsical drawings rendered in the simplistic black-lined, multihued, flat-dimensioned paintings of Putumayo world music album covers, the bright colors suggesting Latin America. One side is the main dining room—that's where women in sunglasses and jewelry eat and gossip while their children play in their weekend sports league. Another room features a long bar that serves mimosas and other elixirs for the early afternoon. A counter next to the bar displays *Mexican Food for Dummies,* its traffic-yellow book cover radiating as a Latina stands nearby, rolling pastries.

One of the two owners of Border Grill, Susan Feniger, approaches the front. She's short, wiry, a kitchen Dietrich mixed with Garland—pinstriped pants, hair pulled back by a bright orange bandanna, and wearing tortoiseshell-framed glasses. Her voice can disintegrate cinder blocks—it's not obnoxious, not domineering, but firm, powerful. Feniger has popped out of her office for about two minutes but has already greeted multiple guests, texted, placed a phone call, and accepted another—and apologized for her lack of time. See, she needs to be somewhere else. She just ventured out on her own for the first time with Street, a restaurant that combines global street food with Hollywood's hip vibe. But Border Grill is her first love, the Mexican restaurant that set her and her business-cooking partner, Mary Sue Milliken, onto the path to television shows and cookbooks—and now a food truck.

Feniger digs through her chips while nursing her sore throat with English breakfast tea and mineral water before marveling how a Jewish girl from Toledo became an authority on cooking Mexican food. The first Mexican restaurant she experienced was Loma Linda's, just outside Toledo Express Airport in the city of Swanton and open since 1955—the first and oldest Mexican eatery in the region. "Terrible," she remembers, "but at the time it was just—we're talking forty years ago—great. I can't even remember the food. My guess was that it was very

Tex-Mex, but I loved the feel of it. It was small and almost cantina-y. People thought back then that that was Mexican food."

Toledo was too small a town for an outsize person such as Feniger, so she set off on a journey of self-discovery—attending college in Vermont, moving to California, learning French cooking, and meeting her cooking partner, Milliken, while working in Chicago. Feniger worked under Wolfgang Puck at Ma Maison, where the Austrian was creating the idea of the celebrity chef. She convinced Milliken to relocate to the West, where the two opened City Café in 1983, a small storefront that became the talk of Los Angeles with its charismatic owners' bold take on California cuisine.

For a vacation they accompanied prep chef Tacho Nielsen to his hometown of Mexico City. "Every morning, his mom took us to the market. We came back to the house and cooked all day," Feniger remembers. When they returned, Feniger and Milliken resumed the daily grind. Most nights in Mexico City ended with the ladies treating their workers to a late dinner at a nearby taqueria. "We'd also go there after lunch and get carnitas tacos, which wasn't something we were too familiar with back in Toledo," she says. "Now you can find them anywhere, but definitely not then. Wrapped in butcher paper, forty of them at a time. Delicious. We asked ourselves, 'Should we open a great taco place, or a noodle house?'"

Kennedy had already introduced Mexican food beyond Cal-Mex and Tex-Mex to the United States, but few had seriously thought that a restaurant offering regional specialties, operated by Americans, might work. Feniger insists that the viability of such a place in those days never entered the conversations of the two. "We'd never gone to that place of whether it could work," she says. "We just wanted to open a restaurant that we love, and food that we love. And that was authentic Mexican food."

Los Angeles's Mexican-restaurant scene at the time was trifurcated: fast food; Mexican-majority eateries with great food but little ambience for non-Mexicans; and El Torito clones with buzzing social scenes but inedible grub. "Maybe you want a cocktail and a scene along with your tacos," Feniger says. "That's what we thought we could create."

In 1985, Feniger and Milliken returned to Mexico City, renting Volkswagen Bugs to reach Veracruz and the Yucatán. "As we drove, we were writing the menu [for our new restaurant]," she says, remembering the street stalls and *fondas* (inns) where they stayed along the way. Finally the two ended up in Valladolid, a colonial city near the ruins of Chichen Itza. They walked through the town until tumbling upon a taqueria with a large window. "There was a big guy with platters of tiny bites. Shrimp, turkey, avocados, radishes, peas. The place was jammed. He'd get a tortilla, stuff it with his ingredient, and do it again. We stood there for an hour, taking notes. Eventually he brought us tacos, beer, and a smoked red bean stew, served with an ancho salsa. It was *fucking awesome.*"

They returned to Los Angeles inspired but hurried, with only a week to prepare a menu. That first Border Grill menu featured not a single Feniger or Milliken creation, but rather recipes collected from their recent trip. One of those items was *panucho,* a specialty of Yucatán yet to penetrate mainstream Mexican restaurants in the United States. "You push [customers] to make them try new things," Feniger says, and they pushed non-Mexican Los Angeles into unfamiliar terrain. Tongue tacos. Cactus salad. Cayenne with jicama, a staple of Mexican households during summertime but one combo that they finally dropped because "no one ever bought it. Literally—no one." Feniger and Milliken weren't too doctrinaire: they introduced a tostada on the menu soon after their opening "because customers wanted it."

Border Grill opened in 1985, in Los Angeles's trendy Melrose district. Then–*Los Angeles Times* restaurant critic Ruth Reichl sparked the buzz with the first sentence of her review: "I knew the minute I looked at the menu at the Border Grill that I was in trouble. I wanted to eat everything on it." The rest of the write-up was no less gushing, with Reichl concluding, "It looks like all the people who keep asking when

Los Angeles is going to get a great Mexican restaurant may finally have an answer."[18]

The careers of Feniger and Milliken soon took off. In 1989, they opened another Border Grill, in Santa Monica, taking their cuisine to the Los Angeles area's ritzier Westside. Their first cookbook, *Mesa Mexicana,* arrived in 1994; two years later, the two became national stars with the debut of *Two Hot Tamales.* ("Tamales can be terrible and most of the time, they are up here," Feniger says, explaining the name. "But it's one of those great dishes—so simple, yet so complicated.") With it, the acerbic Feniger and the reserved Milliken became the Hope and Crosby of the then-fledgling Food Network, cooking regional Mexican food in a populist manner that further demystified the cuisine for the curious. The show ran for nearly four hundred episodes and spawned cooking tours à la Haffner-Ginger and Zelayeta. They even released *Mexican Cooking for Dummies,* part of the iconic 1990s series that explained the obscure to the hoi polloi. The two opened another restaurant, Ciudad, and other Border Grills.

Others took their cues, publishing cookbooks and creating series. *Two Hot Tamales* ended; the cookbooks stopped, along with restaurant expansions. But Feniger doesn't mind. "That's the capitalism thing," she says. "You have French-raised chefs doing Mexican. Once that gets attention, people go into the restaurant. Then they want more than cheddar and jack at home; they want panela or queso fresco. You can influence people's decisions. Then the customers want to make their own guac or margaritas—but the grocery stores don't stock them. They go back to the restaurant to order the salsas. Then they want to make them, but they need tomatillos. And the supermarkets start stocking them, and it becomes an accepted part of the cuisine.

"A young chef of mine once tried to do a *manchamanteles,* this legendary Oaxacan mole," she adds. "He tried to put a spin on it, this hotshot from culinary school. It was terrible. Do it the way it's supposed to be made, or don't do it at all."

"Authentic" flavors are what Feniger, Kennedy, and Bayless purport to practice, and their legion of followers carry their torch. But while the authentic-Mexican warriors rose during the 1980s, a different, home-grown school of thought emerged as a counterpoint, one intent on treating unadulterated authenticity as fool's gold and preferring instead to fuse the ancient with the modern. The Southwestern cuisine move-ment is now nearly forgotten, derided as a bad '80s fad à la hoop ear-rings, but when it was around, it further changed the concept of what America considered "Mexican" food.

Chapter Six

Whatever Happened to Southwestern Cuisine?

About an hour north of Santa Fe is the village of Chimayó, a place revered by true believers because miracles happen there. Every Holy Week, tens of thousands of Catholics come by car and on foot, along roads that wind off U.S. Route 285 toward the Santuario de Chimayó—the town's sanctuary, a humble adobe church built around a hole.

The Catholic Church maintains that in the 1800s, a Chimayó man discovered a cross in the ground while digging for water. He placed it inside the local church, but the cross mysteriously returned to the pit the following morning. The man built a sanctuary around the *posito* (watering hole) to mark this mystery, and it's still there, inside a small room toward the back of the sacred structure. Two hand shovels stay in the small pit so people can scoop dirt to take home. Hundreds of baby shoes, crutches, pictures, and scribbled notes fill a room nearby, attesting that they found cures for their terminal diseases by merely touching the dirt from the posito. The Catholic Archdiocese of Santa Fe freely admits that the redemptive soil isn't self-regenerating, but rather comes from the mountain range that serves as the church's scenic backdrop, the towering Sangre de Cristo—Blood of Christ.

This Lourdes of the Americas is a magical place, and not just because of the location's supposed curative powers. There is food—bags of roasted pecans sold at roadside stands or from people's homes, sacks of piñon (pine nuts) harvested from the fragrant, spindly trees, mounds of dried or fresh chiles depending on the season, Chimayó's other notable cultural product. And a few steps away from the Santuario stands Léona's, a long but narrow restaurant. It seems like a tourist trap—on the wall hang aprons, T-shirts, packaged chiles, chile powder, and even special TSA-approved flight bags to store food in that ensure it won't spoil on the plane home. But man does not subsist on faith alone, and this is where pilgrims retire after getting their fill of dirt for the day.

Owner Léona Medina-Tiede is a Chimayó native who helped her family sell meals every year during Holy Week as a child—tamales, burritos, and steaming bowls of posole (stews of pork and corn kernels), accompanied by huge wheat tortillas. She serves food that most Americans call Mexican: chile stews, enchiladas, tamales, and burritos. But it really is *New* Mexican cuisine, a food developed in isolation over centuries and unlike any other Mexican food in the United States. The chile stews don't just burn; they're fleshy, fulsome, derived from pods cultivated in the nearby valleys over centuries by farmers. Enchiladas aren't rolled tortillas submerged in canned sauce but come stacked like pancakes, made from blue-corn tortillas, glued together with cheese and ground beef, then baptized with a fried egg. Tamales emphasize the masa and the many different kinds of corn grown in New Mexico. If it's Lent, Léona's also sells small containers of a brown sugar pudding called panocha—the Spanish-speaking faithful will snicker, though, as that's the Mexican Spanish slang word for "vagina."

In Chimayó, as in the rest of New Mexico, people find magic. During the 1980s, the flavors on display here were the Next Great Mexican Food in the United States, kindle for hundreds of restaurants that suddenly offered blue-corn tortilla chips or exotic salsas while decorating with howling coyotes and silhouettes of Kokopelli, the humpbacked, dreadlocked, flute-playing fertility god of the Southwest. Chimayó became the name of restaurants from Virginia to Utah to even Southern California, to the edge of the Pacific at Chimayó at the Beach in Orange County. The food, the names, the colors, and the decor: New Mexican culture was used to evoke a sense of awe, of timelessness, for a cuisine that fizzled out as fast as it blazed across the United States.

New Mexico is simultaneously a land where fusion occurs with the ease and frequency of its spectacular skies, but one also stubbornly, beautifully provincial, protective of its heritage. America's dalliance with New Mexican food—about fifteen years—receded into the state's valleys, its mountains and pueblos, shadows and crevices, and the natives don't mind. Even at the height of its popularity, New Mexico's favorite dishes never ventured beyond its borders; they still haven't and probably never will. Trendiness is just not how New Mexico operates, and the Southwestern cuisine movement never understood this, never heeded the warning offered by the writer who warned of the state, "The wide and strange land shaped and reshaped human institutions to its own purposes, and one either learned to live with the blazing sun, the scarcity of water, the dust and interminable distances, and the whispering quiet of empty canyons and mesas, or he admitted failure and moved elsewhere."[1]

The Spanish Crown initially explored what's now New Mexico when they sent forth Francisco Coronado in 1540. He arrived in the territory expecting an alien race but instead found that the Indians made something familiar to the conquistadors: tortillas, the same concoction of maize introduced to them by the Aztecs just twenty years earlier. The Zunis, according to Coronado, made "the best tortillas that I have ever seen anywhere. . . . They have the best arrangement and method for grind that was ever seen . . . one of these Indian women here will grind as much flour as four of the Mexicans do."[2]

Settlers from Mexico trickled into the territory during the seventeenth century, incorporating their food customs with those of the natives; in turn, the Indians used Mexican ingredients and styles and adapted their cuisine to the new order. And that was life in New Mexico for the next two hundred years, an uneasy living between Spaniards and Indians, but an open embrace of each other's food cultures until one was nearly indistinguishable from the other and coalesced into an identity called Hispano. It wasn't until the early 1800s that Americans explored the territory and discovered the region's cuisine. Most didn't take kindly to what the hospitable New Mexicans offered. "Miserable muddy coffee, a stew made of mutton smothered in onions, half-baked *tortillas* . . . and a few boiled eggs, constitute the best meal it pretends to furnish," wrote one scout, adding that he had never eaten a New Mexican meal "without it creating in some degree a sensation of nausea at the stomach."[3]

It took Charles Fletcher Lummis for an American to celebrate New Mexico's cornucopia. This chronicler might have done more than anyone else to create nostalgia for California's mission past, but it was New Mexico that called to his heart the most, a place he described in one of his books as the land of Poco Tiempo—Pretty Soon, a region in perpetual, romantic arrested development. "It is the Great American Mystery—the National Rip Van Winkle—the United States which is *not* United States," Lummis enthused in his book *The Land of Poco Tiempo*. "Why hurry with the hurrying world? The 'Pretty Soon' of New Spain is better than the 'Now! Now!' of the haggard States."[4]

American intellectuals—writers, artists, philosophers, mystics, painters, anthropologists, adventure seekers—flocked to New Mexico because of the hosannas of Lummis and others, to live in a time warp, and published guidebooks and letters on this peculiar American territory. Social scientists authored studies on the region; one of the earliest, a 1904 thesis by New Mexico State student Pearl Cherry Miller titled *Mexican Cookery*, collected New Mexican recipes such as *bizcochos* (cookies made with lard, anise, and cinnamon), *chicos* (dried corn kernels prepared as a soup), and the elusive *panocha*. "Without [tortillas] and without chile, I doubt whether the 'Mexicanos' would consider life worth living," the aspiring scholar wrote.[5]

The state drew more national attention during the Balboa Exposition of 1912 in San Diego (the year New Mexico attained statehood), where the state's exhibit was housed in a Spanish-style adobe. After that, travelers to New Mexico expected everything to look like it originated during the time of Coronado, to the point that one historian felt newcomers "preferred to start with a one-story, three- or four-room Mexican adobe house; if it stood partially in ruins, so much the better."[6] To cope with the expectations of visitors, the Santa Fe City Council passed a resolution aiming to freeze itself in time by requiring that all buildings "conform exteriorially with the Santa Fe style" of architecture, namely adobes.[7]

Attempts at mummifying New Mexico, however, had the opposite effect on Hispanos: the state's opening to newcomers meant that the foods of the native residents disappeared under the onslaught of modern times. Railroads brought jobs, which took villagers away from agrarian lifestyles and toward a consumer-based economy; the abandonment of those family farms left the land barren, and food traditions suffered. A 1942 University of Chicago study discovered that in just sixty years, tiny communities near the artists' colony of Taos had abandoned whole wheat flour for refined flour, fresh cow's and goat's milk for canned milk, and nourishing *atole* (gruel) and *chaquehue* (hot cereal made from blue corn) in favor of coffee and oatmeal, respectively.[8] "Taos culture is inadequate to meet current problems," another social scientist wrote. "When the Taoseño loses his grazing lands and his farm he is unable to fit himself successfully into a new mode of life. His cultural handicaps make him a misfit, socially and economically, in current affairs."[9]

Alarmed at their disappearing civilization, a group of Hispano women created the Sociedad Folklórica de Santa Fe, with a two-pronged purpose: to chronicle their atrophying ways, but to also reappropriate them from opportunistic Americans looking to make money off their heritage. What triggered the group's formation was a 1935 article in *Holland's Magazine* that called for the use of bread flour instead of corn to make tortillas. "How nice and light these must be without yeast or shortening," Cleofas Martinez Jaramillo sarcastically remarked in her memoirs. "And still these smart Americans make money with their writing, and we who know the correct way, sit back and listen."[10]

The Sociedad Folklórico gathered collections of stories, penned memoirs, and engaged in amateur anthropology to counter the growing Anglo narrative of their homeland, and one of their most effective publicity tools was cookbooks. Jaramillo published *The Genuine New Mexico Tasty Recipes: Potajes Sabrosos* in 1939, a collection of foods she made clear weren't Mexican but rather New Mexican. But the most influential member of the Sociedad was Fabiola Cabeza de Baca Gilbert, who worked with the New Mexico Agricultural Extension Service to teach sanitation and preservation techniques across the state. Hispanos lived in some of the poorest, most isolated communities in the United States, and she sought to uplift her community by reminding them of their proud culinary accomplishments.

In 1931, Cabeza de Baca released *Historic Cookery,* the first widely available cookbook on New Mexican food. Her home state, she wrote, was "a land of changes. Its blue skies of morning may be its red skies of evening. They have been changes in its people, in its customs, and naturally in its food habits."[11] She invited readers to try the food, but more importantly remember where it came from: "Try the recipes. And when you do, think of New Mexico's golden days, of red chile drying in the sun, of clean-swept yards, outdoor ovens, and adobe houses on the landscape. Remember the green valleys where good things grow."[12]

The Sociedad published other tracts, held fiestas, and organized workshops on traditional crafts, but the preservation battle was a losing one, and the Sociedad knew it. In 1954, Cabeza de Baca Gilbert published her family's memoirs, *We Fed Them Cactus*. It's a book filled with parties, old customs, and gaiety, and also an overwhelming melancholy. "Through four generations, our family has made a living from this land," she wrote in the introduction, "from cattle and sheep, and lately by selling curios, soda pop, gasoline and food to tourists traveling over U.S. Highway 66."[13]

A proud people reduced to selling Coke to Americans. New Mexico's only chance of survival was by adapting to the new times, by evolving. But the restoration had to wait three more decades and happen far away, on the sunny coast of California.

Rivera seems like the type of restaurant—in a hip, gentrifying part of Los Angeles—that all good people must loathe. The armrests and base of the seats at the bar lounge curve into backward *r*'s in the same sans serif font as the restaurant's name. Electronic music pulses in the background as the beautiful people flirt and flit. Random images of Hispanic glory—bullfights, jungles, Aztec pyramids—flash against the walls.

Meals arrive, simultaneously ancient and future-looking. The tamale tastes like a Mexican household come Christmas Eve, ruddy and hearty, but is as flat and as thick as a regular issue of *Vogue,* and topped with button mushrooms that add a playful, earthy touch; on the plate, in piquant pepper, reads "Stimulus Package," carefully stenciled—funny! Duck *enfrijoladas* skips across four distinct, clashing groups—Oaxacan (enfrijoladas are tortillas smeared with black bean paste) in a bitter Puebla-style mole, stuffed with duck and a block of Peruvian *chuño* potatoes. The tortilla is a proud purple, crafted from the blue corn of New Mexico.

Ah, that tortilla, sweet and chewy, evoking images of adobes inhabited by Anglos wanting to live in the land of Poco Tiempo. This isn't an atavistic offering, however, but a brilliant summation of this magnificent restaurant, which spans the length of the Hispanic world, from Spain to Brazil to Cal-Mex, all under a decidedly Mexican gaze.

The man behind Rivera, both the restaurant and the name, settles into a private room, where the curved helmet of a conquistador acts as a lampshade. John Rivera Sedlar has just returned from Barcelona at the invitation of the Spanish government, eager to showcase their country's chefs to the man whom *Gourmet* once anointed the father of Southwestern cuisine, in the hopes that he might incorporate it at his always packed restaurant.

"Mexican food is so much more flavorful right now than Spanish," Sedlar says. He speaks in waves, long, looping anecdotes, smooth and lulling, yet his descriptions reel in the attentions of anyone nearby, waiter and customer alike. "It was perceived as a second-class cuisine. But it's shoulder to shoulder with all the great cuisines of the world."

Save for a full head of gray hair, Sedlar looks and acts almost exactly like the prodigy who wowed food critics from his Southern California base through the 1980s—except now he's reinterpreting himself as a pan-Latino magus instead of just focusing on the Southwest. Sedlar explains that though New Mexico is his mistress, it's Mexican food that's his *amor*—but there can't be one without the other.

"Without Spain, there is no Mexican food as we know it today," Sedlar explains, pouring shots from a bottle of mescal left to age in barrels that once contained brandy. The finish is sweet, syrupy, caramelized. "And without Mexican food, there is no New Mexican cuisine."

For those who remember Sedlar in his younger days, painting Southwestern cuisine as a godly revelation, his current comeback as an apostle of pan-Latino food seems unlikely, even opportunistic, but it's authentic, the evolution inevitable. His childhood in Santa Fe was one where frozen green beans and canned corn masqueraded as home cooking. But Sedlar, of Hispano roots, grimaced through those "terrible, terrible meals" for the promise of summer, when he'd travel to Abiquiu in the Río Arriba territory of New Mexico, the tiny pueblo that Georgia O'Keeffe made famous by living there. Rivera's eyes still widen at the memories of "*primas* tending woodstoves" for old-style New Mexican dinners. He'd also visit in the late summer and early fall, when all of the state stops life for a couple of weeks to harvest chile and roast it, shrouding the state in its smoky-sweet aroma.

In those days, New Mexican dishes still masqueraded as "Spanish" on the menus of respectable restaurants across the state; combo plates and tacos were still largely rumors. "You'd have two sides on the menu—Continental cuisine and 'Spanish,'" he says. "It was rural lies—it was *New Mexican* food. That was the culture. It's not like you could get away from it."

As New Mexican food disappeared from the homes of the state's longtime residents, their dishes became a commodity for the tourism industry. As early as the 1930s, the Fred Harvey Company offered New Mexican food in its hotels and restaurants in Santa Fe, and published "traditional" recipes in the Atchison Topeka Santa Fe Railroad magazine under its "Harvey Girls" column.[14] Restaurants opened to accommodate the tourists who increasingly passed through the state, whether on the railroads or via automobile; most famous of these is La Posta in Mesilla, which opened in 1939 just a couple of miles northwest of El Paso and remains the oldest New Mexican eatery in the state.

Sedlar moved to Los Angeles in the late 1970s, working at a couple of restaurants before training at L'Ermitage, the Gallic restaurant credited with turning the city into a serious food town instead of a desert of fast food, cafeterias, and diners. He apprenticed there for a couple of years before moving on to the French-inspired Saint Estèphe in the L.A. suburb of Manhattan Beach in 1980. But the call of his homeland pushed Sedlar to try something new.

By the end of 1983, Seldar decided to follow French techniques but also incorporate ingredients from New Mexico. What emerged was sea-bass mousse tamales and salmon-jalapeño terrine. Green chile mayo and American caviar served on small blue-corn tortillas. Dishes painted in sauces to evoke the Puye cliff dwellings. It was a bold move, especially in Southern California, a region that knew a thing or two about Mexican food and lashed out against any newcomers who pretended to teach them. During the 1970s, a nouveau Mexican restaurant in Los Angeles bought hundreds of pounds of blue corn to turn into tortillas, but the results so disgusted customers—who assumed those tortillas were rotten—that the restaurant had to throw away nearly all of their blue corn.[15]

Saint Estèphe, however, set off a revolution. American diners were beginning to embrace regional cuisine—Cajun cooking, California cuisine, Japanese, and others. By the mid-1980s, with Mexican food firmly ensconced in the American diet but having not seen a new trend since the rise of El Torito and Chi-Chi's in the 1970s, the spread of Southwestern cuisine was welcomed—and not just limited to New Mexico. Three years before Sedlar's experiments, Mark Miller had spun off from the world of Alice Waters to open his Fourth Street Grill in Berkeley; its quick success on vaguely Southwestern dishes motivated him to spend the next couple of years serving as a lecturer until the 1987 opening of Coyote Café in Sedlar's hometown. From Texas, a group of chefs—Dean Fearing, Stephan Pyles, Avner Samuel, and Robert Del Grande, with restaurant consultant Anne Lindsay Greer as their girl Friday—decided to turn Tex-Mex cuisine into a petri dish for modernist experiments and called themselves the "Gang of Five." Greer published *Cuisine of the American Southwest* in 1983 to boost her self-appointed revolution; the others worked in their restaurants around Dallas and Houston creating dishes as fanciful as Sedlar's even though Greer had little respect for the source, deriding Tex-Mex as a "mixed-up plate of rice and beans and ground beef in red chile sauce all over an enchilada."[16]

The boy genius, though, remained Sedlar. America's food critics tried to outdo themselves to praise the young chef, with Craig Claiborne perhaps topping all write-ups by writing in 1985 that Sedlar had offered him "some of the most remarkable mixings of food styles I have ever witnessed."[17] That same year, the Gang of Five and others held a weekend conference at the Four Seasons Hotel in Houston titled the "Festival of Southwest Cookery." Nothing particularly earth-shattering emerged from the gathering; Pyles summed it up best: "We didn't come up with any clear-cut definition of what we are doing, but we all agree it tastes good."[18] But the resultant media attention further promoted Southwestern cuisine. By the time Sedlar's first book, *Modern Southwest Cuisine,* appeared in 1987, its initial print run of twenty thousand sold out almost immediately.

Sedlar should have reigned as king for years, yet he felt something lacking. In 1989, Sedlar, Miller, and others traveled to Veracruz to learn from Patricia Quintana, a famous Mexican chef. "None of us had been to Mexico before," Rivera recalls. "She went through all the chiles and herbs of the country. We had never used them. That's when I realized maybe I should play around with the food of my ancestors." Just after opening his third restaurant, Abiqui, in 1994, Sedlar left the restaurant business—"I burned out," he acknowledges. Southwestern cuisine was already descending, anyway. The push by all the chefs in the movement to outdo themselves with nouveau takes meant that all sorts of abominations took place in the name of innovations, most with no connection at all to the Southwest—papaya salsas and the Southwestern chicken salad, a sad collection of greens, roasted corn, and chicken, the sole dish of the era (along with blue-corn tortilla chips) that survives on a nationwide scale to this day.

Rivera is surprised that the movement he helped birth and propagate went as far as it did. "It shouldn't have gone national," he says, "but it was a good door to Mexico. It was baby steps. It taught people that you could offer what they thought was peasant food in an upscale environment, challenge them with new dishes or interpretations of classics. When we were growing up, we ate chile and beans, but we wanted to eat chicken dinners because you thought that was better food. But as you grow up, you realize that *our* food is more flavorful—and it deserves all the praise in the world."

Green surrounds the city of Hatch, at the bottom of New Mexico: fields of chiles that allow the tiny municipality to call itself the Chile Capital of the World. Water from the Rio Grande via irrigation ditches flows through it, but the town itself is dry—just a highway, small houses, and storefronts, all selling chiles by the burlap sack.

One of the most damning indicators that the Southwestern movement's existence was ephemeral was that its practitioners didn't fully embrace what New Mexicans actually favored above all flavors—chile. As Sedlar noted, the state comes to a standstill every fall, when farmers harvest the crop they've nurtured for months. After roasting, the chiles get pealed, then pulverized into powder, dried, dehydrated, diced, and freeze-dried—seemingly everything but eaten, since folks are preserving for the rest of the year. This is not a rarefied ceremony, however; New Mexico's cult of chile is earthy, of the people, unpretentious.

"I've eaten it since I was wee high to a snail's butt, and ah, it has not only counteracted the destructive elements that I have imposed upon my beautiful God-given brain, but given me a genius that I cannot account for except for the chile seed," says Jimmy Santiago Baca, New Mexico's most famous Chicano poet. Chile accompanies breakfast, lunch, dinner—the only debate in the state on the matter is which area grows better chiles, the most famous of which are Chimayó and Hatch. The Chimayó pepper is earthier, drier because of the height, fleshier, but Hatch's is more prominent due to its annual Hatch Chile Festival, the southern, jovial brother to Chimayó's sanctified pilgrimage. Come Labor Day weekend, Hatch's population expands from a bit more than a thousand to nearly thirty thousand for a celebration of everything chile.

Attending almost yearly is Joseph Baca (no relation to Jimmy or Fabiola), a wine writer by trade. "Out of all the festivals in New Mexico I feel that this celebration honors the one characteristic that differentiates us from other states," he says. "It's the cultural zenith of New Mexico and honors everything that we stand for as a unique people in a very Wal-Martized America."

The festival itself is at the municipal airport just outside town; the main festivities take place in a hangar. Across the grounds are booths selling lemonade, straightforward Mexican food, and heaping plates of New Mexico comfort: posole, smothered burritos, and fat sopaipillas. Local farmers set up stalls, displaying their harvest in all states of being—fresh, fat, and green; dried; presented in *ristras*; freeze-dried, wet, and shining. Dehydrated. In powder form contained in bags as small as a cell phone charger, as large as a freezer bag. The roar of propane-fueled flames envelops the field as young men dump bags into giant screen-sided roasters that tumble—some automatically, some cranked by hand—to ensure that each pepper gets properly roasted. The peppers blister after a minute, their dark green hue first turning white, then black, nearly into ash, as the sweet scent of burned chile fills the air.

Nearby, the festival continues, a country fair at its corniest. An elderly man wows the crowd by doing rope tricks with a lasso made entirely of beer cans, jumping in and out of his tin-can rope. A band blasts out country and Tex-Mex classics in English and Spanish, even though all the players are white. When the Hatch Chile Queen, a local teen, arrives in a convertible to greet her waiting subjects, her dress is decorated with red and green chiles. Of course.

A film crew sets up at the edges, readying for a special that will air on one cable show or another, but no one really cares. To get to Hatch requires commitment—either a flight to El Paso, then an eighty-mile drive, or the two-and-a-half-hour drive from Albuquerque. Will the United States come and finally follow the true New Mexican way? Probably not—but who cares? New Mexico is another country—

totally Mexican, totally American, totally its own thing. It's the Land of Enchantment, forgotten and everlasting.

Besides, Americans always toss aside the Mexican food we once loved. Just look at what's happening to Tex-Mex.

Chapter Seven

Is Tex-Mex Food Doomed?

Texas is the second-largest state in the Union, a country unto itself, with enough history, culture, and weirdos to populate a planet—yet the entirety of its most lasting export to the rest of the United States fits in a one-mile stretch of San Antonio's Commerce Street, which connects the Mexican West Side to the African-American East Side by bisecting its *muy*-tourist center.

Near the eastern end of that strip is the Alamo, the monument to Manifest Destiny that political correctness has unfortunately rendered a sad shell of its former glorious Mexican-trashing past. In this old structure, where hundreds of Americans gave their lives to defend the takeover of a foreign land, it's the few Hispanics who sided with them whom docents now play up. You see it in small displays in the surviving dank, dusty barracks, in the presentations prepared by the keepers of the Alamo's memory as bemused Mexican janitors, security guards, and workers look on. Those lecturers now stress it was a *multicultural* ragtag group of rebels who became martyrs for the incipient Lone Star Republic, and you'll even find books mentioning their minor exploits—Juan Abamillo, for one, or José Gregorio Esparza, lionized in Texas lore as the only defender of the mission to have a proper burial. Good luck finding the booklet on Juan Seguín, highlighted in the 2004 Disney-produced film *The Alamo* as a friend to the Lone Star cause; while he's portrayed as a virtuous, civil man, the film doesn't disclose that he was a virtual exile at the end of his life, shunned by the new colonists as a dirty Mexican and rejected by the Mexicans as a traitor, forced to live "as a foreigner in my native land."[1]

Nowhere is there any hint of what might have been the final meal for those who defended and attacked the mission-turned-battlefield. But if you want to remember the Alamo with a hearty Texas lunch, your best choice is a couple of minutes by foot to the south, to Casa Rio on Commerce, "a taste of history on the river," as the menu proclaims. It's a pretty enough place, right on the River Walk, the picturesque banks of the San Antonio River, which snakes through the city. Men dress in white *guayaberas*, the arabesque cotton shirts original to Cuba that now function as the standard uniform for waiters in your finer Latino restaurants; the women flutter from table to table in flapping, billowy tops called *chinas poblanas*, which barely cover the shoulders of the wearer, swing low to modestly showcase cleavage, and have been worn by every waitress at a Mexican restaurant since the days of Olvera Street.

Casa Rio is the caretaker for what's supposed to be America's original Mexican food combo plate, known here as the "Regular": an enchilada, a tamale, refried beans, rice, and chile con carne. The restaurant only dates back to 1946, the first built on the River Walk, but through a twisted chronology it insists it's the genealogical heir to the Original Mexican Restaurant, a long-closed eatery opened in 1900 just up nearby Losoya Street credited with creating the Regular; menus of the era attest to this. But best to buy Casa Rio's version for the history than the taste. The small tamale is more grease than masa; the sauce on the enchilada more gravy than salsa in the favored Texas style, but strangely chalky. The only strong point on this plate is the chili con carne—crisped beef slathered in a red, slightly mephitic sauce. This chili con carne, according to the menu, is "just like the chili queens served in the plazas of San Antonio in the 1800s." But that was more than a century ago; today the only people who frequent Casa Rio are older tourists wheezing as they climb down the stairs to feast at this edible museum. A much more vibrant scene is west on Commerce, at Market Square, the city's attempt to portray a sanitized version of Old Mexico in the plaza where the chili queens once set up shop before getting banned. *Papel picado,* colorful paper cuts featuring elaborate scenes in each vibrant sheet, crisscross the plaza, strung from building to building. Outdoor vendors hawk Mexican curios—sombreros, wrestling masks, more saint statues than in the Vatican.

The center of this bustle is another seeming tourist trap: Mi Tierra Café and Bakery, open twenty-four hours a day since its 1948 debut, and a place former president Bill Clinton made nationally famous by once jogging in a T-shirt bearing its logo (that scene is now immortalized in a painting inside the restaurant) and writing in his autobiography that he "once ate three meals in eighteen hours" there while a young campaign worker during the 1970s. Mi Tierra teems with eaters: out-of-towners, yes, but also locals, foodies, people looking for a great sit-down meal among mariachis or for a quick pickup at their bakery, where dozens of *pan dulces* (Mexican pastries) sit for just hours before getting sold. Inside, huge murals depict Mexican luminaries—Kahlo, Zapata, Rivera—looking on in approval at the diners. Mi Tierra sells no chili con carne; their strength is, well, *Mexican* food: baked goat, gamy and stringy, from the city of Monterrey; fatty Michoacán-style carnitas; and a decadent *mole poblano,* the complex stew enjoyed by Mexicans in Mexico for centuries as the pinnacle of the national cuisine. The waitresses also wear the *china poblana,* but their demeanor is happier than that of their colleagues at Casa Rio, their *mexicanidad* more authentic.

Between the two restaurants is largely desolation on Commerce—an empty downtown, street preachers screeching about the End Times, and the stagnant splendor of the Aztec Theater, a once-gleaming palace of Art Deco, Spanish Revival, and Meso-American architectural fusion that opened in 1926 but that nowadays hosts country music and mariachi concerts. Somewhere between Casa Rio and Mi Tierra lies the first evolutionary steps beyond the tamale and chili con carne for Mexican food's long, slow trek toward accomplishing what the Mexican troops who won the Alamo yet lost the war never accomplished: conquer Americans, specifically their stomachs.

But tell that to the haters.

Tex. Mex. Tex-Mex. A hyphen separates two cultures that faced off in blood but are forever linked around the world. Each exists on its own, each is fine separate from the other, but together the phrase now conjures up something almost universal: culinary disgust.

Platters baked in an orange goop resembling a dairy product. Oily. Gas-inducing. As early as the 1930s, Mexican chroniclers lambasted the cuisine as inauthentic, a gabacho conspiracy created to dilute Americans' perception of Mexican cuisine. Tex-Mex "brought [Mexican food] down to their lowest common denominator," wrote Diana Kennedy, with "an overly large platter of mixed messes, smothered with a shrill tomato sauce, sour cream, and grated yellow cheese preceded by a dish of mouth-searing sauce and greasy deep-fried chips."[2] *Texas Monthly*, the bible of Texas, has defended its native cuisine fiercely—but even they are becoming skeptics. In December 2010 they published an issue on the fifty best Mexican restaurants in Texas but issued a proclamation: the era of Tex-Mex was nearing its end.

"Mexican food is the richest and most dynamic native cuisine in Texas, and it's getting more Mexican all the time," wrote food editor Patricia Sharpe in her introduction. "We will always love our yellow cheese. But as dishes from Mexico's heartland apply for permanent residency in Texas at an ever-increasing rate, we're on the threshold of a new culinary era: the time of Mex-Tex."[3] It was an inglorious obituary for a cuisine that for a century incubated Mexican restaurant concepts that spread across the United States, from the chili queens to the combo plate to fajitas, where Americans first made their peace with the food and learned how to love it.

"Tex-Mex" as a term to describe the cuisine is a relatively new concept; it only dates back to the 1960s, because before that, there was no need to differentiate it from other types of Mexican food available in this country. Mexican is Mexican, right? An enchilada is a taco is a burrito, no? Of course not. But the confusion dates back to the hectic frontier days, when anything of Mexican descent, whether born in the new United States, or recently migrated, was Mexican—not American, not Texan, not Spanish, not even Tejano, but Mexican. There was no fantasy heritage reclamation project à la California; in Texas, as well as with nearly the rest of the United States, you were Mexican or you were not, and anything associated with you was the same.

An example of such thinking is in the existing descriptions of what was perhaps the first-ever Mexican restaurant in the United States to open outside the Southwest, a pop-up eatery run by an unlikely restaurateur: Buffalo Bill.

In 1886, William Cody was already a national celebrity for his Wild West show, which brought to the United States (and soon, the world) the Great Frontier of the young land with a cast of hundreds. Cody brought his cavalcade of the conquered to New York City to close out the year, camping in the first incarnation of Madison Square Garden. Ads taken out in local papers promised "a grand drama of civilization," a "most artistic, enjoyable instructive and gorgeous presentation of the Hurricane Wild West." But at the bottom of the ads lay a curious addendum: "A genuine Mexican Restaurant now open."[4]

Cody never explained what Mexican food had to do with the submission of the West, and the "Mexican ranchers" who populated his show alongside Native Americans and cowboys were more accurately vaqueros, the Tejano riders from which the American English "buckaroo" derives and from whose womb cowboys emerged. But Cody's Mexican restaurant—staffed by Mexicans, with mescal and chocolate shipped in from Mexico to end the meal—became a New York sensation, with lines of Gothamites waiting to taste curiosities, "inflamed and excited by the hot chile peppers and the other condiments which burn like caustic," according to an observer.[5]

Ever the master promoter, Cody arranged for a reporter to join him for an "Alumerzo a lo Mejicano"—a Mexican breakfast, never mind that the correct term for breakfast in Mexico is *desayuno* (*almuerzo* is more accurately the lunch meal). Served by "two swarthy Mexican women," the meal entranced the lucky eaters, including Cody, and as the reporter noted, it "was plain to see that the mysteries of the Mexican cuisine were as much a surprise to him as to his guests."[6]

The only problem was that the menu was what Cody *imagined* "genuine" Mexican food to be. Although some menu items were Mexican favorites (*puchero,* a type of stew that originated in Spain; *picadillo,* beef hash), most of the items were actually the cuisine favored by the Mexican natives of Texas—enchiladas, chile rellenos, tamales, coffee, and chili con carne, which the observer called the "pièce de résistance" of the breakfast.

As tamales and chili spread across the United States, most chroniclers described them as "Mexican" food, not realizing that chili was a wholly Texas invention and that the tamales in the United States differed from those in Mexico. The first scholarly examination that attested to the unique nature of this Americanized Mexican food appeared in "The Folk-Foods of the Rio Grande Valley and of Northern Mexico," a paper published in the *Journal of American Folklore* of the American Folklore Society in 1895. Its author was John G. Bourke, captain of the Third Cavalry for the U.S. Army, a Civil War veteran stationed in the Southwest after its end, and a pioneering anthropologist for his work detailing the customs of the Indian tribes his men had corralled into reservations.

"The Folk-Foods of the Rio Grande Valley" was published for militaristic rather than culinary purposes, as Bourke noted in his introduction. The region he described had been Mexican land for just fifty years, drips in the bucket of time that is the chronology of the American Southwest. France had occupied Mexico only thirty years earlier. If such wars happened again in the region, Bourke thought, "it might perhaps happen that an officer would find himself beleaguered, and supply trains cut off, in which case there would be no alternative of surrender or retreat, unless he could provide food for his troops from the resources of the country."[7]

The paper is mostly a recitation of wild fruits and vegetables native to the region, but Bourke also made sure to devote some pages to the preparation of Mexican cuisine, a subject that he knew already stirred controversy. "The abominations of Mexican cookery have been for years a favorite theme with travelers rushing hastily through the republic, and pages have been filled with growls at the wretchedness and inadequacy of the accommodations offered in the hotels and restaurants," Bourke wrote. He wanted to make it clear to readers who had no plans to rally "to the defence [*sic*] of Mexican cookery in the abstract, or in its entirety; as a general rule, there is an appalling liberality in the matter of garlic, a recklessness in the use of the chile colorado or chile verde, and an indifference to the existence of dirt and grease."[8]

Nevertheless, Bourke felt that despite "disagreeable features," there was "not a few excellences in Mexican cookery which occupy pleasant niches in the memory, and are deserving of preservation and imitation." He urged the American government to create culinary schools and classes in its still-new land grabs. And while in Mexico proper, Bourke confessed that the street life reminded him of the San Antonio chili stands, "once a most interesting feature of the life of that charming city, but abolished within the past two or three years in deference to the 'progressive' spirit of certain councilmen."

Bourke ended with a prophetic warning: "Colonies will always be looked upon, in any country, with a good deal of suspicion and mistrust. Where they do well, the natives feel that they are losing profits which belong to them by the right of prior occupation." In Texas, Americans who enjoyed Mexican food but not the Mexicans learned the secrets and sold the food to their fellow countrymen. Mexican food was on its way to becoming Tex-Mex.

Denison, Texas, is best known as the birthplace of President Dwight D. Eisenhower and for sitting on the Red River. Even today, it's far from the corridors of Mexican immigration in Texas that long ago spilled far from the borderlands and into the rest of the state. But it's here—somewhere—that one of the earliest attempts to open a Mexican restaurant suited for American tastes was attempted.

Its only record is in an 1878 newspaper published hundreds of miles away, in Brenham, under the local paper's brevities section. The brief merely noted that a Denison man—no name—sought to serve "chile con carne, tomales [sic] and other 'hot' dishes" at a to-open eatery.[9] Tamale vendors were just starting to spread across the state; chuck wagons had yet to absorb the fiery sorcery of the chili queens. As Texans accepted the two dishes in the coming decades, the market grew for a respectable way to eat them instead of on the street.

The person who capitalized on this sentiment wasn't a Texas native but rather a Chicagoan: Otis M. Farnsworth. In the late 1890s, he visited San Antonio on business, and his hosts took their guest to a Mexican restaurant on the West Side. A line already wrapped its way around the café when they arrived. Most of those waiting to get in were like Farnsworth: otherwise-respectable people with no business in the city's Mexican quarter save for a fix of culinary crack. Farnsworth figured that if these people were willing to slum it in their finest, they'd probably frequent a more respectable place if it were brought to them.

The Original Mexican Restaurant opened in 1900, just to the west of the Alamo. Each side of the hyphen in Tex-Mex came to fruition through Farnsworth's midwifery. The cooks were Mexican but the owner was white. The place was fancy, but murals of Mexican peons in pastoral village scenes decorated the walls. The dish names were in

Spanish—tamales, chili con carne, enchiladas, frijoles, corn tortillas, and *sopa de arroz* (rice soup, but in actuality the side of rice we know today)—but collapsed into a special Farnsworth called the Regular Supper, the protean combination plate that reigns as the lingua franca of Mexican restaurants in the United States. Instead of the chaos of San Antonio's plazas, here was a refined experience—dining jackets were mandatory for men, and ads advised that within their walls were "elegantly appointed dining rooms in which we serve our appetizing Mexican dishes."[10]

Farnsworth took pride in his Original—at a meeting of the Rotary Club, he told an audience that "his restaurant has never lost its Mexican individuality" despite its Anglo ownership.[11] Others took notice, and the Original concept followed the roads out of San Antonio and onward—an Original opened in San Francisco in 1904, followed by a Houston imitator in 1907, another one in Galveston in 1913, and the Original Mexican Restaurant in Fort Worth, now known as the Original Mexican Eats Cafe and open since 1926. "Regular" suppers also popped up as specials in Los Angeles restaurants. As that experience spread, others thought of delving into the same refined Mexican dining experience—and not just Anglos.

Miguel Martinez was a laborer from Chihuahua, the state just across the Rio Grande from Texas; he immigrated to the Dallas area just after the Mexican Revolution. Picking up odd jobs at a hotel, he graduated to cook's assistant, ably stepping in when the head cook fell ill. For his efforts, Martinez's boss fired him. Unfazed, he opened an eatery in the Dallas barrio of Little Mexico in 1918, calling it the Martinez Cafe. It originally served Mexican and American dishes, but he switched exclusively to the former at the request of customers and renamed the restaurant El Fenix—The Phoenix, the mythical bird that symbolized reinvention. Martinez continued Farnsworth's innovation of offering multiple items on one plate, but added even more combinations. Someone at the restaurant numbered the different options, making it easier for non-Mexicans to order a plate instead of pronouncing each item on the menu, and the—pick your favorite: #1? #5? #15?—numbered combo plate became de rigueur.

Other Mexicans copied the El Fenix concept. Adelaida Cuellar stretched her family's meager farm earnings by operating a tamale stand at the Kaufman County Fair during the 1920s. The Cuellar children, who had grown up working the fields with their mother, opened a restaurant in the city in 1928—really just a long bar and stools. One son, Frank, moved on to open a Mexican restaurant in Shreveport, Louisiana; two others found success in Oklahoma City, learning how to customize Mexican food for all palates, not just their own.

The Cuellars gathered their resources to open El Chico Restaurant in Dallas in 1940. The food wasn't too different from what their competitors offered, but it distinguished itself by the entrepreneurial know-how of the Cuellar family and a sharp ear for what was next in Mexican food; when the taco rose in popularity, they commissioned one of their cooks, Joe Caballero, to create a prefabricated hard shell to expedite orders (Caballero is also credited with introducing sour cream to the Tex-Mex platter). Appearing in ads as "Mama's Boys," the Cuellars offered franchising opportunities with their restaurant concept in 1968; by 1977, seventy-nine El Chico's flourished across the United States, and the chain stays strong through Texas and the surrounding states.

El Chico's efforts inspired others, Anglos and Mexicans alike, to open Tex-Mex restaurants outside of Texas. This was the food that Robb Walsh, winner of multiple James Beard awards for his exhaustively researched, wonderfully written forays into Texas cuisine, grew to long for as a child moving around the United States during the 1960s. "There's something about Tex-Mex that has the American comfort food angle," he says, "and yet it's a bicultural food. It's cuisine without pretension."

Bean dip and Fritos (another Texas creation, which will get its proper analysis in a couple of chapters) were part of the Walsh household cupboard, but "Mexican" food wasn't until they moved to Southern California in the 1960s. He remembers eating tacos created by neighbors in Anaheim, proud to have utilized a taco-making kit at home. The Walshes patronized drive-through taco shops soon after—but when they moved back East, there was no Mexican food, leaving the young Walsh hungry.

That scenario changed dramatically when Walsh enrolled at the University of Texas at Austin and regularly ate Mexican food again. "It was reacquainting myself with a taste I'd fallen in love with years ago," he said. After college he scored a job with the *Austin Chronicle,* the city's alternative weekly, one that had him covering the rise of "authentic" Mexican food and modern Southwestern cuisine during the 1980s. It was a time when Tex-Mex was under assault by the likes of Diana Kennedy, even as most Mexican restaurants introduced fajitas onto their menu, the last charge of the genre into the Mexican-American culinary palate.

Originally, the term "fajita" referred to a cut of steak around the cow's diaphragm known in American butchery as the outside skirt steak (which supposedly looks like a small belt—hence its diminutive, because *faja* means "belt" in Spanish). It was a cut ignored by Anglo ranchers in favor of the rest of the cow, but created into an appetizing meal by the lower classes: pounded until it was little more than membrane, then marinated until the formerly tough strip became succulent. Like chili con carne, the origins of the fajita's rise gets mucked in myth and history, although Texas has generally agreed that it came somewhere from the Rio Grande Valley, the stretch of Texas nearest Mexico, where its Mexicans traditionally lived and where its cattle industry roamed the farthest. Down in this region, near the beef-crazy states of Nuevo León and Tamaulipas, the cut was just part of the cow.

In 1969 a Laredo restaurant called the Round-Up tried something revolutionary: they prepared the fajitas, but instead of serving the dish on a regular plate, it was brought out on a sizzling platter, angrily spewing forth juices. Four years later, a Lower Rio Grande Valley native named Maria Ninfa Rodriguez Laurenzo introduced the concept at her Houston restaurant, Ninfa's, along with another border favorite: tacos al carbón.

Like Farnsworth before her, others took Ninfa's idea, so many that the National Restaurant Association named Rodriguez female restaurateur of the year in 1984. By 1985, *Nation's Restaurant News* wrote, "Until only a few years ago, fajitas—pronounced fa-hee-tas—were largely unknown outside of Mexico and parts of Texas. Today few restaurants specializing in Mexican or Tex-Mex cooking can afford to omit the dish from their menus."[12] At about that time the price of outside skirt steak went from 49 cents a pound in 1976 to as high as $2.79 a pound in the mid-1980s. The reason: Japanese, also fajita-crazy, were buying 90 percent of outside skirts at the time. Coupled with a rising Stateside demand for the dish, South Texans were priced out of the cut they helped pioneer.

The craze for fajitas became such that restaurateurs marketed nearly any meat as fajitas: Shrimp fajitas. Steak fajitas. Vegetarian fajitas, nothing more than strips of sautéed onions, bell peppers, tomatoes, jalapeños, and zucchini. At the Hyatt Hotel in Austin, chefs introduced chicken fajitas—never mind that the meat didn't come from the actual meat around the diaphragm of hens. As long as guests had the opportunity to see a waiter bring a sizzling platter of something to their table and warn them that the platter was hot, that was a fajita. This led to a backlash against the meal by culinary gatekeepers who dismissed it as an inauthentic development instead of acknowledging its Tex-Mex origin. A column in the *Philadelphia Inquirer* snarked that fajitas were "the ideal food for yuppie grazers."[13] A July 1980 blurb in *Texas Monthly* stated in an almost exasperated tone, "Something perverse about Texans inspires them to elevate no-account dishes to cult status. First it was chili; now it's fajitas," even as the column advertised the fifth edition of a Fajita Cookoff, a McAllen festival that continues to this day.[14]

All along, Walsh watched the development from within and afar.

For an assignment, Walsh traveled to Oaxaca in pursuit of a pepper reportedly spicier than the infamous habanero. At a party, the interested hosts asked him about his assignment. When he revealed it, the disbelief became downright uncomfortable.

"A man tells me, 'Salsa? You came down all the way down here for writing about salsa? Pardon me for laughing, but imagine that I'm a Mexican writer and show up to your house to write about ketchup,'" Walsh says. "There was an attitude at the time that there was nothing cool about regular Mexican food to write about. In Mexico, people didn't see value in it. They thought it was *pinche indio* ("fucking Indian") food. And back home in Texas, I realized that Tex-Mex is *pinche indio* food.

"Intellectual Mexicans look down on Tex-Mex because it is a peasant food," Walsh adds. "Intellectuals up here look down on Tex-Mex because it is a peasant food. Until 1972, it was just Mexican food. And it was Mexicans cooking it. It's *pinche indio* food. The people who are opposed to Tex-Mex now are opposed to it for some reason of purity. It's mongrelized, it's bastardized, right? Once upon a time, your Anglo son was going to marry a Mexican girl. It was going to be a weeping and gnashing of teeth with the Anglos and vice versa. If you see the motives of those [intellectuals], it's some sort of cultural purity test, and this kind of aversion to cultural mixing is something that takes you back to terms like 'miscegenation.' The people who are upset with Tex-Mex are upset with miscegenation. To the extent that we're comfortable with interethnic marriage, we're comfortable with mixed ethnic cuisine."

He scoffs at the upscaling of Mexican cuisine that happened during the 1980s, deriding it as an attempt to make tacos "compatible with expensive wine." But his obsession with Tex-Mex is real—after decades of writing for various publications in Texas, Walsh opened a restaurant, El Real Tex-Mex, in an Art Deco theater in Houston, specializing in stubbornly Tex-Mex meals; as a nod to the past, El Real even features the restored chairs from Felix Mexican Restaurant, a Houston

Tex-Mex landmark whose founder, Felix Tijerina, was an important Latino leader during the 1950s who hobnobbed with the likes of Lyndon Johnson.

But can Tex-Mex survive in an era of unlimited Mexican food options? "When that Mario Batali brought that northern Italian food thing to New York, I worried that pizza would disappear, but somehow it didn't disappear. I don't know why," Walsh says in a tone so dry it mimics the Sahara. "My challenge is that every gourmet Mexican restaurant, every new Mexican taqueria take fajitas, chips dipped in salsa, chile con queso and everything else that's identifiably Tex-Mex off the menu, and see how long they last.

"Why do we call it Tex-Mex?" Walsh concludes. "So we won't piss purists off claiming it's Mexican."

While chili is now so mainstreamed that most Americans don't even know its *tejano* origins, while fajitas have become a standard offering at restaurants, Mexican or not, across the country, while the combo platter is standard fare, other Tex-Mex dishes have stubbornly remained provincial, impervious to Yankee malleability or exportation, never making it past their hometown's city limits.

West Texas is the land of the stacked enchiladas, and none are more historic than the ones served at Borunda's Bar and Grill in Marfa. The proprietors are direct descendants of Tula Borunda Gutierrez, founder of the Borunda Café, the oldest standing Mexican restaurant in the United States when it closed in 1989 after 102 years of operation and cited by scholars as the country's first-ever Tex-Mex restaurant. These are not the enchiladas of gabacho renown, but the ones native to New Mexico and Arizona and sort of like a stack of pancakes. On each corn tortilla is smeared some cheese, sauce, and onions until the whole thing is topped with fried eggs, a glorious ode to the days when no one cared how much cholesterol you pumped into your arteries.

Though the chili queens are still celebrated in San Antonio, chili con carne is no longer the city's mainstay dish. The city's minor league baseball team, the Missions (a Double-A affiliate of the San Diego Padres), has two official mascots: the Ballapeño (a giant pepper dressed as an umpire) and Henry the Puffy Taco, an anthropomorphic felt taco of a shell, lettuce, tomato, and cheese that hangs off its chest like the leaves of a weeping willow. It's a nod to San Antonio's favorite meal: the puffy taco, a gleaming meal sold everywhere from doughnut shops to gas stations and sit-down restaurants. Cooks take a freshly made corn tortilla and place it in a fryer for only an instant, so that air pockets enter the masa and puff up the taco until it glimmers like gold. In goes ground meat or a stew, and cabbage; green sauce is on the side. It's like a taco aspired to become a sope mixed with a quesadilla but got scared by the grease bath and quit halfway. The taste is momentous: the slight crunch is reminiscent of a crisped tortilla, while the meat absorbs the grease.

For such a star, only one other restaurant outside Texas in the United States regularly offers the meal: Arturo Puffy Taco in Whittier, California, owned by a branch of the Villa family that helped to popularize the dish (they're behind Henry's Puffy Tacos and also Ray's Drive-in, credited with introducing the puffy taco to the world, but competing Villas helm each business, and let's leave it at *that*). "When I grew up, I was shocked to learn that the puffy taco hadn't spread beyond the city," says Richard Farias, an English professor at San Antonio Community College whose family has lived in Texas since the eighteenth century. "Perhaps it was just that San Antonio's pastoral or provincial nature preserved it as a local, homespun thing and it's remained a unique quality. [Then again], the puffy taco could probably only be invented here—where the grease and the puffiness come together with panache and *panzón* (being fat)."

San Antonio also claims the breakfast taco, but Austin has usurped it as its own child. No matter who created it, its countenance seems engineered with an eye toward the American palate. Instead of corn tortillas, they're made with small flour ones. The ingredients can occasionally be Mexican, but American morning-time stalwarts dominate: scrambled eggs, bacons, potatoes, ham. It seems like such a natural meal would be the next great Tex-Mex hit, but breakfast tacos haven't really caught on across the rest of the United States.

"Austin's breakfast-taco culture is a magnificent milieu of the usually outstanding, the often unhealthy, and the always exciting collision of traditional Mexican fare with everything else," says political consultant Joshua Treviño. He patronizes the city's most famous breakfast-taco place, Torchy's Tacos, but insists that the best in the world come from Nano's Taco Run in Corpus Christi. "They're inventive combinations that drag flavors from Mexico's southern heartland and distant past, ingredients from the American breadbasket, and ingenuity from the Texan culinary mind, and place them on your morning plate—what's not to love?"

Herrera's Café in Dallas doesn't lay claim to any invented meal—it's just a good place to experience *queso*. Remember, this is Dallas, the capital of old-money Texas, so it's pronounced "kay-so" and is cheese in name only. It's melted ecstasy—milky, thick, and served steaming, so be careful to let it cool lest it coat your tongue and burn. Queso is probably familiar to the American palate as an ancestor of nacho cheese, but it stands as its own condiment in Texas—sluiced with jalapeños, used as a dipping sauce more often than salsa.

"It's our bacon: it just makes everything better," says Jesse Sanchez, a writer for Major League Baseball's Web site. "It's also great if you are not worried about your waistline or the front of your shirt. If you don't like it, don't eat it. It just means there will be more for us to dip our entire worlds into."

Farther south, in the Rio Grande Valley, where John Bourne traveled so long ago, what passes as Tex-Mex is even more obscure to American tastes. Meat rules, but not just fajitas—think *cabrito,* roasted kid goat, and *carne deshebrada,* meat baked for so long it turns into a pile of strings. Even tastier is *barbacoa,* the root word for the American "barbecue"; in the Rio Grande Valley, it refers to a pit, some maguey leaves, and a full cow's head, buried to roast for hours, until the face of the cow and the meat are so tender that it looks like a melting Madame Tussaud's statue.

Tex-Mex's national heyday might be gone, and *Texas Monthly* might herald a new era, but its advocates stubbornly press on. In 2008, the Martinez family sold El Fenix to Dallas businessman Mike Karns, who grew up eating at the restaurant and whose parents patronized the place before Mike was even born. The Martinez family had turned it into a Texas institution, but the second generation didn't want to run the restaurants, let alone expand. The clan still runs individual locations, and a Martinez still sits on El Fenix's board of directors: the chief operating officer, John McBride Jr., great-grandson of Miguel Martinez, who explains his seemingly un-Mexican name thusly: "My grandmother married an Irishman."

"Tex-Mex is important to us because it's our bond to Mexico, even for us born in the United States," says Sanchez. "And it's just Mexican food to us. Are we less Mexican or Mexican-American because we are Tejanos? We consider ourselves all part of the 'Mexican food' family and are surprised to hear when people speak of our food—or us—with disdain. The critiques sound elitist to us, and that says a lot coming from a state where we claim everything is bigger and better."

"I love Mexico, I don't wish it ill, the cuisine," Walsh says. "But don't come to my country and tell me there's something wrong with my food either, okay?"

Chapter Eight

What Took the Burrito So Long to Become Popular?

There is a burrito sold in the Los Angeles neighborhood of Boyle Heights that's beyond cosmic, that's as close to touching God while eating Mexican food as finding Jesus on a tortilla. It's the Manuel's Special at Manuel's El Tepeyac Café, a ramshackle restaurant named after the hill where the Virgin of Guadalupe first appeared to the world. A small shrine to *la morenita* sits at the back of Manuel's parking lot; Assumption Catholic Church stands just across the street, its stained-glass abstract mosaic of the Savior looking right at the eatery, like those invariably waiting in line on the sidewalk.

Manuel's Special: five pounds, beans and rice and guacamole and sour cream and your choice of meat—juicy nubs of grilled chicken, carne asada burned into succulent charcoal, or best with *machaca*, shredded beef that sticks between molars for hours afterward, heavily spiced and just grand, wrapped in a flour tortilla that, if laid flat, can serve as swaddling cloth for a puppy. Many brave souls order Manuel's Special with the intent of eating the mass on its own, but this cylindrical god[1] is best enjoyed communally, sliced up and portioned out like the Holy Host.

Manuel Rojas runs the place, opened by his parents in this spot in 1952, serving burritos almost as long, and drawing thousands of visitors over the years. Although a Mexican eatery by genre, English dominates at El Tepeyac—third-generation Angelenos trekking for a post-Mass lunch as they have since childhood, or the children of Mexican immigrants, far removed from the native cuisines of their parents, settling for the Hollenbeck and the Okie, Manuel's other famous burritos, merely as large as a policeman's forearms.

But for all its fame, Manny's giants aren't nationally known. No, the true burrito of renown is in the north, in Los Angeles's eternal civic rival, San Francisco. In a city as self-important as this one, one that residents and outsiders alike consider a beacon for innovation, hedonism, arrogance, and gluttony, it's telling that one of the few restaurants in San Francisco with the audacity to call itself a lighthouse—that most indispensable of structures in seaside towns, the guiding light to safety and shelter for the lost—is Mexican.

El Faro—what else? "The Lighthouse" in Spanish—stands on the northeastern corner of 20th and Folsom Streets, on the edge of the city's iconic Mission District barrio, San Francisco's slice of America's demographic jalapeño, in the area where gentrification has yet to sneak up. Every day at about noon, breakfast, or dinner, people come to sit on its uncomfortable, yellow-and-orange benches. The menu speaks of tacos, combo plates, even *pupusas* in a nod to the Mission's Central American community, but customers come for the burrito—not just any, but the ur-burrito, from the agreed-upon birthplace of the Mission-style burrito, the gift wrapped in foil, hefty and fat, that now dominates the United States.

The original sign still stands outside—orange backdrop, black-and-white lighthouse, with "El Faro" in the searchlight pointing downward, toward the entrance. But the most distinctive part of the restaurant is a tiled mural decorating the wall above everyone. It's a city-wide party. A city celebrates. And on both sides of the wall, a lighthouse beckons the world in. Photos of celebrities ring the wall—

Willie Shoemaker, Hollywood stars, and a complete *charro* outfit worn by *ranchera* icon Vicente Fernandez, intricately embroidered sombrero, belt, and gold-woven suit hanging in a display case like the Shroud of Turin.

You enter through the doorway, go to the end of the tiny, narrow restaurant, and pick up your drink from upright coolers. The kitchen is in plain view, separated from the eating area only by a counter and chest-high glass panels. Place the food order—burrito, of course, and your choice of meat. Everything? A woman places a giant flour tortilla on a press, just enough so it heats and the glutens inside the flour tortilla loosen, allowing the disc to stretch without ripping apart—a necessary attribute, as will soon become apparent. She grabs the tortilla, moves to her right, and lays it flat on the counter, ready to adorn it with toppings—a bed of beans, a tundra of rice, a spoonful of meat, all grabbed from heated trays in front of her. Soon comes a rain of cheese, dollops of sour cream and guacamole, a jungle of shredded lettuce, items in containers laid out in front of her that she scoops up with spoons, as fast as in a game of Whac-a-Mole.

The worker moves east to west through this Station of the Burrito, speaking with other workers but never stopping her benediction, waiting for the worker in front of her to move on to the next step. It's the Miracle of the Loaves, the burrito becomes fatter, bigger, a mount. Edible origami is the finale: ingredients in the center, the worker folds one side of the tortilla three quarters of the way over the other, then tucks it all up like a Windsor knot. The excess folds at the ends of the new creation get poked inside and disappear. She puts the quivering mass in the middle of an expanse of foil and wraps the burrito in it. And again. Your double-wrapped superburrito is ready, placed on a plate, with chips on the side and salsa in a ramekin.

Eating the burrito is like eating a living, breathing organism—you can feel the burrito's ingredients sigh inside with each bite, each squeeze. The foil acts as an exoskeleton that must cover what isn't yet ready to eat—rip it all off at once, and you're liable to eat a burrito plate as the contents explode and the tortilla flops open. Instead, eaters rip off the foil piece by piece, leaving the shimmering petals on the plate.

El Faro is one of more than a hundred such taquerias in and around the Mission. Pancho Villa, La Taqueria, El Castellito, El Cumbre (which claims they created the Mission burrito assembly line)—the rivalries are fierce, the natives argue online, in person, at the taquerias. The Mission-style burrito is a way of life. It's also in danger of disappearing from its birthplace, even as its cult has turned into a full-fledged religion nationwide.

Mayans never ate burritos. Mayans never set up shop in Springfield, Missouri, as far as archaeologists have determined. But a metallic sculpture of one of the ancients, resplendent in flowing headdress, hand stuffing a burrito into his big-lipped mouth, now adorns more than a thousand restaurants across the world.

Some brothers of Tau Kappa Epsilon need to grub. It's closing time at Chipotle Mexican Grill in Springfield, a tiny college town with a baseball stadium for the Double-A affiliate of the St. Louis Cardinals, Missouri State, and little else. This is the type of town where the local business journal runs stories about Indian immigrants who run hotels and must deal with prospective customers who won't stay at their hotels because of their ethnicity.[2]

But Mexicans are okay. The Tekes each order a burrito—one pork, one vegetarian, two shredded beef. "Black beans or pinto?" the worker asks. "Sour cream, guac, or both?" More questions; more answers. The Stations of the Burrito starts again, in Heartland USA. The tortilla press. The ingredients. The bundling of the babe in foil. Except this juggernaut is larger than anything you can find in the Mission. Other changes have happened, too: the salsa is milder. The music is Phil Collins and other 1980s classics instead of *ranchera*. Carne asada is now called "steak"; the meats, all organic and free-range.

Others rush in for last-minute takeout orders. They receive their burrito in brown bags with second-grade doodles. A floating, smiling pig face shouts via cartoon bubble, *"¡Viva la Revolución!"* Long live the revolution, the classic rallying cry of Latin America. But this coup call is different, the porcine Che calling for the humane treatment of his brothers.

Chipotle is now the second-largest Mexican food chain in the United States; in the past decade, its take on Mission-style burritos has come to define burritos in the United States, leaving other styles relatively unknown. It's an unlikely ascendancy, though, because the burrito has been nationally available since the 1960s (the taco empires all served them) and has existed on the borderlands since the 1920s, when small meals known as *burros* crossed into Tucson from Sonora, the name the dish still goes by in that region. Yet we are in the midst of a burrito renaissance, one as unlikely as, well, a burrito in Springfield, Missouri.

Unlike the taco, the burrito wasn't historically widespread in Mexico—indeed, it's known only in the borderlands, and even then more specifically around Sonora and Baja California, where flour tortillas are preferred instead of corn. There is no known etymological origin for the term, or even where it was created—the story bandied around is that the name came from miners in Sonora who nicknamed their portable lunch after the donkeys taking them down into the depths. But Mexican dictionaries from the late 1800s place it as a food term used in the Mexican state of Guerrero.[3]

What is accepted is that the burrito, from its earliest days until just recently, has been a meal of the working class, the simplest of lunches: a tortilla, the morning's leftovers, and nothing else. They were easier to transport than tacos made from corn tortillas, which harden shortly after heating; the flour tortilla, on the other hand, maintains a fresh flavor long after and easily yields to the ravenous incisors of the lumpenproletariat.

The burrito's first widespread audience in the United States was *braceros*—the migrant workers who legally entered the United States from the 1940s through the 1960s under an agreement with the Mexican and American governments. Braceros depended on farmers and government for everything—their wages, housing, clothing, and food. Their handlers found it easy to make burritos en masse and hand out to workers every day to take to the field, relieving them of the responsibility of preparing fresh lunches; just leave it in foil and let the sun bake it naturally, and you have an instant lunch. "They had good housing; they had good food; they had the kind of food that they liked to have," one farmer told an oral historian decades later. "The migrants knew they were going into a part-time job and they did not mind it. . . . It was a pretty fair thing they were getting and I don't think they felt that they were being put upon."[4]

That's not how the braceros felt; for them, the burrito became an object of scorn. Most of them weren't familiar with the item, as they came from central Mexico, where the flour tortilla, let alone the burrito, was exotic. "A bracero is given two burritos for his lunch," noted a chronicler, incredulously noting cheese was added only "as a bonus. Can you imagine eating two bean burritos every noon hour for lunch?"[5]

"They were disgusting!" a bracero remembered decades later, saying the food was nothing like that in Mexico.[6] In other cases, the portions were so meager and disgusting that famished braceros filled them with dog food.[7]

Burritos were personal meals, meals of pain and embarrassment. Stories of Mexican students from the 1950s and 1960s suffering burrito humiliation fill the annals of Chicano literature.[8] Gerard Meraz remembers his mother's embarrassment when her white classmates at Catholic school ridiculed the burritos she brought to class one day. "Because of the shame of eating [burritos], her mom switched to sending them to school with bean sandwiches," says Meraz, a professor at California State University, Northridge.

While Mexicans struggled with their burritos of shame, Americans warmed up to them. It became a staple of Los Angeles's catering truck scene by the late 1950s. Glen Bell included bean burritos in his original

144

1962 Taco Bell menu, and copycats followed. By 1964, the *Los Angeles Times* published its first burrito recipe, noting they were "beginning to be popular in our taco stands"; demands for that recipe moved the *Times* to republish it a year later.[9] Southern California became the country's burrito nexus, and the region's many drive-ins and delis incorporated them onto their menus, whether in Mexican-American neighborhoods or not.

These burritos were straightforward—just beans, rice, some sort of meat, and maybe guacamole or sour cream. But mongrels arose, most famously with the Kosher Burrito, an ungodly concoction of a flour tortilla, heaps of pastrami, and cheddar cheese. Its birthplace is unknown, but logic points to Boyle Heights, a historic Jewish-Latino neighborhood in Los Angeles. It spread in popularity during the 1960s until reaching an apotheosis at Oki Dog, a run-down hot dog stand in West Hollywood that became legendary in punk circles during the late 1970s. Here, Okinawan immigrant Sakai "Jimmy" Sueyoshi created the dive's namesake: two hot dogs, chili, cheddar cheese, pastrami, and grilled onions wrapped in a flour tortilla, grilled and served to hungry punkers and the brave who still stand in lines wrapped around the building for a grease-drenched end to their night.

Other competitors took Oki's cue and served their own variations. Up north during this time, the Mission-style burrito was coalescing. The first one was born on September 26, 1961, a day after Febronio Ontiveros opened his grocery store, El Faro. During lunch, Ontiveros and his clan claim, a group of firefighters from the station a block away asked Ontiveros for sandwiches. He had just arrived from Durango, a state in central Mexico, trying to better his life. With no sandwiches but not wanting to lose business in his first week, Ontiveros asked the firefighters to return the following day, when he'd have something better for them.

He did. Ontiveros had eaten burritos in his youth, and knew that it was a staple of Mexican workers in the fields of California's abundant Central Valley to the south. But he also figured firefighters needed more than a single order. When they returned as promised the following day, Ontiveros had positioned two flour tortillas side by side, spread the ingredients across the duo, and wrapped everything together; the fire-fighters took the creation back to the station and returned soon after for more. Other customers asked for that same remodel, and Ontiveros figured this Siamese twin wasn't a onetime special.

Ontiveros found a tortilla factory and asked them to make a flour version much larger than what was generally available at supermarkets at the time, the better to create his new find. The rest, as they say, is *historia*. El Faro spawned imitators across town and became a multi-million-dollar mom-and-pop still run by the family. "I've been able to demonstrate what can be done in this country with a good idea," Ontiveros told a Spanish-language newspaper years later.[10] Others further innovated the art of burrito-building in the Mission. El Cumbre claims they innovated the assembly line, with owner Raul Duran getting the inspiration to enter the business after "a friend from Los Angeles told him that people there were making money selling them."[11] By the 1980s, the foodstuff was a Mission mainstay; by 1990, more than a hundred Latino restaurants operated in its few blocks, almost all of them serving burritos in the same fashion.[12]

Such a unique, specific means of production inevitably emerged in the Mission, according to John Nuño, a Mission native and reporter. "It's the working-class background of the neighborhood, the ethnicity of the Mission's Mexican immigrants, the scale of the neighborhood, and San Francisco's transformation into a technology hub," he says. Historically, the main restaurant customers were blue-collar stiffs "who don't have time to sit with plate of carne, beans, and rice. And for working people, who often don't have much money to spare, cost is important. A burrito is a full meal that can last a long time."

He also points to the district's compact nature, which forced kitchens to stretch out in their narrow spaces from front to back and offer cheap, fast meals lest impatient customers just walk over to a taqueria next door. But the Mission burrito didn't draw non-Mexicans in earnest until the late 1980s, when a new wave of immigrants—young, mostly white professionals—moved into the barrio, drawn by its cheap rents and vibrancy. Travel guides mentioned them as a regional marvel, drawing more first-timers to the Mission. One of those young migrants was Steve Ells, the founder of Chipotle.

Ells grew up in Indianapolis before moving to Boulder during junior high. His wasn't a family that favored fast food, though he admits to "sneaking out with my dad and eating crispy tacos at Taco Bell." At home, "my mom used to fry corn tortillas for tostadas, with the ground beef and diced tomatoes and slices of avocado and shredded yellow cheese, and that was like the American taco." For seasoning, instead of hot sauce or chilies, the family used cumin or oregano.

Upon moving to Colorado, the family entered an area with its own unique Mexican food. The southern part of Colorado had been colonized by Spain in the 1600s but didn't get settled in earnest until the mid-1800s, when New Mexicans moved into the southern part of the state, in the San Luis Valley. Much of New Mexico's culinary influence made the journey as well—the use of chile, mutton, and an appreciation for *adovada* (marinated pork). From this foundation, Colorado-Mexican cuisine evolved. The chile turned into more of a gravy, almost indistinguishable from nacho cheese to the outside eye but fierce, verdant, a Rocky Mountain ratatouille with pork bits, tomatoes, jalapeños, diced green chile, salt, and red chile powder, a soothing balm to guard against furious winters. The chile rellenos became smaller, sometimes blanketed in an eggroll wrapper and filled not with actual cheese but Tex-Mex–style queso. Burritos also appeared, perhaps most innovatively, in a marvel called the Mexican hamburger: a bean-and-meat burrito with a hamburger patty inside, smothered in Colorado-style gravy, and served on a plate and eaten with a knife and fork.

Unlike New Mexico, Denver's Mexican-American community also featured a large segment of recent immigrants who adapted their tastes to Denver's unique Mexican food needs. In the 1970s, burrito vendors hit the streets of Denver—first in the city's barrios, then on street corners around the multistory offices of downtown. These burritos were more in the Los Angeles style than San Francisco—large but manageable, and wrapped in foil to keep them warm. Some of those vendors asked office buildings for permission to peddle burritos from office to office, a phenomenon that continues to this day.

Ells enjoyed those burritos and the smothered variety while attending the University of Colorado during the 1980s, graduating with a degree in art history. He moved on to the Culinary Institute of America, finishing in 1990, and shortly after scoring a job as a line chef in San Francisco under Jeremiah Towers, one of the pioneers of California cuisine. On his day off, Ells and a friend visited the Mission to try its famed burritos for the first time; he can't remember which burrito spot they visited, but he still remembers his original sin.

"I unwrapped it completely from the foil, and my friend said, 'No, no—wrap it back up,'" he says, laughing. "For me, forever, a burrito was from a plate and smothered in green chile. This was something completely different. It was delicious. And I started to eat them often."

He had ambitions of opening an upscale restaurant back in Denver but had no way to fund it. But seeing the lines snake around the Mission's many taquerias, viewing the Fordian assembly line methodically prepping the burritos without any loss of quality, hundreds throughout the day—"Each one at five bucks, they're making some good money here," he remembers thinking. "That's what I'll do—I'll start one, but put my own twist." Ells returned to Colorado and experimented in the kitchen.

Chipotle Mexican Grill opened for business in a former ice cream shop near the University of Denver in the summer of 1993 with the help of an $85,000 loan from Ells's father, who was so skeptical of the idea that he required his son to draw up a business plan. Ells wasn't the first person to try to introduce the Mission-style burrito to a non–San Francisco audience. In New York, Stuart Tarabour unveiled them at the Kitchen in the early 1980s, a takeout spot on Eighth Avenue; at about this time, another native San Franciscan, Mike Mercer, opened

Harry's Burritos and then Benny's Burritos in 1988, which he promptly turned into a minichain.[13] Chipotle wasn't even the first Mission-style burrito to penetrate Denver. The previous year, Chez Jose introduced them to Denverites, much to their curiosity and annoyance. "When we first opened up, it was kind of funny—we had to explain to people what we were doing," founder Dan Oholson told *Westword*. "They'd come in and say, 'I want my burrito smothered.'"

Chipotle, on the other hand, became an immediate phenomenon. Ells told his father that he had to sell about a hundred burritos a day to make a profit; more than a thousand a day sold after the first month. Another Chipotle opened in 1995, and a third one soon after, with Ells still intent on using their revenue to open a formal restaurant. He dropped those plans after he had ten Chipotles, but people still ask when he'll open his much-dreamed-about "real" restaurant. "I open three real restaurants every week," he now replies.

But as he expanded and continued to experiment, Ells noticed a drop in quality in the products he used. One day in the late 1990s, as Chipotle readied for yet another expansion, he worked on a carnitas recipe but found nailing the flavors he sought hard, if not impossible. "It seemed that pork chops were better back in the day," he says. "I was feeling the same way with carnitas—they really weren't great." He returned home and read an issue of *The Art of Eating,* a literary journal about the culinary world, with a profile of the Niman Ranch, a company that pioneered the promotion of organic, sustainably raised livestock. After tasting a sample—soft, juicy, nearly silky, nothing like what was readily available—Ells told his business partners he wanted to incorporate the meat immediately into Chipotle's menu, but the number crunchers told him it was impossible.

The texture and flavor of the pork obsessed Ells. He visited the Niman Ranch farm in Thorton, a tiny town in the Iowa cornfields, then toured a factory farm. The latter sight horrified Ells. "These animals are so expressive and playful when outside; in these confinement operations, they're just being tortured," he says. "The bottom line was that I didn't want my success or the success of Chipotle to be based on the exploitation I saw."

A year later, Ells bought Niman Ranch pork for Chipotle. To keep the company profitable, he raised the price of a burrito by a dollar; sales not only didn't suffer, they passed all previous records. "What it told me was that customers were interested in sustainable food. Then that begged the question—where did everything else came from?" He incorporated other naturally sustainable products into Chipotle, to the point that the company now serves more naturally raised meats than any food chain in the United States, convincing and pushing competitors to do the same—and endearing themselves even more to hipsters nationwide.

"People love Mexican foods because they're craving exciting flavors," he says. "A typical burger? A patty and ketchup and a bun. People want something different today. They want more. There's something really great about the burrito in that people can make all different types of combinations of things. I can't imagine people going down the service line and making a chile relleno. It doesn't quite lend itself—same with the tamale. They're delicious—I love them, they're wonderful, but they're something different. There is something great about burritos—because they're customizable."

Chipotle set off an American love affair for Mission-style burritos that continues. Its chief rival also is a Denver creation: Qdoba Mexican Grill. Tony Miller was an investment banker for Merrill Lynch who returned home and grabbed a bite at Chipotle. Company lore maintains that Miller proposed a business partnership with Ells, who declined. Knowing a great business idea when he tasted one, the Coloradan opened his restaurant in 1995. Instead of just burritos and tacos, Qdoba plays around with other Mexican foods, such as *licuados* (Mexican-style smoothies) and *mole poblano,* a style they label Modern Nouveau Mex.

"To me, it's such a misunderstood cuisine," says Ted Stoner, the director of strategic product development. It's a long-winded title that means he's the man trusted with keeping Qdoba relevant in an ever-changing Mexican-food landscape. "It took Chinese and Italian a lot longer to morph into regional inspiration because the immigrants didn't saturate the country. With the population boom of people coming over the border, it's allowed people to absorb them much faster."

Qdoba lags behind Chipotle but isn't an upstart, with about five hundred locations and expanding almost as rapidly as Ells. But Qdoba also is an unlikely guardian of the burrito's honor in courts of law. In 2006, it tried to open a location in a Shrewsbury, Massachusetts, shopping plaza. It raised the ire of the Panera chain, which had a clause in its lease that prohibited any restaurants that specialized in sandwiches from opening in its Shrewsbury location. Panera tried to argue with its landlords that Qdoba fell under that category, since burritos were obviously sandwiches. When their landlords didn't agree, Panera took them to Superior Court.

To bolster its case, Qdoba called a former USDA official who contributed an affidavit that stated, "I know of no chef or culinary historian who would call a burrito a sandwich. . . . Indeed, the notion would be absurd to any credible chef or culinary historian." A judge agreed, noting in his decision, "A sandwich is not commonly understood to include burritos, tacos and quesadillas, which are typically made with a single tortilla and stuffed with a choice filling of meat, rice and beans."

The case earned national headlines—who in the twenty-first century still thought the burrito was a sandwich?—and the Qdoba opened in Shrewsbury soon after. "Short story, it looked like a frivolous lawsuit and it was that," Stoner says. Doug Thielen, former manager of nontraditional marketing and public relations for Qdoba, was working with the franchise group in Boston to promote them when Panera filed the lawsuit. "There was a little bit of surprise—people thought, 'Really?'" he says, laughing. "With this country being immersed in Mexican food on a regular basis, you'd figure people would know this already. From a social media perspective, people still bring this up—it was great publicity for us. Legally, burritos now stand on their own."

Burritos, while extraordinary, can bring trouble to those who aren't careful. Hold it wrong, squeeze it a bit much, trust another to fold the flour tortilla that encases any number of ingredients, and the burrito collapses, its contents hopefully falling on the plate in front of the eater but more likely spilling across the chest in a grotesque spectacle of gluttony. Even wrapped in butcher paper, in foil, or some other superfluous sheath, this toothsome torpedo can make grubby kindergarteners out of the most refined men.

On the corner of Alvarado and Sunset in Los Angeles stands Burrito King, its logo a cute little donkey—a burrito—with a crown. Their chile relleno burrito nearly squirts congealed cheese if so much as a finger grazes it; it's more dairy than wheat or even pepper, but legions of Angelenos work off hangovers with its loving caress. Colombian immigrant Julian Montoya bought the stand in the 1970s, tasting burritos in San Diego while stationed there for the navy. He positioned Burrito King during the 1980s to spread Los Angeles burritos nationwide and became a millionaire, establishing more than twenty locations from California to Texas to Colombia. But through a series of miscalculations, and, he says, thieving employees who took his recipes and money, Montoya was just reduced to this one Burrito King.

Los Angeles's burritos never earned regional branding like San Francisco. But the burrito evolution continues. There's the breakfast burrito, as an entity dating back to the 1970s—before then, Mexicans just called it "breakfast." The wrap—a tortilla modified to take on a different flavor, such as spinach, then wrapped around tofu or other non-Mexican ingredients—emerged in the 1980s, eaten by people who wanted a healthier option than carb-heavy sandwiches. And there is another burrito emerging around the American Southwest poised to go national.

If you travel to San Diego, you will notice something odd: a sub-genre of Mexican restaurants with the suffix -berto's. Alberto's. Adalberto's. Nolberto's. Roberto's. Filiberto's. Gilberto's. Hilberto's. All counted, there are more than a hundred such suffixed restaurants in San Diego County alone, with dozens more north, in Orange and Los Angeles Counties, nearly fifty in the Las Vegas region, and fifty more in Arizona and Utah—and this doesn't count derivatives even more outlandish, such as Alberta's, Albertaco's, and Albatros. All are near-carbon copies of each other: a canary yellow/fire-engine red color scheme, a Mexican bandito logo, and a drive-through. Their menus feature tacos, taquitos (known in San Diego as rolled tacos), fries buried under carne asada and fistfuls of guacamole and sour cream, and burritos as sturdy as San Francisco's. No frills, no add-ons, no fancy assembly line, just rapid-fire delivery. These -berto's also prepare and originated the California burrito: the regular burrito, but now engorged with French fries: crunchy. It's coming your way soon.

This informal federation is the legacy of one man: Roberto Robledo, the burrito Brahmin who never was. He was born in 1928 in San Luis Potosí, a state in central Mexico that historically didn't have mass immigration to America like, say, Zacatecas or Sonora and thus didn't influence Mexican food up here. Robledo signed up for the bracero program in the 1950s, bringing over his wife and seven children in 1957. The family settled in San Ysidro, a city right on the U.S.-Mexico border, but used it mostly as a base to follow the harvest seasons—apples, peaches, nuts, and more—up to the Central Valley and the Imperial Valley.

"My dad would always be working," says Roberto's son Rodolfo Robledo. "He always had construction work in the off-season. But all that traveling with [by then] eleven kids made Dad want to open his own business for the family, and a *tortilleria* came to mind, to stop the traveling."

Opening a tortilleria so close to Tijuana and in the city where El Indio had attracted Anglos and Mexicans alike since the early 1940s was a risk. "There were people telling him, 'What are you doing?'" says Rodolfo's brother Reynaldo, who says with a laugh, he "thinks" he's the eighth of his thirteen brothers and sisters. "'Are you thinking right? There are tortillas across the border.' But he was set on it and he did good. He didn't let no one bring him down."

Robledo bought two houses, one behind the other, turning the front structure into a tortilla factory in 1964 while housing his family in the back. Every morning, the children prepared tortillas before going to school; after they returned and finished homework, back to tortillas, with Rodolfo following his father on deliveries he made across San Diego's Mexican restaurants, a large number of which called themselves "taco shops" because they served only tacos and burritos. Intrigued, Robledo opened his first restaurant, La Lomita, in 1968, and others followed. It wasn't until opening the fifth restaurant, Jesse's Place, in 1971 that Robledo's wife suggested he rename the restaurants Roberto's Taco Shop. Most Mexican restaurant owners named their eateries after themselves, so why not Robledo?

From the beginning, Roberto's emphasized fast-food delivery with sit-down flavors. "Fast food was a lot better concept, a lot less overheard," says Rodolfo. The first hit for Roberto's Taco Shop was the Poor Boy: a bean burrito, nothing else, small and steaming, for a dime. Roberto sold so many Poor Boys, and opportunities for expansion emerged so rapidly, that Robledo brought over family, friends, and others from his birthplace of San Juan de Salado, his home village in San Luis Potosí, to work his taco shops. Some he brought over legally; others, not. Robledo taught them how to run an operation and left them to it.

In 1976, Robledo allowed his cousins, brothers Juan Diego and Alvaro Rodriguez, to open their own taco shop using the Roberto's name. But the relationship soon soured—Robledo felt they weren't following his freshness standards of making a daily batch of beans and rice—and he gave them an ultimatum: start following my orders, or stop using my name. The Rodriguezes changed the name, but wanted to keep their association with Roberto's Taco Shop in the minds of customers. They bought a can of paint, changed the cursive R in Roberto's into an A, and the O into an L; everything else was left the same. Alberto's became even more popular than Roberto's, and the Rodriguezes immmigrated more villagers from their hometown; those workers itched to open their own places but wanted the cachet of Alberto's/Roberto's, so *they* modified the name into the constellation of -berto's of today.

And the expansion wasn't limited to San Diego. In 1989, Roberto's relative Filiberto Tenorio transplanted the Roberto's template to the Phoenix suburb of Mesa, naming it Filiberto's. Filiberto's now has more than fifty locations across Arizona and the American Southwest—and this number doesn't include *its* rip-offs. The domino effect emptied San Juan de Salado but brought back hundreds of thousands of dollars in remittances; it was the town the burrito built.

As the -berto's evolved, so did the offerings. The burritos enlarged, to about the size of a Los Angeles version. Fish burritos appeared. Carne asada fries emerged. The Flying Saucer—a bowl made from a fried flour tortilla filled with beans, meat, cabbage, sour cream, and guacamole—was born. Neither Rodolf nor Reynaldo know who created the California burrito—"When I got my first restaurant in 1985, it still wasn't on the menu," Reynaldo says—but both acknowledge that one of the clone -berto's was responsible. The Americanization of the burrito ensured that San Diego's surfers mythologized their offerings and took them around the world, wherever there was a wave to catch.

All told, the number of -berto's across the United States is into the hundreds and represents millions of dollars in annual revenue. But the Robledo brothers claim their father never felt betrayed. "He wanted to better the village," Rodolfo says. "No resentment. I never heard that from my dad or mom. 'There's plenty of customers for everybody,' he'd say."

Not everyone in the -berto's galaxy was as grateful. In 1998, operators of two Alberto's successfully sued the Rodriguezes in San Diego

County Superior Court for a broken contract. That same year, the Rodriguez brothers pleaded guilty to tax evasion and to convincing other Alberto's operators to cheat on their taxes; a judge sentenced them to thirty-three months in federal prison. A couple of years later, Alberto's newest owners sent cease-and-desist notices to all the knock-offs of the -berto's brand, claiming it as their intellectual property. That went nowhere, however, as the deluge happened years before.

Roberto Robledo passed away in 1999 in Las Vegas, where he had opened more restaurants after noticing that the area lacked the Mexican cuisine to serve the immigrants and transplanted Mexican Americans from Southern California who were relocating in droves. Roberto's numbers forty-seven in Las Vegas as of 2011; Reynaldo runs them and continues his father's legacy, hiring people from San Juan de Salado and offering them opportunities to open their own Roberto's. More might be on the way soon—Reynaldo says he gets at least five requests a month from across the country, asking when Roberto's Taco Shop will set up in their state. "San Diego is a military place and a college place," Rodolfo says. "We get young people from all across the United States, some who don't know what a burrito is, or *think* they know what a burrito is. They go to Roberto's, and they realize what a great product we make. And they never forget that burrito, and all the memories they have of them are [from] when they were young."

The burrito, finally, turned into an object of upward mobility for Mexicans. But with more immigration, aspiring restaurateurs discovered that they didn't have to rely on tacos and burritos anymore to ensure a livelihood. Once again, America wanted newer, better Mexican food.

Chapter Nine

When Did Mexicans Start Making Food for Mexicans?

Everything old is new again, and there's nothing new under the sun, to quote Ecclesiastes via the Barenaked Ladies. After a century of mitigated tastes, of tamales canned and combo plates slopped, the United States is crazy about Mexican food anew—and not just for burritos. Now the need is for Mexican food that is, well, *Mexican.* "Authentic"—at least more authentic than companies started by gabachos such as Ells. The 1965 Immigration Reform Act unleashed a historic wave that brought in Mexicans from all across Mexico—but whereas the early immigration of Mexicans to the United States arrived mostly from the northern and central states (reflected in the kind of Mexican food that first spread across their new homeland), the latest exodus has introduced foods from every corner of the Empire of the Sun, from Sinaloa to the Yucatán and Mexico City's many interpretations of masa. These immigrants wanted to bring bites of home with them to their fellow migrants; what they never expected was that Americans might be interested in the regional cuisines as well.

That want of the latest "real" Mexican has also brought back that once-extinct profession: the tamale man.

From the west to the east, the north to the south, Mexicans sell tamales again with a vigor not seen since their previous heyday during the 1890s. But the tune has changed: now, women dominate the ranks. Now, coolers function as the heat-keeping container of choice instead of steam buckets, car trunks the impromptu restaurant instead of wagons or carts. Now the catch call is "Tamales, tamales, ta-ma-les!" shouted in the singsong tone of the Mexican countryside, instead of promises of red hots.

The Keystone Kops routine between health inspectors and tamaleros continues, of course, but a funny thing happened in the century-and-change since the tamale man's last public stand: they now get respect. And it's fitting that the most joyous adoration of modern-day street tamales happens in the cities that iconized tamaleros in the first place: San Francisco and Chicago.

Claudio Velez rules the streets of the Windy City, specifically the Wicker Park, Ukrainian Village, and Logan Square neighborhoods. Most nights, he cooks tamales at home, wraps them in husks, places them in bags, and loads them in a handheld red cooler. Velez goes from bar to bar—not the Mexican bars or the East European immigrant dives but where hipsters roam, where Velez is an icon for his easygoing manner and treasures: chicken or cheese, five for six dollars, selling more than two hundred per shift, bringing warm comfort on frigid nights on an average evening. Starting at eight, winding his way across the area until last call, Velez is more than just a tamale man—he's the Tamale Guy.

He's a modest guy. When I called his listed home number for an interview and asked the man who answered if I might speak with Velez, a man happily replied in the affirmative. When I identified my intentions, the line went silent. "Oh . . . he's not here anymore," he replied slowly in Spanish. "He went to Wisconsin to visit family."

"But you just told me you were Claudio Velez," I shot back.

"Yeah, um, I'm his cousin," he said, now nervous.

"When is he coming back?"

"I don't know—maybe never."

"How is that?

"Wow . . . well, I don't know what to tell you."

"Can I leave a message?"

Claudio hung up.

It's okay; others maintain his devotion. A Tamale Guy Facebook page is in the five figures of fans; Twitter hosts the Tamale Guy Tracker, where followers tweet sightings of Claudio and his copycats that automatically get retweeted to its thousands of followers. The service's creator is Clint McMahon, a Minnesota native who moved to Chicago in 2006 and witnessed the Tamale Guy phenomenon one night.

"These guys came into the bar selling tamales," he remembers. "People around this one guy started whipping out five-dollar bills and people are saying, 'You have to have one, you have to have one.' I told them I never had one, and they looked at me with an expression like, 'What are you saying?' I can't even understand that. How can you not have a tamale?"

Life in rural Minnesota does that to you, although McMahon did patronize Taco Bell and other sit-down Mexican restaurants. He ordered two tamales from Velez that first night—cheese and pork sluiced with red and green salsa. "They were amazing—I had never had anything like that before," he said. "You're not expecting a lot of taste, especially something in a Ziploc bag. But these tamales are very, very good."

McMahon followed the Tamale Guy over the next three years, but he needed more. In early 2009, he and a friend were hungry. It was bar night; the Tamale Guy wasn't around. The friend told McMahon he wished there was a way to track Velez, and McMahon, a software engineer, decided to crowd-source sightings via Twitter. And so it started.

A sampling from the night of July 24, 2011: "Claudio at nick's. You're welcome very much," wrote @matty_ryan. Two hours later, @lifeofswood tweeted "Happy Village. And they're going fast." Two hours pass. "At the Green Eye. Red cooler," noted @moneywitt. Another hour. "red cooler at ten cat ~@jennaaaye." Shortly after, @mariannevelonis tweeted the line of the night: "if you come to deville I'll kiss you on the mouth."

"People love tamales here. It's not like a burrito; you can pass the bag along and share with your friends," McMahon says. "And these guys—people call them legends, they're minor celebrities. Nothing really stands up to it. In San Francisco they have a tamale lady with a cooler on wheels who hangs outside bars for a couple of hours. Instead of a package of five, you get one big one. Good, but not as good as what you have in Chicago."

He's referring to the Tamale Lady: Virginia Ramos, who lords over the Mission District and South of Market, the neighborhood slowly marching into the Mission with its gentrifying blob. Chicken mole, pork, vegetable, bean, sweet potato, cheese, tamales larger in size: Ramos prepares them in her apartment in the afternoon when she's not cleaning houses. Her son runs Ramos's seldom-updated Twitter account, but devotion to the Tamale Lady needs no social media. Worshippers throw birthday parties for her; in 2003, *Our Lady of Tamale* debuted, a mishmash rockumentary following a day in the life of Ramos. It's an inspiring story, but much more interesting is the sound track. The filmmakers put out a call to the Bay Area asking artists to contribute thirty-second musical homages to Ramos; they whittled down the contributions to a sound track of fifty that appeared in the film and in a companion CD, veering from mariachi horns to college a cappella, swamp rock to grrl-rock and nearly every other modern musical genre. *Our Lady of Tamale* went on the documentary circuit, aired on the local PBS station, and lives forever on the Internet.

Of course this happened. We want the most "authentic" Mexican at all times—always have, always will. And if your neighborhood still suffers under the tyranny of Taco Bell and combo plates? Fear not—Mexican food is coming to wow you, to save you from a bland life, as it did for your parents and grandparents and great-grandparents. Again. Like last time—and the time before that.

In 1905, New York's *other* other other respectable broadsheet, the *Sun,* felt there was a problem with Mexican food. It noted how R. H. Putnam's California Chicken Tamale Co. and its imitators had tried and failed to conquer Gotham, as did the second wave of barkeeps who offered tamales free to drunks. "The popularity of Mexican national dishes has had to be 'promoted' in the United States," an unsigned *Sun* article fretted.

The paper maintained hope for the rise of "real" Mexican food, however, since "the darkest hour is just before the dawn." They reported on a Mexican dinner held by members of the Sedgeley Club, a private Philadelphia club, where the women dressed like señoritas and offered a menu of chili con carne, enchiladas, chile rellenos, and rice. Not the most unique items, but a classy appearance for Mexican food in the East, in the halls of the elite, was downright revelatory for the *Sun* correspondent. "This formal recognition of the excellence of Mexican dishes," they raved, "may prove at last the open door to their popularity in the United States."[1]

Mexican food was well on its way to conquering America at that time, but this short dispatch offers a pertinent glimpse into our need. Even though Mexican food of some sort has existed in this country since the Mexican-American War, fans of the cuisine also have known that even better Mexican grub was out there, have hoped that someone might come and deliver it, allowing them to break free of the shackles of their current Mexican dinner. Demand drove Mexican food's easy spread across this country, turning yesterday's new dish into today's mundane choice and dragging novices into their enthusiasm—a circadian rhythm of Mexican consumption.

As this has happened, however, one group has squirmed: Mexicans. As long as Americans have enjoyed "Mexican" food, many

Mexicans have stood back, aghast, that Americans enjoyed what they considered gross mischaracterizations of their cuisine. Typical of such sentiment is the definition of chili con carne offered in the 1959 edition of *Diccionario general de americanismos* (*General Dictionary of American Sayings*), edited by Francisco J. Santamaria, an influential Mexican intellectual. He dismissed the favored Mexican dish of millions of Americans as "a detestable food which, with the false title of Mexican, is sold in the United States from Texas to New York."[2] Hollywood film star Katy Jurado took to preparing tacos in her own apartment off the Sunset Strip for the Hollywood colony wanting authentic Mexican food and urged fans to prepare them for themselves instead of buying them at restaurants.[3] As early as the 1940s, restaurants took to promoting themselves as serving "authentic Mexican food," as if their competitors were somehow inferior even though both served the same foodstuffs that Mexicans in Mexico derided as *agringado*—Americanized.

"Tex-Mex food is a regional cookery, too," Patricia Quintana, a Mexican chef who won acclaim for elevating Mexican food in her homeland into the realm of fine dining, told one food critic, "but the territory had few resources at the time the Americans began to adapt the peasant foods of the region, so it's very simplistic."[4]

Those who decried Tex-Mex and America's other regional Mexican foods as somehow less legit than what existed down south never bothered to consider that the lambasted food was created by Mexicans here for Mexicans here, who considered it Mexican food. But Quintana's views were typical, and the 1970s saw chefs further indulge in the authenticity races. Fonda San Miguel in Austin opened in 1975 with the consultation of Diana Kennedy, who forced the owners not to serve chips and salsa because they weren't up to her authenticity meter. That didn't last long, as patrons complained loudly about the snub. "So we finally gave up and gave them their damn chips and hot sauce," said owner Tom Gilliland. "We just didn't tell Diana right away."[5]

It wasn't until the 1980s, however, that an earnest movement to serve what some called "interior Mexican" food emerged—in other words, Mexican food that hadn't yet penetrated the American market. The most vibrant scene started in the *loncheras*—taco trucks.

Across the Southwest and wherever there was a Mexican, his food, and something on four wheels capable of creaking from place to place, mobile meals played an important part in dispersing Mexican food. As early as the late 1800s, buggies in San Antonio delivered fresh tortillas and other Mexican snacks as a counterpoint to the stationary chili queens.[6] Los Angeles's tamale wagons took that business to the next level. After the tamale wagons' demise in the 1920s, Mexican families took advantage of the rise of the automobile to make meals truly mobile: in the morning, they prepared meals at their homes—the ever-present tamale, but also enchiladas and tacos, still then just a decade old in Southern California, and whatever else migrants wanted. The *familias* drove through their barrios, stopping in spots from early in the morning until the evening; in 1927, a sociologist documenting the Mexican community in Los Angeles noted that they had "come to form a good business."[7]

Such efforts, however, were regular trucks filled with food, not bona fide mobile kitchens. It wasn't until 1974, when an immigrant from Mexico City named Raul O. Martinez first sold tacos out of a former ice cream truck jury-rigged to support a stove and grill, that taco trucks truly emerged. He had immigrated to the United States five years earlier, finding employment as a dishwasher and a meatpacker. One weekend while relaxing at a park, Martinez cooked meat on the grill—carne asada, chicken, and other cuts. A nearby team of soccer players, all hungry and entranced, approached Martinez with money and pleas for tacos.

He decided to open a restaurant but didn't have the funds, so Martinez settled for a truck. Friends thought he was *loco*—hard-shelled tacos still ruled Los Angeles, while those made with corn tortillas and fresh meat largely stayed in the domestic domain. But Martinez pushed on, going so far as to offer cuts that weren't common even in

Mexican restaurants yet—*cabeza* and *al pastor,* the central Mexico tradition of putting beef on a spit, a tradition taken from Lebanese people who immigrated to the region in the early twentieth century. Martinez, his wife, and his father parked next to a bar in East Los Angeles during a weekday night and sold seventy dollars' worth that first time; within a week, his profits doubled. He opened a restaurant, King Taco; today King Taco is a Los Angeles institution boasting twenty locations and is patronized by politicians who need a photo op to show they're down with the brown. Loncheras continue to figure in the King Taco equation, but they now park outside their bigger-brother locations, the better to deal with overflow crowds.

Whether King Taco was the first bona fide taco truck is unknown—in 1966, two New York housewives opened Tic-Taco, a taco shop in the Riverdale neighborhood of the Bronx, and also owned a minitruck with a canopy that they used to cater parties[8]—but its success spurred other enterprising Mexicans to follow its example. By 1987, about five hundred loncheras served Southern California,[9] all introducing the foods brought to the United States by the latest waves of Mexican immigrants.

On the haute level, the regional American movement promoted Zarela Martinez as the queen of Mexican authenticity. Martinez had moved to El Paso from Sonora in the 1970s and ran a catering service to supplement her salary as a social worker. She caught the attention of Paul Prudhomme, who in turn suggested her to *New York Times* food editor Craig Claiborne. He had met Martinez in 1982 when Claiborne was searching for someone to cook Mexican food for a dinner designed to represent the United States to a group of nearly two hundred French chefs touring the country. Martinez impressed Claiborne enough that he invited her to help cater a party that year, which concurrently celebrated his birthday, twenty-five years at the *Times,* and the release of his memoir, *A Feast Made for Laughter.* She enthralled the ever-curious Claiborne palate by drawing more on the seafood-intensive platters of the Mexican coastal state of Veracruz instead of the beef-heavy platters of northern Mexico and Texas; he described a private dinner she made for him in "Memorable Dishes from a Master Mexican Chef."[10]

The following year, Claiborne presented to Martinez a much more daunting task. The previous fall, then-president Ronald Reagan's deputy chief of staff asked the critic if he might help prepare a menu for the coming G-8 Economic Summit. Instead of going the typical state-dinner route, Reagan wanted one planned around all-American foods. Selected to represent the country was Prudhomme, Wolfgang Puck and his California cuisine, representatives from the world of barbecue, delis, desserts, Southern cooking—and Martinez.

"In short, I wanted to show what cooking in this country is all about," Claiborne wrote. "A series of definitive all-American menus without a Tex-Mex meal would be unthinkable," and Martinez was entrusted with the lunch menu for the final day of the conference.[11] The *Times* critic asked her to include nachos, refried beans, chili con carne, and salsa, but Martinez blew away Claiborne with her inclusion of something completely foreign, completely *Mexican*: fish tamales drizzled with a coriander salsa, and filet mignon stuffed with chilies and cheese, a take on the *tampiqueña,* a famous Mexican meal consisting of carne asada, chiles, and cheese.

The G-8 dinner was a winner, and Martinez became the toast of America's chef class. A couple of years later she opened Café Marimba in New York, and later Zarela's, where her pursuit and dedication to teaching Americans about "real" Mexican food continued for decades. Of course, even her creations weren't enough to placate purists such as Kennedy, who argued that Martinez's Gotham places lacked *mexicanidad*—Mexican character—to the *Times* after visiting, to which Martinez replied, "It's not so much a matter of compromise as it is each chef making the cuisine his or her own."[12]

Martinez continued with her restaurants until 2011, when Zarela's finally closed. Her reputation was secure, however. She had shown America that Mexican food was worthy of world leaders. After closing, Martinez told papers she was looking for a new location, that rising rents, not changing food tastes, had shut her down. But Zarela's was old news by 2011—the city and the country were catching up. Hundreds of thousands of Mexican immigrants had moved to New York, specifically people from the state of Puebla, who brought their *cemitas,* sandwiches made with something approximating challah bread and the size of a slightly deflated football. And if Mexicans had reached New York, what do you think they showed the rest of the United States during that time?

Olympic Boulevard in Los Angeles cuts through the heart of Koreatown, the largest enclave of Koreans in the world outside the mother country. Block after block features signs advertising businesses in blocky Hangul script—spas, restaurants, churches, supermarkets, and schools intermixed among signs in Hebrew, Arabic, Spanish, Chinese, Vietnamese, and even English. At 3014 West Olympic stands an ornate, palatial building—blue shingles on the curved roof in classical Korean architectural style, whitewashed regal. It was built to house one of the area's first Korean restaurants, Young Bin Kwan (known in English as the VIP Palace), opened in 1975 and designed by developer Hi Duk Lee to serve as an anchor for his grand vision of a planned Koreatown to rival the Chinatowns and other ethnic enclaves of America. Young Bin Kwan gamely carried on until the late 1990s, when a Mexican immigrant named Fernando Lopez moved in and opened it as a new restaurant: Guelaguetza.

The exterior is the only reminder of its days as a hub of L.A. Korean life; inside, Guelaguetza shocks the senses with vibrant colors, big-screen televisions perpetually tuned to soccer from across the globe, and stunning dishes. Wooden chairs hint at hacienda aspirations; counters near the front sell food to go along with tourist-trap tchotchkes such as colorful shirts and CDs. But this isn't a typical Mexican restaurant. There are tamales, but they come wrapped in banana leaves and are as hefty as bricks. The tortilla chips come complimentary, but most tables nibble on *chapulines*—dried grasshoppers rolled in chili dust, sprinkled with lime, tangy and crunchy. The condiment that bathes everything isn't yellow cheese but one of the restaurant's five types of mole, the legendary stews of Mexico.

Guelaguetza is a Oaxacan restaurant, representing the southern state that's Mexico's most celebrated culinary region, the area that Diana Kennedy and Rick Bayless highlight again and again—Kennedy published a book on Oaxacan food in 2010, while Bayless prepared a mole negro for an Obama administration state dinner. But the palace's more important role in Mexican food history is how it showed Mexicans and Americans alike that there was demand for regional Mexican food—not as high-priced experiences, not as washed-down replicas, but as a Cartesian statement. It serves, therefore it is.

The family responsible for this walks in. Fernando Lopez is in business casual, the cuffs on his light blue long-sleeved shirt slightly rolled up, his hair neatly parted, the top two buttons undone on this steaming day. He's relaxed, cheery, looking every bit the semiretired owner he is. His wife, Maria, wears the floral-flashing blouses customary to their homeland, the blouses signifying a working woman, one as effervescent as she but also sturdy, ready for work; she's the chef at Guelaguetza. Last to stroll in is their daughter Bricia, the one in snug jeans, T-shirt, and wielding a smartphone she checks between every other sentence.

Fernando Lopez came from a family of *mescaleros,* people devoted to the craft of distilling tequila's smokier, harsher relative. Life was good enough in Oaxaca, but "we Mexicans have this idea of *salir para conocer* [get out there to learn and experience]," he says in Spanish. Lopez left his wife and children behind in Oaxaca 1993 and trekked to the United States to see what opportunities were available.

He and hundreds of thousands of his fellow *oaxaqueños* constituted one of the more distinctive immigration patterns in recent U.S. history. While Oaxacans are technically Mexican citizens, the country historically treated the region as a foreign land—its rugged geography had isolated the region for centuries, allowing for a vibrant flourishing of indigenous traditions. But that was the problem: for while the Mexican government officially embraced their contributions, the day-to-day life of Oaxacans was filled with discrimination, since most Oaxacans didn't speak Spanish as a first language and were shorter and darker than other Mexicans. Oaxaqueño became a common slur, a synonym for a dirty Indian—the Mexicans of Mexico—and the Mexican government ignored Oaxaca's infrastructure or modernization needs, preferring to let the state and its people exist as a tourist attraction and little else.

Oaxacans, however, are known in Mexico for their pride and stubbornness, and they emigrated en masse for better opportunities in California during the 1980s. Enclaves landed in either the Central Valley, where most found work in agriculture, or in West Los Angeles, where Oaxacan families settled away from Southern California's established Mexican barrios so as not to suffer further discrimination. Lopez was one of the latter, moving in with his sister Soledad, who worked as a housecleaner for wealthy families. Every month she traveled to Tijuana, which had its own sizable Oaxacan community, to load up on Oaxacan products no one else carried in Southern California, not even at Mexican supermarkets—stringy cheese known as *quesillo,* chapulines, mole paste, peppers, and so much more. Fernando joined in the trips, out of nostalgia.

"It was a dream to eat a *clayuda* up here, to taste quesillo," he said, even now wistful, referring to corn tortillas from Oaxaca as large as a basketball hoop. "And I know I wasn't the only one." The Oaxacan community was tightly knit in Southern California, organizing basketball tournaments, cultural schools, community fairs, and churches. Stalls at events sold Oaxacan food, but no restaurants specialized in the cuisine. Lopez hadn't come to the United States with thoughts of starting a restaurant, but he decided to open a street stall selling tamales and clayudas on the corner of Normandie and 8th, the heart of the emerging Oaxacatown.

Not long after, Lopez secured a restaurant spot early in 1994 with a loan from his sister. Shortly after signing the lease papers, a health inspector came in, congratulated Lopez on his *ganas* (desire), and immediately advised him to sell the business since no restaurant had ever succeeded in the space. These warnings didn't deter Lopez. He named it Guelaguetza, after an annual summer festival in Oaxaca that has no American equivalent, knowing the name's cachet among homesick Oaxacans. The name is what drew in their first customer, a woman who ordered a tamale de mole negro, a brick of masa tinted darkly due to the chocolate used in the mole. Lopez hadn't yet decided what to charge, so he asked her how much she wanted to pay. "Since there's no other restaurant that sells tamales de mole here, I'll pay four dollars," she replied. The customer ate one, then ordered twenty.

Lines promptly formed once Guelaguetza officially opened, almost all Oaxacans eager to try an unmitigated menu. Friends and family urged Lopez to sell hamburgers, tacos, and other Southern California meals to ensure financial success, as the thought of Oaxacan food was still foreign in Southern California, but Lopez refused. "Everything was here for Oaxacan—the ingredients, the customers. If I'd make hamburgers, I'd have to compete against McDonald's. I didn't want to sell to the Americans, I wanted to sell to Oaxacans. But if Americans came? Welcome!"

Guelaguetza wasn't the first restaurant to offer Oaxacan food in Southern California. Oaxacan men had long worked as line cooks in the city's finer eateries; one of them, Celerino Cruz, had opened Tlapazola Grill (named after his hometown of San Marcos Tlapazola) in Santa Monica in 1992, and wowed critics with a refined Mexican menu promising hints of Oaxacan flavors and a couple of appetizers. El Texate in Santa Monica also served Oaxacan bites, but included Mexican-American favorites to ensure crowds. But Lopez's unapologetic flavors created a phenomenon, and it wasn't just Oaxacans who waited in line for one of its three tables. Many Oaxacan women worked as nannies for wealthy families and had treated their employers with Guelaguetza's tamales. Soon Mercedeses and BMWs parked near Guelaguetza, domestic workers inviting their employers to see how they lived.

Rich Americans and Oaxacans constituted their core base, though; non-Oaxacan Mexicans ignored it (tellingly, *La Opinión*, the city's largest Spanish-language daily, wouldn't review Guelaguetza for years), along with Americans raised on enchiladas and hard-shell tacos. But a couple of months after Guelaguetza opened, Jonathan Gold—then a critic for the *Los Angeles Times*—reviewed the restaurant. They sold out of food that day. "When Guelaguetza came along," Gold reflects now, "it wasn't that local Oaxacan food had never existed, or that regional Mexican cooking had never existed here . . . but that the cooking was fully formed, and available in what seemed like all of its stunning range. It's one thing to make a mole verde and quite another to make *that* mole verde; county-fair-quality clayudas are good, but Oaxaca-quality clayudas are something else entirely."

Now successful, Fernando sent for his wife and three children from Oaxaca; all immediately helped out. "I was scared of coming but my husband said he needed the help," says Maria. Soledad opened a Guelaguetza in the Palms neighborhood of Los Angeles, closer to all those rich families, while Fernando expanded the original location and opened in Koreatown. He started a newspaper, *El Oaxaqueño,* published in Los Angeles and Oaxaca, and raised funds with other Oaxacans for their hometowns in their native land.

Meanwhile, his daughter Bricia and her siblings tried to assimilate into a Southern California where the idea of Mexican food was foreign to them. "I remember the first time I had Taco Bell," Lopez said, laughing. "My dad said we should try this foreign food. We had no idea what they were serving us. Hard-shelled tacos? No. Fajitas? I had never heard of them. *Nada que ver con el México* [nothing to do with Mexico]. But that's how people sold it here."

The Lopez clan at their Guelaguetza restaurant in Los Angeles. They
helped popularize regional Mexican cuisine prepared by Mexicans for
Mexicans by offering their native Oaxacan food. *From left:* Paulina,
Maria, Bricia (*seated on bar*), Elizabeth, Fernando Jr., and Fernando Sr.
(*Photo by Rene Miranda*)

National acclaim followed, and a network of Oaxacan restaurants
and other regional Mexican eateries opened in Los Angeles and beyond.
Other chefs aimed higher: in the city of Bell, chefs Jaime Martin del
Campo and Ramiro Arvizu opened La Casita Mexicana, a restaurant
devoted to highlighting the greatest hits of regional Mexican cuisine via
a professional kitchen. Their efforts and shaved heads earned Martin
and Arvizu a devoted following in the Spanish-language media. The
success of others, however, meant that the Lopez family became victims
of the movement they helped to start. The locations in Palms and the
original closed; Bricia and Fernando Jr. opened two offshoots, Cemitas
y Clayudas Pal Cabrón ("For the Bad-Ass" in Spanish) and Natura, a
fruit-juice bar, but eventually shuttered those as well. Fernando now
serves mostly in an advisory role, while Bricia and her siblings have
concentrated on righting the family's ship—an unlikely development

for Bricia, considering she didn't want to work in the restaurant industry. "I was so jaded with them, having grown up in the business, and I wanted to stay away as long as possible," she admits. "But I didn't want to see our locations close—I just thought it was wrong." Now Bricia is royalty in Southern California foodie circles; more than a dozen L.A.-area bars have named mescal-based cocktails after her, and she became a spokesperson for the ubiquitous "Got Milk?" campaign of California's dairy industry.

"That's the difference between Oaxacans and everyone else," Fernando concludes, making the same point again. "Other Mexicans eat what's here. Us? I'd die for chapulines—all of us Oaxaqueños would. We Oaxacans are stubborn like that, but that's how we're tied to our traditions. No modifications. Always to the original. We didn't try; we did. We do."

In the summer of 2010, a scene developed in Los Angeles that is almost never repeated: Mexican immigrants created dishes, while white servers jumped to their every command.

The scene happened in the city's Angeli Caffe, a mainstay on Los Angeles's chic Melrose Avenue, a Fellini flick come to life complete with plates of Italian dishes, and a garrulous, charismatic owner: Evan Kleiman, a nice Jewish girl internationally known for her by-the-books interpretation of regional Italian cuisine. She's also the host of *Good Food with Evan Kleiman*, a program on KCRW-FM listened to religiously by thousands of foodies across Southern California and beyond.

Kleiman focuses mostly on the concept of slow food, of sustainable practices and agriculture, but she's also a champion of ethnic cuisine, especially Mexican food, which she fondly remembered from growing up near East Los Angeles, in the bohemian neighborhood of Silver Lake and its standby, Burrito King. For this afternoon's dinner, she's one of the servers, wearing an orange T-shirt that complemented her curly locks and smart glasses emblazoned with "Nina's Food."

"It's great to see my producers work the floor," Kleiman said with a laugh as the clatter of dozens of forks meeting plates and conversations about the FIFA World Cup filled the crowded Angeli. She decided to hold a fund-raiser for Nina Valenzuela, a Mexico City native who had originally set up a stand in a parking lot in the Boyle Heights neighborhood of Los Angeles, selling the specific cuisine of her homeland. Other unlicensed vendors quickly followed her, and soon weekends attracted hundreds of curious eaters who blogged its existence.

That was the problem: law enforcement caught the Breed Street food scene's fragrant wind and shut down the operation. Kleiman immediately stepped in and offered her restaurant for an afternoon to a vendor, in the hopes of drawing crowds that might raise enough funds to let the street vendor open her own eatery. Nina won an invitation for her *pambazos* (French rolls soaked in red chile, then grilled before getting slathered with a mix of chorizo and potato) and a salsa *seca,* a sauce composed solely of chile seeds, slightly oily but with a furtive, toasty fire.

"You *have* to get the pambazo," Kleiman repeated to everyone, correcting people's mispronunciation of the dish occasionally, but in the tone of a kind Old World aunt. The cheese on the pambazo was yellow, but only because the red hue of the *bolillos* and the chorizo had tinted the creamy quesillo Nina used. The roll was almost as sweet as bread pudding, with a heat that gently singes. On the side were simple garnishes—*cotija* cheese, *crema fresca,* repollo—and everyone washed down the meal with an *agua fresca de fresa*: pureed strawberry mixed with water, nothing more, nothing less.

Nina, tired but also jubilant, barked orders in the kitchen. "I'm glad people like my food," she said. She had toiled anonymously in Boyle Heights and other Los Angeles areas since the 1980s, but word of mouth has turned her into Los Angeles's own icon: the Pambazo Ma'am, or something like that. "I never thought Americans would like this type of Mexican food. I'm glad they do, because it's delicious!"

The customers were almost all non-Mexican, and the idea of eating regional Mexican at a fancy restaurant tickled them. "Will you be having your pambazo on the terrace?" someone cracked while affecting a Jeeves tone, to the pambazo-muted howls of his table.

Mexican food had arrived to wow customers, to save them from a bland life, as it did for their parents and grandparents and great-grandparents. Again. Like last time—and the time before that.

Thus concludes the history of Mexican restaurants in the United States. Of course, Mexican food has never limited itself to the realm of diners—as long as there has been a restaurant selling Mexican food, there's been a food producer trying to figure out how to replicate those flavors and have households buy their product instead. And those stories are just as colorful as those of restaurants, if not better.

Chapter Ten

How Did Mexican Food Get
into Our Supermarkets?

Indianapolis, Indiana—home to the Indy 500, Hoosier values, the Crossroads of America—is now becoming irretrievably, beautifully Mexican.

In just twenty years, the city's Latino population increased more than 500 percent, from about 8,500 in 1990 to more than 50,000 in the latest census, with the majority of those residents Mexicans. The population is still relatively small—about 8 percent of the city's total of more than 830,000—but Latinos are the fastest-growing ethnic group in Indianapolis, with fertility rates ever exponential, as we're wont to do.

Halfway through this population boom, Samuel Barrera saw an opportunity. In 1999, he opened Tiendas Morelos, a Mexican grocery store that was among the first in the city. A second one soon followed, but the demand for Mexican food products in Indianapolis was so strong that Barrera kept opening them on an almost yearly basis. Now Tiendas Morelos has eight locations through Indianapolis, and there are plans for more.

Indianapolis has brutal winters, snowstorms alien to most people south of the border, so entering one of Barrera's stores on a frigid February morning is as comforting to a *mexicano*'s soul as the smell of a mother's tortillas. A butcher cuts meat on order but also keeps already marinated cuts to make tacos in neatly arranged stacks in the refrigerated display case. Gnarled slabs of pork fat and skin called *chicharrones* bake under a hot lamp, looking like pre-Cambrian fossils in a museum exhibit or rutted timing belts. Freshly baked bread sits on trays; bags of chiles hang from hooks. Mexican music blasts on the speakers, sometimes CDs but also one of the metro area's three Spanish-language radio stations. Aisles feature magazines from Mexico, tortillas made in Chicago, piñatas from God knows where, California-produced canned menudo, corn husks, candies, even Mexican detergent. Anything and everything Mexican.

The Tiendas Morelos company is just one of more than thirty stores across Indianapolis that specializes in Mexican groceries. And those *mercados* aren't the only markets in town that stock Mexican food. That mighty Midwestern grocery giant, Kroger, stocks shelves of Mexican products, but the offerings are a bit different: Tiendas Morelos doesn't stock frozen burritos or canned chili like Kroger, nor do they carry Kroger Refried Beans or Mexican-Style Shredded Cheese, whatever that is. Tiendas Morelos is but a speck compared to the Kroger conglomerate—yet Kroger wants in on Morelos's customer base.

The same situation now appears across the United States—has, actually, almost as long as Mexican food has enticed Americans. Where there has been the rumor of Mexican food, there have been mainstream supermarkets selling it—first chili con carne and canned tamales, then chiles, taco sauce, tortilla chips, and tortillas, until one shelf became two, two became the "International" section of the market, and that melded into the Latino aisle. Americans have never contented themselves with just eating Mexican food from the streets or at restaurants or cooking it at home; they also wanted prepackaged meals, and that desire became as important and influential a factor in popularizing Mexican food in this country as any Bayless or Taco Bell.

The following are the most important companies of the batch, though hardly the only. Someone put them on the Mount Rushmore of the American food industry, because they deserve it.

Downtown New Braunfels, Texas, has seen better days. It's a charming enough town, about half an hour north of San Antonio, with a turn-of-the-twentieth-century downtown centered on a roundabout. But life in this municipality is moribund—on an August Sunday afternoon, with the promise of Cowboys football weeks away, the Phoenix Saloon is nearly empty. It's a former floor of a department store that's now a cantina, with a long wooden bar, high ceilings, bad acoustics, and as dank as you'd expect any 1870s-era building to be. On a stage, a warbling man sings a song of cheating hearts—"She's a looker and a hooker" is the line he enunciates with particular scorn—strumming his acoustic guitar to tepid applause from the audience.

Once visitors get past the bad music and dead atmosphere, the Phoenix is a great place. The drinks are stiff, the beers cold, the bartenders perky in many ways. A menu is minimal—really just burgers, salads, and sandwiches—but it also promises "True original Texas red chili. Made with sirloin not ground beef. No beans!"

The dish is simple and spectacular—lean, large chunks of beef, minimally decorated with freshly chopped onion, cheese, and little else. It's not exactly spicy, but heat lurks somewhere in that bowl, that cauldron of comfort. Still, after the drinks and the food and even a trip downstairs to a basement pulled out of Prohibition (which, incidentally, was used as a bootlegger's hideaway during that time), this Phoenix ain't exactly rising.

Outside the bar, in a building across the street, is a more colorful scene—a wall-tall mural documenting New Braunfels's birth as a German colony in the 1840s. It's a much prettier mural than the one painted on the side of the Phoenix, an old, WPA-style insignia for Gebhardt's Eagle Chili Powder. A stylized eagle holds a banner and sits on a wreath that, upon closer inspection, is festooned with red chili peppers, a testament to the saloon's most famous tenant: William Gebhardt, the father of America's Mexican produce *and* home-dinner industry.

A picture of a Gebhardt's Original Mexican Dinner Package, circa 1920s. German immigrant William Gebhardt pioneered prepackaged Mexican dinners and recipe booklets for home cooks *Courtesy of Gebhardt Mexican Foods Company Records, MS 44, University of Texas at San Antonio Libraries Special Collections.*

Gebhardt was a German immigrant who landed in New Braunfels in about the 1880s, part of the settlement's second wave from Deutschland, and opened a café in this building, back when it was Mittendorf's Saloon. Chili con carne was in the early days of its stomp through Texas, so it was natural for Gebhardt to sell it in New Braunfels and for the German-majority citizenry to use it. But preparing peppers for every pot of boiling chili must have grinded on Gebhardt, because he started to experiment with ways to turn peppers into a powder. After dozens of attempts, the German settled on a recipe that he promptly put into bags and offered for sale.

Gebhardt wasn't the first white Texan to try to capitalize on Mexican food products. In 1884, William Gerard Tobin launched construction on the first-ever factory in the United States devoted to canning chili con carne. He was a San Antonio institution—a former Texas Ranger, city marshal, a Confederate, and part of a U.S. Army unit that quelled a Tejano rebellion in South Texas during the late 1850s. After the Civil War, Tobin returned to open a successful hotel in San Antonio, but sold that business in 1879 to concentrate on canning chili con carne because through his military connections, he won a contract with the War Department to stuff soldiers with his concoction;[1] he secured the same with the navy in 1882, winning the endorsement of the department's surgeon general, who gushed in a letter that it was "eminently adapted for use under" military circumstances and that the chili "confers valuable savory qualities."[2]

At the time, Tobin had his chili con carne canned in Chicago but wanted to expand business locally. Tragically, he never saw his company grow farther than its first contracts: as Tobin prepared the opening of his factory, he died of a heart attack. The Tobin Canning Company gamely continued for one more year before getting repossessed by creditors; at the end, ten thousand empty cans and boxes that never saw chili con carne in them, ready to get packed to other points, gathered dust in the factory, offered for sale to any and all.[3]

Others took Tobin's lead. In Fort Worth, D. C. Pendry marketed chili powder he prepared as early as 1890. T. Bailey Walker opened the T. B. Walker Manufacturing Company in 1901 in Austin to sell chili powder and canned chile con carne and tamales. Marketed under the name AusTex, the brand traveled nationally. But Gebhardt took Tobin's ambitions the farthest. He moved to San Antonio in 1898, receiving a patent for his chile powder machine, and started selling it around town. In New Braunfels he called the product Tampico Dust in 1896, when he first packaged it; in San Antonio he rebranded it Gebhardt's Eagle Chili Powder, using the logo that now adorns the exterior of the Phoenix Saloon, and became popular almost immediately.

Gebhardt wasn't content with just selling powder, however. In 1911, he expanded into the chili con carne canning business (along with tamales and beans), and also released *Mexican Cooking,* a cookbook for customers of his products on how to achieve, as the pamphlet's cover stated, "that real Mexican tang." Prophetically, *Mexican Cooking*'s subtitle was *The Flavor of the 20th Century.*[4] However, 1923 proved to be the company's most momentous year.

In the summer, they printed 250,000 copies of *Mexican Cookery for American Homes,* a thirty-six-page update to their initial 1911 pamphlet, and opened a restaurant in Manhattan called El Rancho, which featured their products. The former was mailed around the world, soliciting orders as far away as China; the latter did "a surprisingly large volume of business," according to Gebhardt's general manager.[5] That year they also debuted a "Mexican Dinner Package": a bottle of chili powder; two cans of deviled chili meat; one can each of chili con carne, eight husk-wrapped tamales, pinto beans; and a copy of *Mexican Cookery for American Homes.* The dinner was big enough to feed five, sold for a buck, and came in a gorgeous colored box featuring a pueblo scene of a man and woman harvesting in the fields, the rolling mountains behind them. Markets sold the package across the United States, but Gebhardt's company also allowed customers to request them via mail. "You may never have the opportunity of visiting the [Alamo]," initial ads swore, "but you can enjoy a genuine Mexican Dinner right in your home."[6]

Cognizant of the stereotypes Mexican food had even then, Gebhardt assured customers that *his* cuisine wasn't like the dangerous stuff Mexicans sold. Ads for his tamales assured, "Rigid Government Inspection insures Quality and Cleanliness," placing those words next to a cigarette-smoking Mexican damsel looking coyly at the reader, her blouse seductively dropped halfway down her arm. It was almost line for line like some of the illustrations San Antonio papers used to romanticize chili queens back in the 1890s.

Gebhardt's company dominated Mexican food products sales for decades. *Mexican Cookery for American Homes* went through multiple reprints through the 1950s, partly because Gebhardt's distributed them free to anyone who requested them and because they included the booklets in every packaged dinner. As for the founder, Gebhardt retired in 1936, passing away twenty years later. Three years after his death, Beatrice Foods acquired the brand. Gebhardt's was now just a company, nothing else, and slowly retreated from the American pantry as other brands eclipsed it. "I really don't know too much about

Mexican food," a Gebhardt's manager confessed to a reporter in 1976. "Before Beatrice transferred me, I worked for La Choy."[7]

Downtown Ventura, California, is as picturesque a clash of chronologies as you can find in the United States. It's right off the 101 Freeway, the old El Camino Real, the trail that connected California's twenty-one Spanish missions, one of which is in Ventura and for which the city is named. To enter this district you exit the 101 on California Street—to the left is the Ventura Pier; a right leads to the city's historic City Hall, a Beaux Arts gem standing on the hill built by the money of agriculture, on the backs of thousands of Mexican laborers who picked the crops from the region's fertile soil.

Several miles away, just before Main ducks under the Ojai Freeway, stands a tiny, sad adobe house surrounded by a water-bottling plant and other industrial buildings. It's so unloved that no parking stalls are marked in its lot, and the parking lot itself is bigger than the three-room structure. Every morning at nine, a worker opens its three wooden doors, behind which stand wrought-iron bars that prohibit the curious from actually entering the adobe. Not that there's much to look at inside: a bed, some pottery and religious icons, and weathered metal plaques that speak of the family that lived here, one of the old Ventura clans. Unlike the rest of historic Ventura, the Ortega Adobe has no docent, no champion. The scene is supposed to represent how Californios lived, but the sight of cobwebs filling window corners and snaking up chairs sullies the romance. There are no brochures, no interactive displays. At 5:00 P.M., the worker returns, closes the door, and closes the gate that separates the Ortega Adobe from the world.

There is one sign, however, that reveals the structure's importance. "In 1897, Emigdio [Ortega's] son, Emilio, started the 'Pioneer Ortega Chili Company' in this house. He developed a successful canning business that still thrives today." This tiny spot is the birthplace of the mighty Ortega empire, an octopus of taco shells, bland refried beans and salsas, cheery cookbooks, goofy commercials, but most important, canned chiles, which the company introduced to the American market. Emilio had initially tried various businesses, to little success: a clerk at a silk house, a stint at a business college, a grocery store owner, a rancher in San Diego, a superintendent at a railroad in New Mexico before finally returning to Ventura due to ill health.

While in New Mexico, Ortega tried the state's saintly chiles. He took seeds on the trip back home and grew them in his parents' adobe in 1894. Away from the harsh, dry climate of New Mexico and in the fecund soil of Southern California, Ortega's harvest was so large that he had to give peppers away. That pleasant surprise repeated the following year; the third year of growing these New Mexico chiles in California produced so many that Ortega couldn't give them all away, letting some rot.

Those fleshy, mild peppers were too delicious to just let waste, and Ortega figured that preserving them was necessary. In 1896, according to family legend, Ortega salvaged scrap iron from one of the decaying buildings near the Mission and had an idea. He fashioned that piece of metal into a sort of cylinder, complete with mesh top, and fashioned it into a tumbler that allowed the chiles to roll inside and roast evenly before falling out of a chute; the tumble separated the pulp from the skin without sacrificing any flavor. This same basic roaster is the one now used by thousands of New Mexicans every chile season, and its basic dynamics remain the most efficient way to roast chiles.

New Mexicans had long roasted them on grills to shrink the peppers or dried them in the sun, but preserving them for commercial sale hadn't been attempted. By 1899, Ortega created the Pioneer Ortega Chile Packing Company, California's first commercial food operation to sell whole chiles and salsa; on the label was a sketch of the Ortega adobe. The following year he moved to Los Angeles, opening a canning facility near downtown, and "proposed to can not less than 500,000 cans of chili sauce," a fivefold increase from the 110,000 cans from the previous year.[8] Ortega's canned chiles spread across the Southwest, allowing families to use them year-round. The surplus also allowed Ortega to be among the first producers of salsa in the United States, advertising it as "Tru Salsa."

Ortega didn't just revolutionize the canning industry. To meet the demand of his products, Ortega contracted with farmers across Southern California to grow chiles using his seeds, with a large concentration in Anaheim; enough farmers there grew them that the New Mexico chile Ortega brought to the Golden State became known as the Anaheim chile. He also cheated Mother Nature by convincing growers to stagger the time when they grew their crops by planting two weeks apart from each other, to stretch the season from late August to late September to the beginning of August into October, a strategy that worked magnificently and was copied by Southern California's farmers.

The cannery grew in Los Angeles, never returning to Ventura. After Ortega's death in 1942, the new owners moved the cannery to Oxnard, just south of Ventura. The Ortega adobe occasionally appears in the company's promotional literature, but that's the only tie left between the city that gave Ortega birth and the prodigal son that will never return.

In 1972, Rosalind Oliva found herself in a moment of desperation living in Worcester, Massachusetts, and did the unthinkable: she tried canned tortillas.

Oliva was a Southern California native, from one of the barrios in the San Bernardino area, and grew up eating fresh tortillas prepared by her grandmother daily. But Oliva was a dutiful wife, and her then-husband had just found a job as a radio newsman at WORC-AM, Worcester's flagship rock station (it's now a Spanish-language station). Oliva was one of the few Mexicans in Worcester at the time, which meant there were no bagged tortillas in the markets, let alone tortillerías that milled masa daily. A care package from her mother was on the way, tortillas and chilies and other essentials, but her husband had invited his boss and a fellow deejay to their house with the promise of an authentic Mexican dinner.

One part of the meal was accounted for: the chile rellenos. Oliva had insisted on bringing a case of Ortega chiles on the three-thousand-mile drive from Southern California to Worcester, despite protestations from family members who assumed Ortega products were available back East. She also wanted to serve chicken taquitos, but the only tortillas available in the Worcester area were canned, which she had never before heard of in her Mexican-American life. Oliva can't remember the brand but recalls that they came a dozen in a can, upright and rolled in one multilayered S, each separated by wax paper so they didn't stick together.

They were terrible. "The tortillas were thick and grainy and fell apart at the ends when I rolled and fried them for chicken taquitos," Oliva now says. "They were not very pliable. To me, they tasted like chalk. They would not have been edible even warmed up with butter inside."

It didn't matter—her dinner wowed the bosses. "They didn't know any better," Oliva says. "They called the food 'exotic' and told me I should open a restaurant! It must have been my grandma's slightly modified recipe for chile rellenos that did the trick."

Tony Ortega suffered a similar dilemma a decade later. He was a new student at Columbia University but already nostalgic for the Mexican food of Anaheim, where he was raised. He couldn't locate a Mexican restaurant in New York City, let alone a grocery store, and visited a bodega in Morningside Heights out of desperation. There he came across Old El Paso products—refried beans, enchilada sauce, and canned tortillas.

"I'd never seen anything like that in my life," says Ortega, now the editor of the *Village Voice*. "The can was a funny shape, wide and short, and sure enough, when you opened it up there were several mini–corn tortillas inside. What could I do? I had no other choice." Ortega made enchiladas with his products for his roommates back in their dank dorm room. "[They] were curious about what I was doing, but they looked horrified at the beans in the pot," he says. "Why the hell was I heating up a can of dog food on the stove? Well, they shut up after they had a bite."

Today the idea of tortillas in a can sounds preposterous, even deceitful. *How? Why? Who? What?* But for nearly half a century, the only tortillas available to the majority of Americans were exactly that—sometimes placed in long tin cans so the tortillas lay flat in their natural state, or stuffed into cans like the one Oliva had, sold by dozens of companies that wanted to capitalize on the growing American taste for tortillas but didn't have access to local tortilla factories. Canned tortillas are almost extinct now, manufactured by only a handful of companies for survival purposes, a testament to America's desire for Mexican food of any kind, no matter how foul.

The man responsible for this curious artifact was George N. Ashley of El Paso, whose place in the pantheon of Mexican food in this country is secured even if the memory of canned tortillas leaves the annals of history for good. For it was Ashley who advanced Gebhardt's idea of Mexican dinners: instead of just offering ingredients and giving customers recipe books on how to cook them, Ashley was the first to can whole dinners—enchiladas, chile rellenos, refried beans, and other treats—and also to freeze them for easier keeping. The Ashley's brand stood for decades as the best choice for Mexican food whenever there wasn't a Mexican restaurant around.

Ashley was a railroad engineer by training who found himself out of a job in 1929, as the Great Depression gripped Texas. He opened a dairy store the following year, but wanted to serve Mexican food, partly because he and his family had long enjoyed it but also because he thought Americans preferred a cleaner environment than the one offered at a typical El Paso Mexican restaurant or across the border in Ciudad Juárez.

"Some Mexican restaurants [in the city] still had dirt floors, live chickens in the kitchen, and no refrigeration," his son George Jr. told a reporter. "My dad decided then and there that he could make Mexican food and serve it in more sanitary surroundings."[9]

Ashley's wife knew how to make tacos and chili; George built tables and painted their restaurant. He also bought an electric fan, to blow the aroma of their dishes onto the street.[10] Ashley's sold dinners, tortilla chips, and meals to go, proudly disclosing in ads that the restaurant's Mexican dishes were "made 100% by American women working under NRA."[11] By 1935, Ashley's gave up selling dairy products to focus on Mexicans; the following year, they expanded with a new dining hall. Fifteen years before Juvencio Maldonado earned the first patent for a taco fryer, George fashioned one capable of cooking six hundred shells per hour, allowing George to sell tacos in even larger quantities than before and much faster than any competitors.[12]

Mexican food, of course, was already popular in El Paso, but Ashley masterfully positioned his restaurant to attract Anglos. It also helped that the restaurant had a guaranteed, almost limitless supply of new customers because of Fort Bliss and Biggs Army Airfield—thousands of army men and women had their first taste of Mexican food at Ashley's, more so once World War II drew American draftees through El Paso on the way to the Western Front. Through this relationship, Ashley secured a contract with the military in 1938 to supply it with Mexican food.[13]

That same year, Ashley's made the move to push beyond El Paso. The military's experience at Ashley's ensured that the taste of Mexico traveled the country, leading to letters from veterans asking George if he might ship them some Mexican dinners. Intrigued, George experimented with canning Mexican foodstuffs—enchiladas, chili, and tortillas. When he felt comfortable enough to go public, Ashley took out an ad in one of the city's daily newspapers to trumpet his accomplishment of canning tortillas, announcing their imminent arrival. "Send a can to your friends in distant points with the assurance they will have the same flavor as if eaten in El Paso," Ashley's ads read.[14]

Requests for Ashley's products poured in from across the globe within months. In November of that year, a letter came to the restaurant from Awali, Bahrain, from a Standard Oil Company employee. "We feel [Ashley's canned tortillas] may be the answer to our longing for good Mexican food," William R. Gentry wrote. "There are four families of us here from El Paso along with several other Texas families and a number of people from Southern California. Our mouths simply drool at the thought of Mexican food. We have made several attempts to make tortillas with more or less luck." Ashley immediately sent Gentry two cases of his canned tortillas, damn the seventy days it'd take for the Americans to receive the taste of home.[15]

El Paso was a hotbed of product innovation in Mexican food because of its proximity to military bases, and the chile fields of southern New Mexico. Ashley's main competitor was the Mountain Pass Canning Company, founded in 1907 in Deming, New Mexico, as a tomato-packing factory before relocating to Canutillo, Texas, just outside El Paso. Ashley's beat them in the canned Mexican dinner game, also in offering frozen Mexican food (pioneered in 1949 by George Ashley with enchiladas), and (as mentioned earlier) in fashioning the country's first taco-frying mold for household use. But once Mountain Pass bought out the Valley Canning Company in 1955, and their Old El Paso label, the company overtook Ashley's to become the largest producer of canned Mexican food in the United States. The Holly Sugar Company bought out Ashley's in 1975, and the brand disappeared from American shelves soon after, its logo of a silhouetted, dancing Spanish señorita forgotten in the onslaught of other, newer, more authentic competitors.

One of those was Rosarita, founded by Pedro W. Guerrero after years of many setbacks pursuing an unrequited dinner dream. He was born in the mining town of Florence, Arizona, in 1896 to a Mexican father and a white mother whose father detested Mexicans. As a young man, Guerrero bounced from Arizona to Los Angeles, finding jobs as everything from tunnel digger to hog slaughterer, store clerk, lumber-yard worker, and even boxer, finding a career as a sign painter. Along the way, he married Rosaura Castro despite her father's warning that his daughter wasn't much of a cook.

In 1927, Guerrero moved his family to Southern California and he took a job with a sign company, but was fired on his first day. It was a humiliating experience, but Guerrero welcomed it in a way because the setback offered him a chance to pursue full-time his Mexican food dream. Four years earlier, Guerrero, his wife, and friends had set up a tent during a Holy Week fair in the town of Guadalupe, nowadays surrounded by Phoenix. Although the area had a sizable Mexican community, only one Mexican restaurant existed in the Phoenix area during the era, meaning most Anglos relied on street vendors or personal cooks for their Mexican food—or this festival, with which Guerrero was familiar.

"I was fascinated," his granddaughter quoted Pedro as saying years later, "by the throngs of people, mostly Anglos, who mobbed these huts. In those days, people thought Mexican food was dirty. But I had an idea: if tamales were selling like hotcakes from little huts, what would happen if you sold them in a clean, pretty place?"[16]

Rosaura made tamales along with hamburgers and hot dogs to hedge their bets just in case customers patronized the other Mexican food stalls; Pedro and his friends served as hawkers. They dressed in immaculate white aprons and wrapped each tamale in a napkin to emphasize that they ran a clean operation, unlike their competitors. Within one day, they sold a thousand tamales at ten cents apiece; the hot dogs and hamburgers barely moved.

"Now I knew I was right about the demand for Mexican food, served in an appetizing way," Guerrero told his biographer decades later. "My mind was racing with ideas—Mexican food in restaurants, Mexican food in grocery stores, Mexican food in huge quantities by machines. I couldn't wait to put those ideas to the test."[17]

But Guerrero failed to convince investors about the viability of selling Mexican food in American markets in the Phoenix area at the time. That didn't stop him, however, from *imagining* he had a food company. In 1931, he commissioned his son to draw the logo for the imaginary Rosita Mexican Products Company, and the son produced the logo they still use: a raven-haired beauty wearing a sombrero, her hair in braids, ruby-red lips encasing a pearly white smile, and a rose in her hair; the name and logo were based on Rosaura. Logo finished, Pedro ordered ten thousand parchment-paper wrappers emblazoned with it, and even made neon signs in the expectation that his hypothetical company needed them for advertising. Throughout that time, Rosauro sold tamales around town during Christmas to help out the family.

For fifteen years, no one wanted to believe Guerrero's dreams, even after he sneaked his way into a Los Angeles tamale factory to figure out how to produce them on a mass scale. Finally, in 1945, Guerrero convinced a Mormon lady named Ann Petrie to sell Rosaura's tamales at one of her restaurants. Before even receiving that first batch, Petrie suggested to Guerrero that they start a company, and also recommended that they allow a returning World War II veteran named R. G. Scarborough to invest.

They hired a Mexican woman, Maria Méndivil, to cook a batch of tamales based on Rosaura's recipe and wrapped them in the logoed parchment paper Guerrero had commissioned so long ago. Petrie dropped them off at Mesa stores; within hours, one demanded more, since their stock of four dozen sold out. Soon afterward the company branched out to sell tortillas and bought a tamale factory in Phoenix and made hot sauce as well. By the late 1950s they expanded nationally, changing the company's name to Rosarita after discovering that someone else already held the copyright for Rosita on nationwide sales.

Guerrero convinced his partners to start offering packaged Mexican dinners after seeing Ashley's succeed in the field. He also pushed for them to offer refried beans, something Mountain Pass had pioneered decades before. By the time Rosarita went public in 1959, Scarborough had become a millionaire, while Guerrero's original $5,000 investment netted him a healthy $231,000 (Scarborough had bought out Petrie years before). Scarborough, however, died tragically in a plane accident that year.

The company immediately reshuffled its board, and one of the moves was promoting a sales executive named Paul van Cleve Langston to sales manager. Under Langston the company evolved from selling all types of Mexican foods—including frozen dinners and "cocktail tacos," bite-sized shells filled with a splotch of ground beef—into the nation's most popular purveyor of refried beans. At one point in the 1960s they were selling more cans of refried beans than Campbells was selling pork and beans. Yet before joining Rosarita, the only acquaintance Langston and his family had with Mexican food was visiting Olvera Street.

Rosarita's success under Langston earned his son Brian the nickname the Bean Prince while attending school in the Phoenix area. "It was kind of exotic, to eat refried beans out of a can at the time," says Brian. "My friends thought it was cool. We didn't own Rosarita, but we ran it." Rosarita struck a deal with Frito-Lay to produce gigantic sombreros with the crown of the hat dipped in; on the brim went Fritos and Doritos, in the crown went Rosarita's beans. At the Rosarita factory was a three-story machine developed by Langston to sift out the stones from the beans before they went into the fifty kettles devoted to boiling beans. Overseeing the chaos was a photo of Pedro and Rosaura Guerrero, no longer involved with the company but still appreciated for their efforts.

Those refrieds first went on sale in Arizona and California, then nationwide, although the East Coast proved a hard sell. "Dad always said he could never sell in Boston and New York because they thought Mexicans were dirty," Langston says, a perception Cleve allayed whenever possible. Once, someone sent a letter to Langston complaining that they found a stone in a can of beans. Langston personally drove from Phoenix to Tucson, a trip of about two hours, with a box filled with canned beans and a personal apology. "This is back when corporate America was actually trying hard," Brian now says with a garrulous laugh.

At the Langston house another innovation arose during the late 1960s, Brian claims. "My [then girlfriend, now wife] was a strict vegetarian, and she asked Dad why he wouldn't make refried beans that were vegetarian," he remembers. "He said they needed lard, but sure enough, she made him some, and of course they were great. They sold the first ones six months later. One of Rosarita's product lines was developed by a cute blond girl practicing the Sikh religion as an impulse!"

In 1971, Brian found himself backpacking across India and Afghanistan after college. He entered a market in Kabul and found a can of Rosarita's salsa with a recipe for something called Dip de Brian: salsa with grated cheese, a concoction Brian had created during college. On a lark, he had asked his father why Rosarita didn't sell his dip; instead, Cleve published it on millions of labels and sold it worldwide. "My friends made fun of me about the label of the salsa when I came back. I was embarrassed, but more like flabbergasted," Brian said. "How the hell did Mexican food get all the way over there?"

Downtown Riverside, California, is a mix of the suburban, the decrepit, and the regal, a city once home to the citrus barons of Southern California, then engulfed by waves of suburbanites who abandoned Los Angeles and Orange Counties for the endless developments of the Inland Empire. In the middle of it all stands the Mission Inn Hotel and Spa, a sprawling complex mixing Spanish Revival architecture with mosaics, rotundas, towers, hidden passages, and too many glorified paintings of California history to remember.

Despite its quirkiness, the Mission Inn was closed during the late 1980s, its structure not seismically sound. In came the frozen burrito to pour millions into the building and save it from destruction—or rather, the frozen burrito's father, Duane R. Roberts. Roberts was raised on Mexican food while growing up in Riverside, son of a meat wholesaler who provided barbecue cuts and hamburger patties to restaurants across Southern California, including the McDonald brothers. Duane helped with the family business, Butcher Boy, as a high schooler, joining full-time after attending college for a spell at the University of California at Riverside and finding that academia wasn't his forte.

As fast-food restaurants increased during the late 1950s, Roberts and his father held a strategy session in 1956 on what other food items Butcher Boy might make to get a piece of the action of the market. Nothing came out of it. Duane mentioned the impasse to a butcher of his, a Mexican (Roberts can't remember his name) who suggested that Butcher Boy produce burritos.

"What's a burrito?" Roberts remembers asking.

"You take a flour tortilla—" the butcher started to explain before an impetuous Robert interrupted him. "Stop right there," he said. "I've only seen corn tortillas. What's a flour tortilla?"

But after Roberts took a crash course in burritos, he became a quick convert. "It was a great idea," he now says. "It'd be portion-controlled—you just put in some ingredients and spices." Roberts found a tortilla factory in Santa Ana that specialized in flour tortillas and spent the next two days making burritos, settling on a beef, bean, and chile colorado blend. He flash-froze, then thawed out the burritos to ensure that they remained edible. After much experimentation Roberts found that the flavor was magnified when the burrito was thrown into a fryer, which gave him the idea to sell burritos to fast-food restaurants; all they had to do was fry them, and an entrée was born.

When he was satisfied with the results, Roberts prepared a sales pitch to Butcher Boy management. "I didn't know burritos," he repeated. "At that stage of the game, in those days, people called tacos 'tay-cos.' I got a photographer to take pictures of the burrito, and created a poster board to describe what it was. I even spelled it out phonetically—'boar-i-to'—so people could pronounce it."

Unlike the other frozen Mexican foods available, the frozen burrito needed no utensils, no plates, not even extra seasoning. Butcher

Boy marketed their burritos under the Mar-kes brand, which Roberts Hispanicized to Marquez. A contract was reached with 7-Eleven convenience stores; they sold so many that the company severed ties with Butcher Boy shortly after they built their own frozen-burrito plant in Utah. More important, Roberts secured contracts with schools across the United States to serve frozen burritos as cafeteria lunches; schools found them cheap, novel, flavorful grub—and the schoolyard loved them.

"The pitch for them was simple," Roberts says. "Our burritos were very tasty, portion-controlled, easy to handle. You didn't have to worry about spoiled food—they had a long shelf life, and you bring them out when you're ready to make them. You had an item that was something that was new and different. Kids loved them. Easiest sell of my life."

Roberts made so much money off frozen burritos that he sold Butcher Boy in 1981, just after reaching the high point of producing one million burritos per day. "It was a heartache, the [bids for my company] got up so high that I had to look at it," he admits. "When I got out of it, it was like selling a child. It wasn't quite the same. I was so known as Butcher Boy, my whole identity was that. You could say the frozen burrito transformed an industry. That burrito of ours? You can just put it in the microwave, and it came out perfect."

There are so many other Mexican-food products stories, so few pages. In 1968, George de la Torre Jr., son of a Mexican-American father and a Japanese-American mother who married in Mexico to avoid California's miscegenation laws, took over his father's fish-canning business in the working-class L.A. district of Wilmington and switched to canning Mexican food instead, renaming his company Juanita's Foods. He was the first to can menudo, the Mexican tripe stew, and mole, both full-fledged meals most thought impossible to can—but it was done. People wanted it.

Gilbert de Cardenas wasn't a Mexican but rather a Cuban refugee who noticed how Mexicans ached for their homeland's cheese. His family were cheesemongers back in Cuba until Castro took away their livelihood. De Cardenas started Cacique in 1973; the company became the largest makers of Mexican cheeses and crema in the world. It was done. People wanted it.

In the 1940s, Henry Steinbarth opened a butcher shop on Chicago's South Side, a European ethnic neighborhood that became Puerto Rican and Mexican. The latter demanded chorizo, the spicy pork sausage, and the Steinbarths complied. But that wasn't enough; Henry's son, Ralph, packaged chorizo as well and sold it around Chicago as La Preferida—The Preferred. Today La Preferida sells more than two hundred Mexican-food products and is a perennial staple of mayoral bets during sports playoffs, representing Chi-Town. It was done. People wanted it.

Germans, Cubans, Japanese, Americans, Mormons, even the occasional Mexican, all vanguards of Mexican foods in the United States, ambassadors of our most exportable native grub. But two items deserve separate chapters, for their influence on American eating habits went beyond the realm of Mexican and into our fundamental selves: the tortilla and its children, and salsa.

Chapter Eleven

Is the Tortilla God's Favored Method of Communication?

The famed Catholic theologian St. Augustine of Hippo had a thing for miracles. Most of book twenty-two in his classic *The City of God* is devoted to explaining, documenting, and arguing for and defending their existence, insisting that there was a natural logic to occurrences that had no terrestrial explanation: the hand of the Lord.

He listed just some of the supernatural acts he had heard about, many involving foodstuffs—salt that turned into liquid when tossed into a fire yet crackled with electric jolts if sprinkled on water; fountains that spewed water at varying times of the day either too hot or too cold to drink; apples that turned into ashes and dust when someone touched them. "And consequently, as these present marvels are not nonexistent, though human reason and discourse are lost in such works of God," he wrote, "so those things we speak of are not impossible because inexplicable."

Miracles happen, whether people want to believe in them or not. When Maria Rubio cooked a burrito of pinto beans, scrambled eggs, and green chile for her husband, Eduardo, before sunrise in October 1977, she knew not to dismiss the burned spot on the flour tortilla she had just cooked as mere skillet burns, the tortilla she had just rolled up into Eduardo's breakfast. Maria was a maid living in Lake Arthur, New Mexico, a tiny settlement in the state's southeast, where one of the taller structures in town is an obelisk commemorating the Ozark Trail, decorated with the distances to other, better places. She asked her daughter, Rosie, to describe what she saw in the tortilla's crackled, thumb-sized spot. The answer was the same as what Maria had thought: before them was the face of Jesus, bearded and crowned in thorns.

Mother and daughter went to a neighbor, who made the sign of the cross upon seeing the tortilla. The following day, they took it to a priest in neighboring Dexter, a town three times larger than Lake Arthur—which is to say it had a population of about fifteen hundred. The priest didn't want to believe, tried to convince the Rubios that the charcoal flakes were a simulacrum of Christ's face, the standard statement from the Catholic Church to dissuade the faithful from seeing God in everyday settings. He nevertheless blessed it, but warned against believing.

"A miracle, therefore, happens not contrary to nature, but contrary to what we know as nature," *The City of God* also stated. The Church was helpless against this miracle. Thousands came to pray at the Rubio household, to offer flowers and well-wishes. From across the globe letters poured in, which Maria kept in a binder that she showed to pilgrims. Maria quit her job as a maid; Eduardo stopped drinking. Donations came in to build it a proper shrine, but the Archdiocese of Santa Fe told them to stop; instead, the Rubios constructed a shed in their backyard and placed the Miracle Tortilla there.

"I'm not too impressed with that kind of miracle," Father Joyce Finnigan scoffed to the press nine months after Jesus appeared. "Since Mrs. Rubio came to me, I've fried a lot of tortillas, and I've found that if you do it often enough, you'll get a lot of things."[1]

But Maria Rubio kept the faith. She welcomed visitors into their home; when the Rubios left, they'd leave a note on their unlocked door inviting people in to see the Miracle Tortilla. "I tell them my message," Maria said. "I believe I must show my faith because I believe the appearance of Christ is a message for all people to unite with each other and become brothers and sisters."[2]

The world snickered, but the Rubios never stopped. They appeared over the next decades on national television shows and granted interviews to the global press. Other heavenly tortillas tried to rival the Rubios', but all fell out of favor. The Miracle Tortilla became an icon of roadside America, dismissed as the hallucinations of funny old Mexicans—no less an authority than God Himself, at least as portrayed in *The Simpsons,* once excused himself from talking to mankind by stating, "Now, if you'll excuse me, I have to appear on a tortilla *in Mexico.*"

Still, the Rubios and thousands of others knew what they saw. Of course God chose to appear in a tortilla, in the vessel of masa, in Mexico's greatest comforter after the Virgin of Guadalupe. This humble disc, whether made from corn or flour or wheat or even New Age spinach, transmits heritage, race, class, and beauty within its circular border with each filling bite, with each crisped fleck. The tortilla is the essence of Mexico, what unites the country from Tijuana to the jungles of Chiapas to outer space, even if geography stretches or condenses it, fries them or rolls them or—*shudder*—puts them into cans, as previously discussed. Without the tortilla we have no taco, no burrito, no enchilada, no nachos or tortilla chip stranglehold on our sports viewing, no transmission of essential nutrients, no way for the poor to stretch out a meal by sprinkling salt on one and calling it a lunch, or cook gooey, slightly burned quesadillas. In short, with no tortilla, there is no Mexico. There is nothing.

It's now essential to the United States as well, a multibillion-dollar industry exponentially expanding. In 2009, the U.S. Department of Commerce estimated that tortilla makers in *los Estados Unidos*—from megacompanies such as Mission Brand to regional brands to mom-and-pop shops—shipped $3.18 billion worth of their cash creation, a nearly threefold increase from 1997, when the total was a mere $1.1 billion.[3] That number is conservative, according to the Tortilla Industry Association, which estimates annual sales at $8 billion in the

United States alone. And that figure doesn't include the tortilla's other children: tortilla chips, tostadas, corn chips, Fritos, and so many of the snacks that Americans now claim as their own yet resonate with a continental collective unconscious shaped over millennia.

Other flatbreads exist around the world: the pita of the Mediterranean, the chapati or roti on the Indian subcontinent, the spongy *injera* of Ethiopia, Iran's fabulous *sangak* bread. Those are delicious—important even—but none is connected to a country the way the tortilla is ingratiated to Mexico. Since time immemorial, Mexicans have greeted their morning with the simultaneous sensory wallops of the scent of fresh cornmeal hitting the *comal* (a Mexican griddle made of cast iron) and the pat-pat of the hands of a mother—perhaps a sister or a grandmother, but always the female of the house—shaping another tortilla into birth. Somnolent boys and men woke up, enticed by the sweet smell and sound of a mass of spongy corn dough formed into nearly neat circles. This was the daily miracle, what made being a Mexican and all of its burdens worth it.

Pat-pat-pat-pat. Hands clapped on the masa—left fingers smashing the masa on the right palm, a quick toss onto the other hand, then right fingers switching to smack the left palm—for a good minute, moving the growing creation in a clockwise fashion to spread the cornmeal so it became uniformly thin, as thin as a quarter. Once splayed, never stretched out too big lest it tear, the new tortilla hit the already heated comal, releasing an earthy, burned scent, one reaching into every synapse formed to identify pleasure. Another chunk torn off from the mother masa, rolled into another ball, then patted away.

Then came time to turn the tortilla, to ensure that both sides cooked. But instead of using a spatula, nimble Mexican hands, thick hands inured to the heat of cast iron over generations, flipped it with ease, with a pinch of the thumb and index finger. The same again. And again. The immaculate, handmade tortilla became sturdy enough to wobble without breaking, dun in color but also flexible enough to roll up. The flip had to happen at the right time—too soon, and masa remnants stuck to the comal, ripping the delicate entity, leaving scraps suited for dogs; stay too long, and the tortilla burns, wrinkles, rendering nourishing masa into little more than carbon. Once done and bitten into, the reject shatters into useless, inedible bits—a waste, a blasphemous waste.

Pat-pat and flip, *pat-pat* and flip: the steps repeated again and again until the day's tortillas were set. Those that weren't immediately rolled up by grateful family members made their way into a cloth or a wicker basket; the warmth of the just-made tortillas kept them ready for immediate deployment. Leftover freshly made tortillas were unknown; they're too delicious, too nourishing to leave alone, and too quick to spoil in the days before refrigeration. Besides, the masa Mass happened again the following day, at the break of dawn.

It's a beautiful rite; it's a historical one, a sumptuous pat-down. It's now almost extinct.

Unless a Mexican is straight from the *rancho,* or unless a family is holding a special occasion, most Mexican families in the United States now buy tortillas the same way as Americans—from a grocery store, prefabricated, cardboard imposters riddled with preservatives to ensure a shelf life. Even those Mexicans who do make them must buy the masa from a local *mercado,* where creating masa—once so crucial to Mexican identity that it was said a woman wasn't suitable for marriage unless she knew how to make a tortilla from nixtamalization to placing it in the wicker—has been reduced to machines and automatons.

Tortillas now sell in the billions of dollars. And they're barely edible.

The pogrom against home tortilla making launched in earnest during the early twentieth century, when the rule of Porfirio Díaz was at its height. Once a Mexican national hero—he was there at the Battle of Pueblo on May 5, 1862, and later captured by French occupying forces, escaping to lead the counterinsurgency against the reign of the Hapsburg emperor Maximilian—Díaz became president of Mexico in

1876, promising to eradicate the wrenching poverty of a nation that had suffered two foreign invasions within fifteen years.

But over the next four decades, Diaz launched political reforms that increasingly privatized land and sought neoliberal reforms that welcomed foreign capital and ideas, all in the name of progress. The Porfiriato (as his regime came to be known) was a firm believer in positivism, the social ideology that spread across Latin American in the late nineteenth century seeking to wean the land from its indigenous heritage while looking across the Atlantic for inspiration. And the movement's archenemy was maize.

Francisco Bulnes, one of Díaz's senators, published a book positing that Mexicans would underachieve as long as corn was a mainstay of their diet. He divided the world into three races: those who preferred wheat, the people of corn, and those favoring rice. "The race of wheat is the only truly progressive one," he affirmed, and "maize has been the eternal pacifier of America's indigenous races and the foundation of their refusal to become civilized." The Aztecs, in Bulnes's mind, "appeared powerful, but [were] in fact so weak as to fall victim to insignificant bands of Spanish bandoleros."[4]

The popular press and intellectuals parroted Bulnes's views, but masa nevertheless ruled Mexico. While one set of elites tried to eradicate maize from the Mexican diet, another tried to eliminate the rigors of tortilla making in a good-hearted attempt to modernize peasants. Disregard the romanticism I described at the top of this chapter; making tortillas, historically, was a brutal task. The corn had to be shucked, then left to soak overnight for the process of nixtamalization. From here, women—and, yes, always women—ground the flattened, blanched kernels in a metate. Ever ground corn? Not fun, and women had to get up hours before sunrise just to make enough masa to feed the family for that day. The masa didn't keep well, rapidly fermenting and thus impossible to use.

Ingenious Mexican inventors set out on a three-pronged task—to create nixtamal mills where villagers brought corn they picked and leave with masa, automate tortilla making, and achieve the Holy Grail: dried masa safe to be stored away for use later, a product that eliminated the need to make fresh masa before every sunrise and eradicate what a tortilla machine inventor described as "the slavery of the metate."[5] The first *molinos* to mill masa appeared in Mexico by the 1890s; tortilla factories appeared in the early parts of the twentieth century, along with simpler apparatuses that flattened masa balls into tortillas. But the much-mythologized *masa harina*—masa turned into flour that reconstituted with the addition of water—didn't happen in Mexico, but rather in the United States, in that grand crossroads of Mexican-food innovation: San Antonio.

Tortilla recipes already dotted American cookbooks and home journals by the 1890s, almost all contributed by non-Mexicans and usually, laughably wrong. A 1902 *Los Angeles Times* recipe offered by a reader called for beef lard instead of the customary pork and instructed readers to "bake slowly" on the stove instead of constantly flipping them.[6] Another manual asked for regular cornmeal to be used instead of masa, an error even its readers knew was wrong.[7] May E. Southworth, author of one of the first-ever published cookbooks devoted exclusively to Mexican cuisine, called for tortillas to be cooked by getting thrown into a frying pan filled with angry lard, "enough to float the tortillas, but not so hot as to brown them" and leave in until blistering commenced.[8] Southworth's recipe—like the recipes of so many others until the middle of the century—called for flour to be used instead of masa. Flour tortillas were the daily bread of northern Mexico, preferred by the natives since wheat was easier to grow in the region than corn, but the choice of flour for American audiences was also obvious: flour mills were common in the United States, and American housewives didn't dare subject themselves to the metate's backbreaking demands.

Tortilla making in the United States, to the extent there was one, depended on the feminine daily household grind. Producing masa on a mass scale simply wasn't feasible, not that inventors weren't trying; as early as 1877, John H. Pendleton of Brooklyn received a patent for grinding what he called "tortilla" instead of maize. The American tortilla industry changed, however, in 1899, with the opening of the first-ever masa mill in the United States. Its founder was José Bartolome Martinez, a native of Mexico raised in Texas. He opened the mill to immediate success, but Martinez wasn't satisfied. All of the money Martinez made from his mill went into experimenting with dehydrating masa, nearly driving him into debt. He persisted, and finally debuted in 1908 with what he called *masolina* but trademarked the following year as Tamalina. He sold his product in five-pound sacks; all a woman needed to do was add water, and masa emerged.

Martinez incorporated the Tamalina Milling Company in 1911, opening a new factory two years later that had the capacity to mill sixty thousand pounds of Tamalina per day, along with sixty thousand pounds of fresh masa for immediate sale. The mill—which housed huge silos capable of storing seventy-five thousand bushels of corn—stood next to the railroad tracks, the better to move Tamalina across the United States. For the San Antonio market, Martinez commanded a fleet of more than twenty wagons to take to the streets of the Alamo City, delivering masa, Tamalina, and tortillas.

Among his company's directors was none other than Otis M. Farnsworth, owner of the Original Restaurant, the father of the combination plate. It's from the collaboration between Farnsworth and Martinez that another landmark in tortilla history most likely emerged: the offering of tortilla chips with each sit-down dinner, along with a side of guacamole or salsa. Such chips, contrary to the assertions of the Diana Kennedys of the world, weren't unknown in Mexico, where they were called *tostados* and feasted on as snacks. But they functioned as *antojitos*—"little desires," almost superfluous, considering any masa at a household or restaurant's disposal was used for the far more important task of making tamales and tortillas.

Tamalina's large-scale production, though, meant excess masa amassed daily, so Martinez used it to produce tortilla chips. After much trial and error with shapes, Martinez settled between strips and triangles, according to grandson Roy G. Martinez. "Finally, after he obtained feedback from friends, he decided to cut them in a triangle shape of medium thickness," Martinez wrote. "The reason was that this shaped chip was better when used with dips. The strip chips kept breaking with the thicker dips such as bean dip or guacamole."[9]

Martinez gave away samples to his many San Antonio customers; they asked for more. Tamalina proceeded to sell corn chips in bags colored like the Mexican flag, with a logo of an eagle gripping an ear of corn, a bearer of a new era where the national birds of Mexico and the United States no longer warred with each other but united under the spell of masa. They debuted under the Tamalina brand in 1919 but didn't apply for label protection until 1932; in a document filed with the Texas secretary of state, Martinez's son Wenceslao wrote that the label was used for "corn products consisting of: Tamale and Tortilla meal and corn flour; plain tortillas and toasted tortilla chips."[10] Competitors had muscled into the tostados market, and the snack spread across Texas and even beyond: in 1937 Maury Maverick—the San Antonio mayor who had driven out the chili queens but was now a congressman— hosted a party in Washington, D.C., where tostados were the snack at hand; curious easterners promptly called them "cornies."[11]

After Martinez suddenly passed away in the 1920s, Tamalina Milling reincorporated under B. Martinez Sons Co.; it still exists. Their contribution, however, was almost completely forgotten. When Rebecca Webb Carranza died in 2006, many American newspapers (including your humble author in his "¡Ask a Mexican!" column) referred to her as the inventor and innovator of the tortilla chip. Carranza, daughter of an American and a Mexican, had partnered with her husband to operate El Zarape, a tortilla factory in Los Angeles during the 1940s that earned praise in a 1950 *Popular Mechanics* article for automating their tortilla making. Years later, she'd tell the story that those early days of production resulted in many misshapen tortillas; rather than toss them, Carranza took them home, fried them, then thought of selling them at El Zarape for a dime under the name Tort Chips. She switched her business plan to making tortilla chips, and was successful enough that in the 1990s the Tortilla Industry Association awarded her with a Golden Tortilla in honor of her innovations.

In a letter to a doctoral student who included the Martinez story as part of her dissertation, Roy G. Martinez expressed his gratitude that someone, *anyone,* remembered his family's innovations. "I am so pleased to have someone like you present my story of the corn chip," he wrote. "And especially give credit to a Hispanic and not an Anglo. Our people are always left out and others are given credit. For some reason they always hate to give Hispanics credit for the good things they do."[12]

Martinez had every right to be bitter. The momentous commercialization of masa harina is universally credited to Roberto González Barrera, the man behind Gruma, the world's largest producer of tortillas and masa harina. In 1948, according to company lore, an eighteen-year-old González traveled to Reynosa, Tamaulipas, a city right on the U.S.-Mexico border, to sell off the stock of a grocery store he and his father ran. There González saw a masa harina machine that intrigued him. Although masa mills were now common in Mexico, and automated tortilla factories also were rising, masa harina was a phantom in Mexico—an inventor filed for a patent in 1912, but nothing ever came of it. He asked the mill's owner about his product; the entrepreneur replied that he only used it during cotton-picking season, when migrant workers bought fifteen tons of their masa harina per month.

González took the flour back to his father, who approved. "We felt we had an industry. . . . My father taught me something valuable—investigation is the mother of the development of a nation, of a company, and of people."[13]

Father and son went on to open Molinos Azteca (ironically, the name that Bartolomé Martinez gave to his original masa mill) in 1948, and branded their masa harina as Maseca. The company has spread like a virus ever since, helped out in large part by their deep connections with the Mexican government. Maseca owns at least three quarters of worldwide masa harina sales and a huge portion of tortillas in the United States (including the top seller, Mission tortillas, which hit the American marketplace in the early 1980s). Under González, Gruma bought Australia's largest tortilla maker and opened plants in China, Japan, and even Russia. And all along, they bought out their American competitors, one by one, until the point where the tortilla you recently ate most likely came from the Maseca monopoly. In America alone, analysts estimate that Gruma owns 50 percent of the market, while commanding 20 percent in Europe.

But Martinez was more upset about the lack of recognition his family has received for the humble tortilla chip, and his object of ire wasn't Webb Carranza, but one of his family's former clients: Elmer Doolin, the founder of Fritos. Doolin was a Kansas City native who, by 1932, was looking for a new product to distinguish his confectionary shop in San Antonio from the rest of the field. He stopped in one afternoon to eat at a Mexican restaurant, where alongside his sandwich sat corn chips.

The chips—not triangular, like tortilla chips, but curled, denser, more redolent of corn—intrigued Doolin, and he set out to find their maker to secure a shipment for his shop. As fate had it, the maker had already put out an ad in the *San Antonio Express* announcing, "CORN chips business for sale, a new food product, making good money. Must sacrifice."[14]

Gustavo Olguin was a native of Oaxaca who had moved to San Antonio during the 1920s. Most of his fame around town was earned on soccer fields, where he coached teams to league championships. As a side job, Olguin had fashioned a potato ricer to create corn chips, and sold bags to San Antonio restaurants. But for reasons lost to history, Olguin wanted to move back to Mexico and sold off his business, recipe, retail accounts, and equipment to Doolin for a hundred dollars.

Doolin, his mother, and his brother quickly set to fry as many of the corn chips from their San Antonio home as possible while plotting for national dominance.

Within a couple of months of acquiring Olguin's business, they had created a name to put onto their bags—Fritos, derived from the Spanish adjective for something fried—and received a trademark for the name the following year, 1934, which also saw Doolin apply for and receive a patent for Olguin's business, calling it "my invention" in paperwork filed with the U.S. Patent Office. Two years later he received a patent for a bag rack, the better to differentiate his chips from the others, which hid behind the counter, available only on request.

In San Antonio, however, Fritos were just one of many brands of corn chips. Times were tough; Doolin traveled the Midwest in his Model T Ford, trying to convince stores to stock his Fritos and even taking a cook's job for the graveyard shift in St. Louis just to make enough money to return home, according to his daughter Kaleeta. Just as soon as the Doolins incorporated Fritos, he relocated to Dallas and opened a plant. By the late 1930s, they opened another plant in Tulsa—and that was the beginning. "Our wedding was scheduled for eight o'clock in the morning," Katherine Doolin told NPR decades later. "The reason I was given is that we have to be on the road by ten, on the way to California and open [a Fritos] plant."[15]

The brand spread across the Southwest, a region familiar with the earthiness of fried corn, but it wasn't until after World War II that Doolin made a national push for domestic conquest, buying ads in *Life* and other national publications and passing off his product as a must-have for the intrepid housewife. In the pages of *Life,* in a year-long advertising campaign, Doolin printed just some of the 145 recipes the Frito Company had concocted, everything from a Fritos Ham Loaf to Fritos Fruit Salad Mold to even a dressing they claimed was "ideal for stuffing all fowls."[16] Also included was Fritos pie—a bowl of corn chips smothered underneath chili that Doolin's mother created;

the dish never really spread across the rest of the country but joined the day-to-day diets of Texans and New Mexicans almost immediately.[17]

In 1948, Doolin introduced Chee•tos—made from the same cornmeal used for Fritos, but now fried into gnarled sticks and possessing a cheddar cheese flavor. But he wanted more than to merely fill the households of America with bags of his stuff. Just months after Disneyland opened in 1955, Doolin convinced Walt Disney to let him open Casa de Fritos, a Mexican restaurant in Frontierland. The Mexican food was straightforward Tex-Mex—a combo plate, tamales, chile, Frito pie, enchiladas, and the "Ta-Cup," the standard fast-food taco about to colonize America but in a Fritos shell, the ancestor of the modern-day taco salad. Fritos came complimentary with every purchase.

Casa's first location was in a strip of attractions called New Orleans Street; nearby was Aunt Jemima's Pancake House. Marquees outside Casa de Fritos simultaneously announced that they sold "authentic Mexican" and Spanish food. Ethnic confusion aside, the restaurant exceeded all expectations, swarmed by tourists who sought to taste Mexican for the first time. Doolin relocated Casa de Fritos to a larger location in 1957, dropping the French Quarter architectural feel for a new building designed to look like an adobe, complete with faux peeling whitewash that revealed faux brick. Guitar players strolled around the grounds, while peppy workers dressed in Mexican peasant dress carried baskets filled with bags of Fritos for sale.

But the Frito Company, for all of its innovations with corn, didn't make the tortillas or taco shells at Casa de Fritos; they contracted that to the Alex Foods Company of Anaheim, whose factory was just about ten minutes up the street from Disneyland. In 1906, Sonoran immigrant Alex Morales sold his wife's tamales from a wagon he commandeered through Anaheim. Morales, a ditch digger by trade, grew the concept into a restaurant, then a tamale factory, then Alex Foods. It's now known as Don Miguel Mexican Foods.

"I never saw our original tamale wagon," says Michael Morales, Alex's grandson and president of XLNT Tamales, a Southern California classic that spun off from Don Miguel long ago and still uses Alex Morales's original 1906 recipe. "That was before my time." Asked if he knew its fate, Morales laughed and said his grandfather "probably burned it."

By the 1950s, Alex Foods had a fleet of thirty-two shiny trucks that delivered their tamales and other food products across Southern California, along with distributing produce that wasn't Mexican food. It was the latter operation that won the company a contract to service many of the food venues within Disneyland, among which was Casa de Fritos. One day in the early 1960s, one of their route salesmen saw discarded tortillas and told the cook to make them into tortilla chips instead of just tossing them in the trash. Tortilla chips at this point weren't part of the Frito family, so the restaurant had no use in offering them as other Mexican restaurants did at the time. The throwaway snack was a hit with guests, so Casa de Fritos put them on the menu—without the knowledge of the Frito Company.

About a year later, Arch West, marketing vice president for the new Frito-Lay Company (spawn of a merger between Fritos and H. W. Lay & Company in 1961), passed by Casa de Fritos and noticed customers eating the chips. He asked the Morales family to mass-produce them. West presented his bosses with a plan to market tortilla chips for national release, with Alex Foods its makers. Frito-Lay bought all the equipment the Morales family needed to make the chips, to be called Doritos ("little golden things"). They debuted in 1966 to immediate sales.

"We were running our plant seven days a week, twenty-four hours a day, to make the chips," Michael remembers. "We just couldn't stop, they were selling so fast." But the success meant "they took us out of the picture." Frito-Lay transferred the production line to their Tulsa plant, and opened a plant in Birmingham as well. Alex Foods didn't seethe; instead, they produced their own line of tortilla chips, and also became a copacker for most of the supermarket chains in Southern California.

"Losing Frito-Lay was a big deal," he admits, "but it didn't kill us."

Doolin passed away in 1959 of a heart attack, at fifty-six years old. The previous year, sales of his chips exceeded $51 million.[18] Doolin—a health fanatic who kept his family on a vegetarian diet—had hoped to see his product become more than a chip, but that never happened. Doritos joined Fritos in being relegated to junk food status—popular, of course, but still junk.

Meanwhile, unflavored tortilla chips climbed in popularity, driven by the rise of salsa, refried beans, and another dip: guacamole, a side almost as old as the tortilla. The Spaniards claimed that the Aztecs ate the exalted fruit as an aphrodisiac—the Nahuatl name for avocado is *ahuaca cuahitl,* tree of testicles, so maybe they had a point—and they largely shuddered away from it (although one Englishman insisted "this Fruit provokes to Lust, and therefore is said to be much esteemed by the Spaniards.")[19] Avocados warrant few mentions in the writings of the Mexican conquistadors, which reflected how little they cared for the fruit.

As a result, *aguacate* never made much of an impact in the Old World. Instead, avocados first gained traction in Asia, with the pits of the quick-to-rot fruit following the Spanish galleons from Acapulco to Manila; other traders spread the fruit across Indonesia and into Vietnam by the eighteenth century; from there, avocados continued westward through Australia, Africa, and the Middle East, infiltrating the cuisines of those lands.

In the United States, the avocado industry didn't begin in earnest until the creation of the California Avocado Society in 1915. Growers had cultivated the tree in Southern California since the 1880s, but it was more of a boutique cultivar than a plant for profit. Avocado magnates formed an organization to mimic the mighty Sunkist coop-

erative that had made millions of dollars for orange growers by specifically branding California oranges as the best in the United States and
then shipping them in refrigerated railcars eastward, stacked in crates
adorned with gorgeous label art. The growers united under the name
Calavo (short for California avocados) and launched an aggressive marketing campaign to highlight the avocado as a healthy fruit for the Jazz
Age; by the late 1920s, Calavo ads appeared in *Vogue* and the *New
Yorker*. Most of them at the time emphasized its roots as anything but
Mexican: Spanish, or even Mediterranean, despite the fact that it didn't
reach those shores until late into the nineteenth century. Calavo's efforts
to nationalize their cash crop proved largely fruitless despite arduous
promotional efforts—even to this day, avocados in American cuisine
don't get past beyond being an ingredient in salads and sandwiches.[20]
The growers nevertheless made their sales in the western United States,
thanks to guacamole. It had existed at Mexican restaurants since at
least the 1930s in Texas, and in Mexican cookbooks even before then
as a salad.

Guacamole and other dips required next to no preparation; tortilla chips, Fritos, and Doritos required none at all other than the
effort of couch potatoes to open their traps and chomp. A dish
inevitably married the two attributes: nachos. They were originally a
Texas phenomenon, most likely created in Piedras Negras, Mexico,
in the 1940s by a chef named Ignacio Ayala, who whipped some
up for Texas military wives who named them "Nacho's Special,"
"Nacho" being the nickname for Ignacio. It wasn't until 1959 that
they migrated west to California, where Carmen Rocha from San
Antonio introduced the meal at El Cholo, where she worked as a
waitress. Recipes filtered into magazine and newspaper articles over
the next two decades, but nachos didn't become nationally accepted
until another San Antonian, Frank Liberto Jr., and his Ricos Products set up a nacho stand in 1977 outside Arlington Stadium before a
Texas Rangers game. Liberto was a concession-stand supplier for the
Rangers who sat down at the end of the 1976 season with the city

of Arlington, which ran the stadium. They wanted a new snack; they wanted nachos.

"I didn't think it would work because it'd be too labor-intensive," Liberto said years later. "I remembered going to a restaurant and ordering nachos, and you'd wait thirty minutes and they'd bring you a plate of twelve chips and an expensive bill, but we encouraged them to go ahead and try—and I held my breath."[21]

To expedite nachos making, Liberto developed a cheese sauce, not unlike Texas queso, easy for concessionaires to heat in seconds, then pour over nachos. Crucially, Liberto also made sure to include jalapeños in the nachos even though the pepper was not yet popular across the country. Stadiums initially balked at selling nachos, fearful they'd cut into sales of popcorn and hot dogs, but the opposite happened: the jalapeños' heat made people buy more soda or popcorn in a fruitless effort to mitigate the burn. Three years later, Liberto tested the nachos at five other baseball stadiums; today every Major League Baseball and NFL stadium stocks the snack, and they're the third-largest concession seller overall in the United States after popcorn and soda, outselling even hot dogs.[22]

The rapid rise of nachos and guacamole convinced Frito-Lay to pioneer their final innovation in Mexican food that doesn't include flavor changes to Fritos and Doritos: the introduction of Tostitos. Instead of being flavored like Doritos or heavy like Fritos, these were light, airy, pure tortilla chips marketed as "authentic" to distinguish them from their Fritos and Chee•tos brothers. In 1978, Frito-Lay test-marketed Tostitos in the Midwest, and hired Fernando Escandón to star in a series of commercials to ensure that their stab at authenticity stuck. The Sonora native had moonlighted in bit roles on television during the 1970s but was a familiar voice for Latinos in Southern California, having served as a reporter for pioneering Spanish-language television station KMEX-TV in the Los Angeles area. He also owned two Mexican restaurants—all the requisites needed to establish Tostitos as authentically Mexican.

With a syrupy, slightly accented baritone, a full head of luxuriantly black hair, and a brush for a mustache, Escandón stood in deliberate contrast to the Frito Bandito, the infamous mascot Frito-Lay used in the 1960s until protests from Latino civil rights organizations pressured the company to drop it. In one commercial, Escandón stands in a restaurant kitchen next to a Mexican chef named Pedro. "It is not easy for Pedro to accept the fact that *my* favorite Mexican snack does not come from Mexico," Escandón states suavely. "Me-ji-co!" Pedro interjects, flustering Escandón. But the actor continues, praising the "authentic tortilla taste" of the chip, and finally making a convert out of Pedro. The campaign worked: in its first full year of national distribution, Tostitos topped $100 million in sales, by far Frito-Lay's best-ever debut for a product.

But when the *Los Angeles Times* asked Escandón to prepare his version of *chilaquiles*—the Mexico breakfast dish that gathers tortilla strips and fries them into tortilla chips, the same product commercialized by Tamalina, modified by Doolin, and turned into a multibillion-dollar industry by Frito-Lay—he forsook Tostitos, instead using fresh tortillas. For that authentic tortilla taste.

In the spring of 2010, I drove to Lake Arthur in the hopes of seeing the Miracle Tortilla.

The easiest way to visit is by taking a flight to Roswell, where aliens descended to offer the world an apparition from the skies, and take U.S. Route 285 south for about forty minutes. But this penitent takes long routes for his sins, so I rented a Pontiac in Tucson and drove east—through the Arizona desert as it turned into a New Mexico sunrise, the purple clouds pregnant with hope, through Las Cruces, past the White Sands Monument, where a Border Patrol officer waved me to the side for a thorough inspection because he had never heard of a Lake Arthur (but confessed to having heard of the Miracle Tortilla on a television show—"I think it was on Fox," the young white man said with a laugh), through the dilapidated military town of Alamagordo, through winding mountains covered with snow, sun-blasted plains where no cars pass for hours and where the wind whips furious storms and honest-to-goodness tumbleweeds cross the road. Seven hours of driving, seven hours of reflection on why I was driving seven hours to go see a tortilla.

I arrived in Lake Arthur just before noon, and parked across from the Rubios' house in the parking lot of Our Lady of Guadalupe Church, the patron saint of Mexico and another miraculous celestial visit initially derided as the visions of a lunatic. The Rubio house was easy to spot—it said "Rubio" near the door. A well-kept place on the front, with lawn chairs present, seemingly ready to welcome stragglers from afar.

But no one was home—there was no need anymore. In 2006, Rubio's granddaughter took the Miracle Tortilla to her kindergarten class for show-and-tell. At some point there was a fumbled handoff, and the tortilla shattered. *Abuelita* didn't reprimand and kept the shards, just in case anyone might ask to see them.

When Christ appeared before the Rubio family in 1977, the tortilla was still exotic, but times were changing. His masa materialization was necessary back then, the final push for America to realize that the tortilla was more than just a vessel—it also offered deliverance, nutrition possibility. The country knows that now; we no longer need reminders, nor the Rubios to keep the faith.

In the backyard, the shed that functioned as an illicit shrine, against the wishes of the Catholic Church but to the comfort of thousands, still stood, boarded up. Weeds filled the dried lawn, along with random equipment and strewn items. Winds whipped, shaking the power and telephone lines. A dirty diaper was rolled up near the back door.

I waited for an hour. I wanted to see even the relics of the Miracle Tortilla, but it wasn't happening that day. A truck rumbled by—someone else. A hotel room waited for me in Albuquerque, four hours away, right next to a Taco Bell that folded flour tortillas as if the existence of man depended on it. Back into the Pontiac. Seven hours to go see a tortilla, with four more hours of driving to go. Four hours of desiccated lands, of lonely people walking God knows where along bleak highways, abandoned towns, and angry, gorgeous skies.

Jesus now appears on grilled cheese sandwiches. His work with tortillas is *finis*.

Chapter Twelve

How Did Salsa Become America's Top-Selling Condiment?

It's fine and all that Americans eat so much Mexican food, in all sorts of plates and cans and buffets and microwaveable trays, but they're smart, too. They could have easily just stayed with the food and left it at that—but they've also incorporated the Mexican love of the hot stuff: salsa, from red-colored water to lava capable of dissolving concrete.

Those salsas are at Serrano's on an early, blazing Sunday August morning in Austin. It's a beautiful restaurant, sectioned off into a main dining room, a large patio, and a clubhouse toward the back that's attracting a parade of people. These are no mere eaters; a solemn, important task awaits them: the tasting and judging of salsa.

The occasion is the *Austin Chronicle* Hot Sauce Festival, one of the oldest and largest in the United States. Every year, thousands of people head to Waterloo Park, right in downtown Austin, within walking distance of Serrano's, with a view of Darrell K. Royal–Texas Memorial Stadium, to hear music, feast on food, and bake on the prickly lawn of the trodden park. But the most popular draw to the fiesta, naturally, is the salsa. In tents better suited to a Pentecostal revival, long lines of people crawl down rows of tables and taste the salsa before them. Green salsas and red ones. Some spiked with fruit, others with tomatillo, pepper, and little else. Hot sauce and pepper sauce. Chunky, mild, scorching, bland. Smaller booths ring the main tent, barking out deals on T-shirts and salsa bottles, but the majority of the action is in those big tents: the people's winner will emerge from here.

The juried competition begins at Serrano's clubhouse. A good thirty or so food critics and restaurateurs, farmers and businessmen, Texans and a couple of stray Californians (who get teased about their state's strange interpretations of spicy condiments—this is the land of Tex-Mex, after all) sit at a table with high-backed wooden chairs, a setting better suited for war negotiations, which is exactly what's about to happen.

They divide themselves into groups of four. On another table stand dozens of salsas in various containers: Tupperware, bottles, jars. Dozens more appear every fifteen minutes, brought in by a brigade of volunteers. Each group of judges gets a batch of entries, broken into categories (green, red, hot sauce, other). If three people like a particular salsa, the entry moves on to the second round; if three people don't like it, it joins the losers' table, which starts piling up like Longhorn defenders on a fumble.

Baskets of chips lay on all tables, along with water pitchers. The judges are ruthless. "I can tell liquid smoke from a mile away," an older man remarks, referring to artificial flavoring that amateur chefs use to bypass hours of cooking in an effort to re-create the magical tang of smokiness. His lips curl after tasting one of the green-salsa entrants. Its sickly hue and fuzzy consistency are akin to mold. "It's a shortcut—and shortcuts get you nowhere in salsa except the sink."

"It's not that difficult to roast peppers and tomatoes to achieve natural smokiness," adds another judge, munching through a bright-orange mango salsa, fruity yet fierce, that passes on to the next round.

Another dips a chip into a frothy number, takes a taste, and grimaces. "This isn't even a gazpacho," she says, spitting it out.

There's lobbying, laughing, gasps of glee, groans of disgust. Whenever entries arrived in tubs, snickers inevitably arose about the big ego of the entrant—this, in Austin, in Texas, where large egos are required by state law. Salsa begins staining the tablecloths, the shirts and pants and skirts of judges; no one notices. The difference between a winning and a losing salsa can be a misplaced Serrano pepper, too much tomato. Some of the better salsas were milder than vanilla, yet exhibited a well-rounded symphony among heat, citrus, and other flavors. Some of the hottest salsas were the most loathed, not because the judges feared scorchers but because there was no depth other than heat—"If all I want is fire," quips one lady, "I'd put out my cigarette on my tongue, then throw in Tabasco."

Then Robb Walsh strolls into the chaos. He helped create the hot-sauce festival back in the 1980s, back when he first defended the merits of Tex-Mex in the *Chronicle*'s pages. He's a large man, bearded and Falstaffian, with a booming voice, the archetypal Texas gentleman, respectful but boastful, and he thanks the judges, reminding them of the importance of their duty. Later in the day, Walsh and a second round of judges will do the heavier lifting of determining the official winners from those that are currently passing.

"Hello . . ." Walsh begins, but notices no one pays attention. "Hey, y'all!" he drawls. That's better—the room snaps to attention and erupts in applause. "Welcome one and all. We're eating hot sauce already—hallelujah!"

He notices the stacks of the approved. "These are the yeses?" he asks a volunteer. She nods; Walsh smiles and grabs a tub. "I need something for my eggs."

How to make your food taste better with a tasty sauce: it's been a conundrum in this country for centuries. Ketchup, mustard, and mayo were the classic answers, with a trail of others following. But at some point in your American life, you must have heard the following truism: salsa is now the top-selling condiment in this country, even more than ketchup. It's partly true: salsa does bring in more revenue for companies than ketchup, $462.3 million to $298.9 million in 2007, according to one research firm. But ketchup moved more units, and Americans purchased more of it in raw volume than its Mexican cousin by far, 329.8 million pounds to 184.6 million pounds.[1]

It doesn't matter: the legend has become fact. "Here's a fact about American life that may illustrate as much as any census finding," NPR *Weekend Edition* host Scott Simon stated in his clipped, stentorian voice one February morning in 1992, as sales figures released earlier that year disclosed the country's new normal. "Salsa—as in picante, enchilada, and taco sauce, English for salsa—now outsells ketchup in the United States."[2] People repeat this as an article of faith and amazement—how is it that something so un-American, so Mexican, now outsells ketchup, that condiment as American as chili?

Such thoughts ignore the obvious: the world has loved the heat of Mexican food ever since its first encounter with it. It was the promise of peppery spice that drove Columbus across the Atlantic. It was the salsas of the Aztecs that captivated the Catholic Spaniards with their hellish temptation. It was the many capsicums traded across the globe after the Conquest that changed world cuisine, arguably more than any other food from the Americas besides the tomato.

Salsa's dominance in the American cupboard, then, was inevitable. Commercial hot sauce in this country has existed since at least the 1800s, and became popular in the 1860s with the rise of Tabasco Hot Sauce, which is Mexican only in the appropriation of the name of the Mexican state and the pepper. It wasn't until the 1880s, however, that commercial American producers marketed their sauces as explicitly Mexican, under the name "chili colorow," a mangling of *chile colorado*, Spanish for the red peppers used to create salsa. The term was popular enough that one packager, William Railton of Chicago, tried to trademark it to corner the market; the U.S. Trademark Office declined. Many American cookbooks, meanwhile, offered recipes for hot sauce under many names, both in Mexican cookbooks and collections written by women's groups. By 1908, the Ortega Company of Los Angeles canned salsa under the name "Tru Salsa" and sold it across the American Southwest; a competitor, Santa Ysabel, offered its concoction under the name Salsa Pura ("Pure Salsa").

But salsa's march to American dominance didn't start in earnest until 1947, when a transplant to San Antonio discovered what the company he formed still calls the "syrup of the Southwest." David Pace was a son of Monroe, Louisiana, born into a syrup-producing family that expected him to continue the family business. World War II took him to the Alamo City, and here Pace espied Mexican-style hot sauce for the first time: not relishy like most salsa, but concentrated into a thick liquid and not as vinegary as American-style hot sauces. Intrigued by the business opportunities, especially for Anglos such as he reticent to indulge in the hot stuff Mexican restaurants offered, Pace figured he'd bottle his own concoction, call it "picante sauce" (*picante* being the Spanish word for "spicy"), and stock it in grocery stores.

The original picante sauce wasn't much, more pureed tomato than pepper. In a city such as San Antonio, where Mexican families and restaurants made their own salsas at home, the public met picante sauce with indifference. Luckily for Pace, the country was preparing to love the taco.

Tacos are delicious things, but they demand a condiment. Mexicans have always drizzled salsa on their tacos, but the condiment's fiery nature wasn't yet ready for American palates. Mexican food in this country has been, if anything, eminently mutable to match demand, so some wily businessman concocted "taco sauce": salsa shorn of its heat. It was first marketed in 1948 by the Mountain Pass Canning Company, an El Paso firm that turned it into the name we know it by today: Old El Paso. It's biggest competitor was La Victoria, created by the Banda family of Los Angeles in 1917 but not entering the national scene until 1951, when German immigrant Henry C. Tanklage assumed control. He switched the focus of La Victoria from the Mexican market to the American market, taming his company's offerings to ensure that Americans who were just familiarizing themselves with tacos didn't scorch themselves.

Tanklage expanded La Victoria across the United States, with many imitators following. Like Taco Bell, taco sauce served as a gateway to hook people into moving on to something stronger. Back in Texas, Pace kept at it with his picante sauce, content with making a profit and with no real dreams to expand farther than the Lone Star State. There just wasn't a need—taco sauce largely fulfilled America's Mexican condiment needs, whether in a taco or on a combo plate.

As late as 1977, the *Washington Post* still felt the need to describe salsa to readers as "a piquant relish used extensively with Mexican foods."[3] But the 1980s saw the exponential ascendancy of salsa in the American market, a rise so sudden that American food companies were caught off guard and forced to play catch-up. It just wasn't the continued immigration of Mexicans into the United States or even the spread of Chi-Chi's (which bottled its own salsa and sold it commercially starting in the 1970s): that decade saw the rise of an informed American gastronome more accepting of ethnic flavors than ever before, and willing to replicate them at home. Also important, however, was the health-food craze, which took to salsa like aerobics: in the freshness of a proper salsa—its many vegetables, the low use of sodium, the lack of preservatives—was a reflection of a lifestyle. Its enlivening taste was almost beside the point: here was a new condiment, one much better than sodium- and sugar-heavy ketchup. "The business exploded when the hippies came along," Pace told reporters years later. "No question but this health stuff made the whole category explode."[4]

The trendiness of salsa convinced bigger players to enter the market. Campbell's Soup introduced their own line; even Chesebrough-Pond's, most famous as the manufacturers of Vaseline, debuted Montera salsa in 1983 with a $20 million advertising campaign larger than Pace's profits that year. The company, however, was unfazed. "We just have to keep up our quality," remarked Kit Goldsbury, son-in-law to David Pace, as the big boys invaded Texas.[5]

And they did. In 1979, only Goldsbury and Pace worked the day-to-day operations of the company. Under the guidance of Pace's daughter, Linda, and her husband, Goldsbury, the company strategized to further their sales and reach. They added other flavors—mild, hot, and thick and chunky—to expand from the classic picante-sauce recipe. Pace created special-order six-pack containers, urging purchasers to "send someone the taste of Texas."[6] The company also secured a contract with the armed forces as the military's salsa provider, ensuring a customer base that sought the stuff upon returning from their stint.[7] By the mid-1980s, Pace became America's top-selling hot sauce, a position it has rarely relinquished since.

As Pace succeeded, so did its competitors. The Southwestern food movement also encouraged people to experiment with fruit salsas, sweet salsas—anything involving tomatoes and heat. Even Heinz entered the salsa game, since its own numbers showed the market was taking over the country; in 1988, 16 percent of American households purchased salsa; by 1992, a third of the country did.[8] That was the year when analysts surmised that salsa became America's top-selling condiment; one reporter called the victory over ketchup "the manifest destiny of good taste."[9] And in the ultimate indicator of its victory, Campbell's bought out Pace for $1.15 billion in 1994 after years of courtship, a move and a price that sparked national headlines. The Pace paterfamilias did stick around long enough to see his company dominate the market. "In '47, my sauce bottles exploded all over the grocery shelves because I couldn't get the darned formula right," Pace told the *New York Times* a year before his death in December 1993. "It just tickles me to see [salsa sellers] take the ball and run with it."[10]

His legacy remained with the company, most notably in a memorable television campaign launched in 1995 to push Pace into the New York tristate area for the first time. Incredibly, Pace had reaped millions of dollars in revenue from selling mostly in the Southwest and hadn't yet penetrated the rest of the country. Company execs gingerly tested their product for a national audience in the form of commercials that tweaked all the Johnny-come-latelys who had followed in Pace's wake.[11]

In the ad, cowboys sit around a campfire. One of them spoons the last chunk of Pace's sauce and asks the cook for more "picante sauce," pronouncing it with the nasal *a* of a Chicagoan, garbling his Spanish so the word sounded like "pecany." The white-haired cook tosses him another brand. "This ain't Pace Picante sauce!" the younger cowboy exclaims.

"What's the difference?" the coot mumbles. The younger cowboy launches into a soliloquy extolling Pace Picante, most importantly because it's "made in San Antonio . . . by people know what picante sauce is supposed to taste like!"

Another cowboy reads the alien sauce's label. "This stuff's made in New York City?!" he exclaims.

"New York City?" everyone yells, now surrounding the old cook. The commercial ends with another young buck looking directly into the camera, deadpanning, "Get a rope."

It played for laughs, but the Pace commercial also served as a powerful allegory. Gone were the days of taco sauce masquerading as authentic Mexican salsa. Americans expected heat and authenticity, even if its producers were Americans. Pace's commercials became wildly popular, helping the company earn record profits. And across the country, other salsa-savvy entrepreneurs dreamed.

There are no indicators that the Tapatío Hot Sauce company is based in the industrial city of Vernon, California, until you walk into their small lobby. Save for the poster that screams "Tapatío WANTED" in the style of Old West outlaw posters, a fake chile plant featuring ripe peppers, and a place mat with the company's name on it, its lobby looks more like the waiting area of a dentist's office. That medicinal appearance carries over when Luis Saavedra opens the door to greet a guest. Tall, bespectacled, with a mustache and the personality of a children's librarian, Saavedra wears a lab coat and carries a notepad. "Welcome to our factory!" he exclaims before entering a conference room where bottles are stacked against the wall and artwork featuring their bottles hang—four pastel-colored Tapatío bottles à la Warhol, on posters, on mouse pads, in promotional literature.

His sister Jacquie walks in, followed by the patriarch: José-Luis Saavedra, also wearing a lab coat and with heavy glasses. Though in his early eighties, he has hair that is movie-star thick and only now graying. José-Luis's gravitas is unquestioned—he sits at the head of the table, his children looking toward him at all times, following his cues and laughing at his jokes. He insists on speaking in accented, though impeccable, English: Ricardo Montalban comes to mind—that is, if Montalban wasn't a Latin lover but instead a rough-hewn scrapper like Saavedra carries himself.

Saavedra starts talking about the logo for his company, immediately familiar to lovers of Mexican food. It's a *charro*—a Mexican cowboy— wearing a yellow riding jacket; a red handkerchief tied around his neck; a helmet of brown hair; a thick, though not obnoxiously bushy, mustache; and a sombrero with arabesque stitching snaking around the brim. The illustration is proportioned so that the hat is as large as the charro's torso, but this isn't another stock bandito caricature. The Tapatío man is smiling, proud, exuding *mexicanidad.*

"This is a real Mexican," Saavedra states emphatically. "We started to represent the charro like a human being instead of a cartoon."

If there is a trusted brand among Mexicans for their hot sauce, it's Tapatío—assertive, thick but smooth, immediately peppery, chiles reduced to their fiery essence. It's not as big a seller as Pace or any of the other brands trotted out by multinationals in the past decade—Tostitos, Herdez, Newman's Own, and many more. Tapatío, however, is a family-run Mexican operation, a company that doesn't release sales figures but is ubiquitous in Mexican homes, and increasingly in American homes—and it's only beginning to become a national brand.

Saavedra was born in 1929 in Mexico City, moving to Chicago

in 1954. With a background in accounting and sales, he found work proofreading for a magazine geared toward doctors in Latin America. But Saavedra didn't enjoy the Windy City's harsh weather and moved to Los Angeles in 1957. Chicago had a large Mexican population but not so much that jobs were at a premium for a Mexican male; in Southern California, center of the Mexican diaspora in the United States, Saavedra's skills relegated him to sweeping floors at a manufacturing plant.

Saavedra's pride didn't allow such a station; within a couple of months he switched to an office job at the same company, using that position to move up with another corporation to head their shipping and receiving. His job took him far from the catering trucks that fed most of working-class Los Angeles at the time, and Saavedra didn't have much of a taste for the Mexican-American restaurants and fast-food taco stands then in vogue. Instead, he brought homemade lunches to work, always packing a bottle of hot sauce from a recipe he concocted while growing up in Mexico. Saavedra's coworkers asked for some; it was such a hit that they suggested he cook up a batch for everyone. The year was 1971.

Mass-produced hot sauce had yet to penetrate American cupboards, and Saavedra visited stores to see who his competition might have been. He found taco sauce "nothing to worry about" and was only able to find two others: an unnamed Mexican brand and Tabasco, which he cryptically refers to as "the Louisiana sauce. There was no real Mexican sauce on the market." After the company he worked for shut down, he had another impetus toward making commercial hot sauce. Saavedra rented a kitchen in the city of Maywood, on the outskirts of Los Angeles, for sixty-five dollars a month, a cubbyhole twenty feet long and twelve feet wide, with three tables to chop peppers, a sink to wash them, and a hundred-gallon tank to create the hot sauce. He turned a meat grinder into a red-pepper grinder, and chopped all the peppers with the help of two part-time workers and his children—on weekends during the school year, and all week during summer vacation. Saavedra did everything else, even gluing labels onto the bottles and screwing on caps late into the early morning.

He produced a couple of boxes and named it Cuervo Sauce, with its logo the modern-day Tapatío man, but with a crow's head (*cuervo* means crow in Spanish) instead of a human. Saavedra tried to stock it in small stores in Southern California's Mexican neighborhoods, but "no one wanted to buy it. People still made their own salsas. It was hell for the first five years."

His wife and friends urged him to quit, but the stubborn Saavedra refused, even mortgaging his home to secure a four-thousand-dollar loan to continue the business. "I continued because I knew I was going to have success," he says. "When, on the other hand, I didn't know." On top of all this, Saavedra received a cease-and-desist letter from José Cuervo, the manufacturers of tequila, whose founding family were distant relatives of Saavedra's wife. Saavedra flew to Mexico City to negotiate with the Cuervos, offering to sell his hot-sauce recipe to them; they refused, wanting only that he stop using their name. He dropped the name and the crow's head from his logo but didn't have enough money to create a brand-new theme. Instead, he found a stock image of a Mexican man and affixed it to the old Cuervo logo. Saavedra thought of naming his new business Charro Sauce, but instead chose Tapatío in 1974 to honor his children's birthplace: Guadalajara, Jalisco, whose residents go by the nickname *tapatíos*.

"It has charisma and phonetically it sounds good," he says.

"Even when people mispronounce it," his daughter interjects, "it sounds good."

But Saavedra is savvier than he lets on. Southern California has received hundreds of thousands of immigrants from Jalisco for more than a century. Calling his new hot sauce Tapatío was a genius ploy that ensured Saavedra almost instant success upon starting anew in 1975. Buying a bottle didn't merely satisfy taste for customers, but also a longing for cultural validation.

"The name has appeal to them," he grudgingly admits. "You appeal to the Jaliscans, you immediately have an audience. One bottle is like a walking billboard for us."

Tapatío started with five-ounce bottles, graduating to ten-ounce versions in 1988, thirty-two-ounce monsters a year later, gallon-sized buckets in 1999, and seven-ounce packets in 2000 that allowed them to become beloved components of the MREs of military personnel, just like a previous generation enjoyed tiny bottles of Tabasco to mask the flavor of their provisions. But their expansion plans aren't just limited to the size of their containers, or even multisized versions of their sauce. In 2010, the Saavedras entered into an agreement with Kraft for food service distribution, ensuring that Tapatío enters even more markets as part of the American condiment giant's galaxy of ketchup, mayo, and salsa. Kraft had commissioned a marketing study asking what condiments people preferred; so many mentioned Tapatío, which shocked the company because officials had never heard of it, that they requested a meeting with the Saavedras. In 2011, they also entered into a partnership with Frito-Lay to produce Tapatío-flavored chips (Fritos, Doritos, Ruffles, and Lay's) that didn't require the Saavedras to give up their recipe and also gave them final say over the finished product. "It is a blessing that others want to make our company grow," José-Luis says, "but it's *our* company. Expansion, yes, but not at the loss of our honor."

José-Luis has assumed a smaller role in his august years, delegating most of the responsibilities to his children, but he still shows up to work every day and "we all report to him," says Jacquie. Jacquie is the office manager. Another sister does the legal work, while their children work at the factory during the summer, as they did in their youth. They all work out of Tapatío's facilities, a thirty-thousand-square-foot factory and warehouse they constructed in 1996 that is starting to feel crowded.

"We've seen other brands cut on the quality—their bottle of five years ago isn't the same today," Luis says. "We want adults to remember the same flavor they first experienced as five-year-old kids. It's not just a hot sauce. It's a table sauce. It goes with everything. It's an international flavor. Tabasco is like Big Ben. We're a Swiss watch."

The heat. That quick tweak of the tongue, followed by a rush of endorphins, a splash of sweat. Salsa and hot sauce are addicting—they make men enter competitions to see who can eat the most, drive them to spend tens of thousands of dollars just for the privilege of saying that they, too, can make hot stuff like a Mexican, even if it doesn't earn them a profit. Lynyrd Skynyrd have a brand, as do Patti LaBelle and Van Halen bassist Michael Anthony; there's even Joe Perry's Rock Your World Hot Sauce. Cheech Marin makes a pretty peso with his line of salsas. And the late Paul Newman—Cool Hand Luke!—made a mint on best-selling, quite delicious Newman's Own salsa, the label featuring the Oscar winner wearing a sombrero, a thick mustache, and a smile.

But the best celebrity Mexican-style hot sauce of them all comes from Dexter Holland, rhythm guitarist and singer for the iconic punk band the Offspring, and owner of Gringo Bandito. Everything about it seems to scream "clueless gabacho," a cheap publicity ploy. The sauce's name, of course. The logo—the blond, spiky-haired, fair-skinned Holland bedecked in bandoliers, revolvers, sombrero, and shades—that apes a bandito, the Mexican archetype that has intrigued and terrorized Americans since the days of Pancho Villa. The promotional pictures on the sauce's Web site—Gringo Bandito superimposed on the Virgin of Guadalupe, standing next to a Chihuahua statue, being poured on an unsuspecting drunk—look like slides from a frat-boy visit to Puerto Vallarta.

"I hope you enjoy the adventurous flavor and tingling tantalization of my not-so-famous pepper sauce," Holland explains on the Web site in a half-serious, mostly mocking tone reminiscent of carnival medicine men. "For over two years, I have searched far and wide for the perfect combination of spices to make your next dining experience a zinger. And I tried to make it easy on the pooper, too. Try it on tacos, burritos, eggs, pizza—it's like a party in your mouth. I personally guarantee it."

But what started as a joke is becoming an unlikely success story. Gringo Bandito is now available at grocery stores across the United States; in health-food markets and at taco stands; in dozens of restaurants across Orange County—and increasingly, the Southwest. Warped Tour used the sauce in 2009 during catering, and Metallica takes it on tour. It won two Scovie Awards in 2009, one of the longest-running hot-sauce contests in the country, for its recipe: flavorful but not salty, like too many commercial hot sauces, packing proper but not hellish heat, with chile seeds left intact and no preservatives to muck up its charms. Gringo Bandito isn't selling at Tapatío levels yet, still largely a Southern California phenomenon, and Holland hasn't left his day job recording with the Offspring—but then again, *Smash* was supposed to be a local indie release and ended up selling 16 million records. And Holland hopes—knows—his product's best days are just beginning.

Holland understands, even appreciates, the bewilderment most people feel about the idea of a gabacho, a punker, a kid from Orange County selling his own brand of the manna of Mexican food. "I realize the inherent contradiction," he says. "It's unlikely. It's unexpected. It was wrong to make it, and that's the fun of it. It's a challenge."

Between recording and touring with the Offspring early last decade, Holland experimented with different blends of hot sauces at his house—just him, some knives and pots, a cutting board, and a stove. He relied on a master's degree in molecular biology from the University of Southern California to determine how to make hot sauce smoother, how to bring out certain flavors, but mostly he relied on trial and error. Once Holland was completely satisfied with a batch, he poured it into bottles and handed them out to workers at his Nitro Records label as a gag Christmas present in 2005.

"They came up to me after tasting it and said, 'Dude, this is good,'" he says. "Yeah, yeah, whatever. 'No, we're serious. We're addicted to it.'

I thought they were just being polite." But once workers finished Holland's hot sauce, they asked when the next batch was coming.

"That's when I realized I might have something," he says. "From there, we just went with it. 'I need a label—hey, it'd be funny if I dressed up like Pancho Villa, how silly would that look?' And then the name—someone said 'gringo,' someone rhymed it with 'bandito.' Then someone else suggested we should sell it, and it just clicked."

Helping him run the operation is Florencia Arriaga, a stout woman with stylish eyeglasses who says with a laugh, "My kids are very proud that their mommy works for the guy from the Offspring." Arriaga is the quality-control director for Hungry Punker Inc., the official company that produces Gringo Bandito. More than anyone working for Gringo Bandito, she's the least surprised at its existence. "I've been seeing Dexter eat for more than ten years," says a family friend. "My God, he loves salsa! I would always see him tasting different salsas, looking at them, studying them. Eventually I would hear him say, 'I want to make salsa. Will you help me?' Of course. Over the years, I'd tease him—'So when are we going to start?' He'd always say he's too busy. Finally, one day, he asked me, 'I want to make a salsa. Can you help me?' Of course!"

In 2009, Holland stopped giving away bottles to restaurants; most continue to carry it because of demand. "It's nice to have a hobby, but it's nicer if it can turn a profit," he says. "I probably should've started a clothing company, something that made more sense. I should've picked something that sells for more than two bucks per bottle. But we do it because we love it. It's just fun."

"My nephews in Mexico say, 'Gringos don't eat chile,'" Arriaga says. "Oh, this one does."

Chapter Thirteen

Tequila? Tequila!

Just off the Interstate 40 exit for Weatherford, Oklahoma, stands Lucille's Roadhouse, a gleaming, white-beamed edifice with two vintage gas pumps outside serving as homage to its former life as a Route 66 landmark. It's now two restaurants, a diner and a steak house, with memorabilia heralding the Mother Road's glory days displayed on the walls and in the gift shop that serves as the waiting area for the two. Seems like a tourist trap, but their chicken-fried steak sandwich is as wide as the Great Plains and just as magnificent, the breaded cut almost twice as large as the bun that futilely tries to contain it, and that alone is worth a stop. Oh, and the fried pickles: crisp, glorious crunch bombs.

But what most of the out-of-towners order is Mexican: nachos, big quesadillas, fried jalapeño poppers that scald, chips with Texas-style queso, even a taco salad. And the drink of choice to take the edge off an hours-long drive through the vast, scenic nothing of the Sooner State is the margarita. They're not the best you'll ever taste: on the rocks, Day-Glo green, with too much triple sec, not enough tequila, and salt clumped around the rim of the bowl-shaped glass like warts on a finger. But those margaritas hit the tables as often as water, sipped or chugged and ordered two at a time. Lucille's can't make a proper Manhattan—request one, and out comes a tumbler filled with ice, water, Jim Beam, and a cherry—but a Mexican cocktail? Of course!

There's Mexican beer here as well, and no one blinks. Americans imported $500 million worth of Corona, Negra Modelo, Bohemia, and other cervezas in 2011,[1] but that's a tiny figure compared to our thirst for tequila. Revenue from U.S. sales of Mexico's most popular spirits—José Cuervo, Patrón, 1600, Sauza, Herradura, Cazadores, and those are just the ones somewhat popular among Americans—has nearly doubled in the past decade, from $962 million in 2003 to $1.7 billion in 2010, and shipment of cases, 6 bottles per order, have increased more than 500 percent in about 35 years, from just 2.3 million in 1975, a year when the *New York Times* reported tequila was "gaining U.S. favor," to 11.56 million in 2010.[2] Actors now shill for premium brands, the drink's many strains serves as a muse for singers from Jimmy Buffett to the Eagles to every third country song, and we all become Mexicans on Cinco de Mayo by communally bathing in a sea of Coronas and bottomless margaritas while wearing sombreros and filling up with chips and guac.

Mexican alcohol is a Virgil in our winding journey through Mexican food. And while cerveza is popular, and high-end tequila bars now serve shots from three-figure bottles in many revitalized downtowns, such acceptance would have been impossible without the margarita, and a specific one at that, one that has fallen out of favor in recent years: the frozen margarita, created from a prefabricated mix, either unwinding out like a frosty snake from a spigot on a percolating machine or served straight from a blender at households across America. If the end result looks like an adult Slurpee, that's because it is—desperate to figure out how to save his business, a Dallas man stumbled upon an idea that allowed tequila and Mexican alcohol to finally, truly conquer American livers.

In the early 1960s, Mexican singer Eulalio González recorded a track called "Chulas Fronteras" ("Beautiful Borderlands"), the latest in his career of parodies of life in the U.S.-Mexico borderlands. He went by the stage name El Piporro ("The Bassoon" or, conversely, "The Tippler"), a mestizo Alan Sherman who tweaked Mexican standards with half-spoken words, half-sung riffs on them. "Chulas Fronteras" was his original composition, though, a polka-esque jaunt about a self-described former wetback who now has his papers and proudly drives drunk. It's really a funny song, and doesn't translate well into English due to the many idioms and double entendres El Piporro throws out, but any American can understand the climax of the song, when a highway patrolman pulls El Piporro over for his inebriated state.

"Hey, *tu mex-sicano, tu eres mojado?*" ("Hey, you Mexican, are you a wetback?"), the patrolman (voiced by El Piporro) asks in the most stereotypical gabacho accent imaginable. El Piporro responds in English, spieling about his working life in el Norte and disclosing that he's now a legal immigrant.

"Well, yes, but you're drinking," the nameless patrolman shoots back, again in bad Spanish.

"Have a drink," El Piporro responds. The patrolman refuses.

"I have whiskey and tequila!" El Piporro says in perfect English.

"Oh, my my. Te-*kaila*!" the patrolman giddily blurts out. Of course he'll have some. Coughs and barks erupt—the gabacho loves it.

"*Este tequila mucho caliente, mucho picoso!*" he responds. El Piporro offers another one, but the patrolman begs off, promising, "*Otra vez* around" ("Next time around").

"Well, I wait for you, or you wait for me," El Piporro concludes. *"Mejor,* you *güey!"* ("Better yet, you're a dumb-ass!).*"*

It's hilarious, but only partially right. El Piporro's point, that Americans were weaklings with tequila, ignored the growth of the distilled liquor at the time across the United States—it still wasn't as popular as whiskey, but the liquor was already a standard at bars on the borderlands and made it into the arsenal of the more imaginative bartenders elsewhere. Already, another set of musicians had immortalized tequila as the embodiment of a good time in the song "Tequila" by the

Champs, a saxophone-driven, party-hearty roar where the sole lyric uttered was—all together now—"Tequila!"

Though representing completely different genres, "Tequila" and "Chulas Fronteras" preached to Americans and Mexicans alike the same gospel: tequila was alluring and fun, dangerous yet irresistible. But what Americans didn't realize—and still don't, really—is that tequila became Mexico's national spirit through a targeted campaign by proponents at the expense of other boozy drinks that had existed in Mexico almost as long as tamales. It was masterful propaganda, since the United States is now the largest consumer of tequila in the world, and the margarita has supplanted all competitors to become the best-selling cocktail in the United States—while almost all other Mexican liquors remain mostly unknown here.

Although Americans associate certain alcoholic beverages with Mexico—tequila and beers, of course, but also Kahlúa and Presidente brandy—alcohol in the country has a long history, one predating the Spaniards and brands. In the north, the Tarahumara Indians prepared *tesgüino,* beer made from fermented corn, and also *sotol,* a liquor derived from the stems of the Desert Spoon plant that's still produced. Other beverages included coconut beer and wines produced from cornstalks, pineapples, bananas, and plums, all drinks that long faded into obscurity, if still existing at all.

The premier precolonial alcohol in Mexico was pulque, a frothy, milk-colored beverage created by fermenting the sap of the maguey, known in Spanish as *aguamiel*—honey water. Pulque was concentrated in the central region of the country and predated Mexico's great empires, almost all of which incorporated the drink into their mythologies upon assuming power. For the Aztecs, Olmecs, and other tribes, pulque became holy, restricted to the priestly classes, imbibed only in moderation, and used specifically to connect with the gods.

After the Conquest of Mexico, pulque left this sanctified realm and entered the day-to-day life of Mexicans, leading to the opening of thousands of *pulquerias* across the Mexican territories. The Spanish conquistadors and subsequent Mexican elite despised the drink for its proletarian roots, but they needed booze. From this need for more distinguished firewater, tequila was born.

How tequila was invented remains in dispute. A still was needed, of course, to distill the alcohol, but whether it came from Spain or from the Philippines via the Manila galleons remains a mystery. No one exactly knows what genius thought of forgoing the aguamiel for the heart of the maguey, known as the piña, baking it, then pressing out its juices and letting them ferment before distillation (from this same process comes tequila's smokier cousin mescal, which is distilled only once to tequila's double distillation; the other main difference between the two is that mescal can be made from any agave plant grown anywhere in Mexico, while the Mexican government has limited tequila production to be solely derived from the blue agave plant and allows it to be produced only in five Mexican states). No one even knows tequila's etymological roots. But production of the beverage was well under way in the 1600s, with larger-scale distribution not starting until the latter half of the nineteenth century.

Even then, a thirst existed in the United States for Mexican alcohol. As early as 1882, shopkeepers imported tequila to Los Angeles, boasting that "the popular beverage of the Mexicans and now so highly appreciated by Americans" was now available Stateside.[3] Four years later, at his pop-up Mexican restaurant outside Madison Square Garden, Buffalo Bill Cody offered mescal as the capper to his multicourse Mexican breakfast. An observer noted, "In appearance mescale [*sic*] is like gin; in taste, a combination of the flavors of gin, rum, and rheubarb [*sic*], and in effect, in small quantities not unpleasant but in repeated doses it is said to have the power of all other intoxicants combined."[4]

While mescal didn't take, tequila trickled into the United States over the following half century. There was enough of a demand that San Francisco venture capitalists drew up plans in 1907 to build a tequila distillery in the nearby city of San Rafael, although construction of the plant never went through.[5] During the 1920s and Prohibition, thirsty Americans traveled across the border to the bars of Ciudad Juárez and Tijuana, which stocked all the banned American favorites but also pushed tequila onto the curious. Enough of a taste developed that moonshiners distilled their own version in Los Angeles, much to the consternation of authorities.[6] Paralleling the narco-traffickers of today, smugglers on the border tried every trick possible to elude American customs enforcement, from building extra gas tanks inside cars to store bottles, to trying to pass off the liquor as "Sonora water." But demand for tequila was simply too much to ignore: at the height of Prohibition, the *Los Angeles Times* even published a tutorial on how to properly drink a shot, advising readers to sprinkle salt on a lime, chew on it "vigorously," then sling back the shot, after which the drinker "gasps a little, blinks his eyes three or four times and indulges in a convulsive shiver."[7]

From that era arose the first popular tequila cocktail: the Tequila Daisy, a mix of tequila, citrus juice, and grenadine over ice. Some maintain it was the ancestor to the margarita, not just because of the similar composition but also because *margarita* is the Spanish word for daisy (and it's a much more plausible origin story than the dozen or so circulating in the historical tradewinds that alternately credit crafty bartenders, showgirls, American doyennes, and even Rita Hayworth, whose first name was Margarita). The drink remained mostly a borderlands sensation during the 1930s and into the 1940s, but did become popular enough that a B-24 bomber built in San Diego was named after it; the plane flew eighteen missions, including on D-day, and featured as nose art a Vargas girl–esque dame snapping off her bra, ready to party.

Meanwhile, the movement to elevate tequila above all other Mexican alcohols was reaching overdrive thanks to its two ruling families. In 1758, the Spanish Crown granted a land deed to José Antonio Cuervo for distilling tequila; from this act came the magisterial José Cuervo company, and the family took control of millions of maguey plants in Jalisco, the birthplace of and main industrial base for tequila, effectively monopolizing the industry. Cuervo's only real competitors were the Sauza family, whose patriarch, Cenobio Sauza, opened his own distillery in 1873 after leaving the Cuervo company. After the Mexican Revolution, the rival clans used their influence with the Mexican government to cultivate an image of tequila as emblematic of Mexican identity.

It was an easy sell. The Sauzas owned radio stations in Guadalajara, the second-largest city in Mexico, which guaranteed access to listeners and the corridors of power. And the acknowledged birthplace of tequila was where their holdings were: Los Altos de Jalisco, the state's northeastern highlands. In the Mexican national psyche, this region (also the birthplace of mariachi) functions like Texas does in the American imagination, a badlands of tough hombres who tamed the wild land with honor and culture. "The mythology of Los Altos," wrote one scholar, "created a horse-riding people who were devoutly Catholic and capitalistic, had never intermarried with Indians, and played Mariachi music."[8] These were the Mexicans that the ruling party of Mexico, the Partido Revolucionario Industrial (Industrial Revolutionary Party, or better known in English and Spanish by its acronym, PRI), wanted to showcase as the country's romanticized self during the 1940s, a time when the PRI was using the country's nascent film industry to burnish Mexico's image abroad. What was once a regional liquor suddenly became as essential a part of Mexico as the tricolor flag and the Virgin of Guadalupe.

Sauza and Cuervo launched their tequila brands in the United States in earnest during the 1950s, when a tourism boom to Mexico whetted American palates for Mexican booze anew. By the 1960s, the Sauzas consciously tried to tame tequila's taste and potency, with an eye for Americans, to give it "prestige and status."[9] It became a rite of passage for American visitors to stay at a seaside resort—Acapulco, Puerto Vallarta, Rosarito, and others—lounge near the beach, sip margaritas, buy a bottle of tequila as a keepsake, and . . .

"My dad would get a lot of customers who'd come back with the bottle and say, 'What do I do with it?'" says Mariano Martinez, the man who invented the frozen margarita machine. "He'd promptly make them a margarita."

Margaritas sold well enough nationwide that by the mid-1960s, the *New York Times* announced it was "competing with Bloody Marys at cocktail hour" in Manhattan bars.[10] But it took Martinez's innovation to catapult the cocktail and tequila into its current popularity—and that's how we get back to the tale of the Slurpee machine.

Mariano Martinez pouring a frozen margarita at his Mariano's Mexican Cuisine in Dallas during the 1970s. His invention of a frozen margarita machine popularized the cocktail and led to the mainstreaming of tequila.
(Photo courtesy of Mariano Martinez)

In May 1971, Martinez faced a mutiny. The twenty-seven-year-old had just opened his first restaurant—Mariano's Mexican Cuisine, near the east side of the campus of Southern Methodist University in Dallas— to almost immediate success. Coeds, oil men, society ladies, and wave upon wave of singles crammed into the eatery, starting at a cantina where rock 'n' roll bands intermingled with mariachi music, with nary a puzzled look on anyone's face, then stumbling into the dining room for an evening of classic Tex-Mex—combo platters, crispy tacos, and enough queso to cover Big Tex himself—before ending with a nightcap back at the cantina. At the center of it all was the dashing, immaculately goateed Martinez, frequently in a bandito outfit, the better to let his gregarious personality charm customers into their fifth or sixth drink.

But the customers had complaints—actually, only one. The margaritas were terrible. Before opening, Martinez convinced his father, a longtime restaurateur, to lend him a margarita recipe, convinced that its use ensured Mariano's success. He was right: the drink sold easily—too easily. The cantina's harried bartenders had to prepare two hundred of them a night: slice the limes individually, then squeeze the juice into an ice-filled blender along with splashes of Cointreau, tequila, and simple syrup. Cocktails are an exact science, an algorithm of ingredients, and a perfect margarita must be tart, but not too much; sweet, but not cloyingly so; polite, but potent. Martinez had nabbed a couple of veteran bartenders from a nearby steak house with the promise of making much more money from the tips earned on margaritas at Mariano's.

The sheer volume of margarita orders overwhelmed the crew. In private, they prepared them to Martinez's liking; on the floor, the product didn't even reach the heights of sloppiness. After receiving too many complaints, Martinez asked for one and retched. He confronted the head of his crew, who admitted demand for margaritas was so great that they mindlessly tossed ingredients into the blender, pushed the on button, and poured the resulting sludge into a cup.

"Look at my hands," the bartender told Martinez, over the shouts of the crowd, who despite their complaints about the margaritas, never stopped ordering. They were pruned, scarred, and bleached from the lime juice's acidity. "I'm so tired of slicing up these limes." He threatened to leave, to return to the steak house, where the most bedeviling cocktail was bourbon and Coke, heavy on the bourbon, with the Coke bottle given to the customer to make the drink himself.

The last thing Mariano's needed was a bad reputation, especially so early in its career. Martinez left his restaurant late that night but slept little. He awoke early and drove to a local 7-Eleven for a cup of coffee. There he saw a Slurpee server, tumbling and churning with its frosty promise. The idea popped into Martinez's mind: prefabricated frozen margaritas, available at any time. That would save the hands of his beleaguered staff, ensure that the same product spouted from the machine order after order, and allow Mariano's to serve margaritas nonstop, all night, with nary a hiccup.

He called 7-Eleven's main headquarters, asking if they might sell him a Slurpee machine. No go—the contraption was proprietary. Martinez was undeterred. He called around town trying to find a machine like the Slurpee one and kept pestering 7-Eleven for a lead, any lead. The 7-Eleven people kept warning him not to copy them— and besides, everyone knows that alcohol doesn't freeze, so how the hell do you think you're going to find a machine that will produce frozen margaritas? He tracked down a used soft-serve ice cream machine for two hundred dollars even though the seller felt that Martinez's plan was unreachable with the contraption.

Machine in hand, Martinez found a man named Frank Adams, who was trying to sell a device that made frozen daiquiris. "The machine was the easy part," Martinez now says. He was speaking to me from his summer home in Pebble Beach, California, the fruit earned from four decades of selling frozen margaritas. Adams would soup up the machine to produce what Mariano's required, and Martinez would figure out how exactly to make an all-purpose mix for the perfect frozen drink.

After some days of experimenting, Martinez lugged the machine back to Mariano's, opened up the spout, and let the slushy, frozen result coil itself into the glass of a waiting patron. He had struck gold— Cuervo Gold, to be specific. Over the next couple of months the frozen margarita machine was modified and improved until it became the toast of Dallas, of Texas, of the United States. The frozen margarita machine came just as the sit-down Mexican restaurant scene was taking off—really, the surge Chi-Chi's, El Torito, and others experienced during the 1970s wouldn't be possible without alcohol to lure in people to casually try the Tex-Mex–Cal-Mex platters the restaurants served almost as asides. The cocktail fueled happy hours, disco nights, the go-go 1970s, and remains how America best loves its Mexican booze.

It couldn't have happened to a more unlikely guy, even though restaurants were in Martinez's blood. His maternal great-grandmother was Adelaida Cuellar, whose sons founded the El Chico restaurant chain; his mother worked as a cashier and bookkeeper at their first location, where his father—a San Antonio native—found a job and married her. Together the couple opened the second El Chico, in Lakewood, a wealthy Dallas suburb where they became the first Mexican family on the block, and spun off from the chain to open their own restaurant, El Charro.

But the rebellious son came to dislike the restaurant industry—"It was a very blue-collar business. We didn't have celebrity chefs then. I wanted to go experience life." And he did, dropping out of high school in tenth grade and playing electric bass for a succession of garage-rock bands before earning a high school diploma at twenty-one. During a visit to a men's clothing store in Denton (where he attended college) in 1967, Martinez heard the owner talk about a new shopping center planned for a city, and how he wished a good Mexican restaurant might open there. Martinez still wasn't much into restaurants, "but I also knew a business opportunity when I saw it." He drew up plans for an eatery with a cantina and a dining lounge, but had to shelve those ideas after the center never developed.

A couple of years later, Martinez heard about a new development in Dallas. He used those same plans to open Mariano's in 1971, finding funding from his own savings and a bank loan earned after dozens of rejections. He was adamant about not using the Cuellar name to open doors, but found he couldn't even use his paternal surname, since Martinezes were the founders of Dallas's other Mexican sit-down powerhouse, El Fenix. "Shortly after I opened the restaurant, one of the girl servers told me that the rumor around Dallas was that I was from the wealthy Martinez family, and they gave me a million dollars so I could make friends and party," says Martinez, who isn't related to that branch. "That went deep into my soul—to hear that someone gave me a million bucks because I was lonely? So I quit using my last name and just went by Mariano."

Mariano's was designed with the goal of getting people as soused as possible while toeing the law. In those days, Texas didn't allow the sale of liquor by drinks—any establishment that sold alcohol operated under a membership program, in which patrons bought memberships to ostensibly store their liquor on the premises for their use only. Because of that law, Martinez made the cantina a membership club, and constructed it so that people had to walk through the raucous scene to enter the restaurant.

"I designed it like this: when couples went to El Chico, they'd take the kids, they'd eat, and they'd have a beer," he said. "When they came to Mariano's, they'd hire a babysitter." But shortly after Mariano's opening, Texas lifted its peculiar law, and sales of the margarita—already high—exploded. It was the perfect time for the dawn of the machine.

Somewhere in the vast holdings of the Smithsonian's Natural Museum of American History stands Mariano's original frozen margarita machine. It's a simple thing: a spigot with a lever, a steel cupholder in which to place a glass, some buttons, and vents. He retired it after ten years of faithful service, having tinkered with it so many times that it finally gasped out some drops one day and just stopped. After giving it a proper farewell—a fiesta—Martinez covered the contraption with fake wood, screwed in a faux-silver placard that proclaimed it "The World's First Frozen Margarita Machine," and had a pedestal built near the bar to jokingly showcase it. The frozen margarita business at Mariano's was so great, however, that Martinez put his baby near the front door to make way for a new machine. The original stood there for nearly twenty-five years, until the Smithsonian asked Martinez to donate it for their collection.

"There are two times in my life where I thought [people] were punking me—when *Nightline* interviewed me, and the Smithsonian wanting my machine," says Martinez, his Texas drawl as syrupy as one of his margaritas. "I grew up the only Mexican kid in my neighborhood, and there was discrimination. I was made to feel like a third-rate citizen. But I used to read about the Smithsonian, think about what an amazing place it is—and now they have my machine."

It's a better fate than what his nephew suggested upon hearing the archival request: putting it up on eBay. "But if they put it in the Smithsonian," the wise uncle reasoned, "that's a million dollars of publicity."

"The invention of the frozen margarita machine is a classic example of the American entrepreneurial spirit," museum director Brent D. Glass said in a press release announcing the acquisition in 2005.[11] Martinez is allowed to see it whenever he wants—but it's now in a climate-controlled room, and he must wear white gloves when handling it.

Not everyone is a fan of Martinez's contribution to American gastronomy, even in Dallas. On the day *Nightline* aired a segment on the man to celebrate his machine's fortieth anniversary, the *Dallas Observer* called the holy day "The Day the Margarita Died." See, to make the margarita mix work, Martinez replaced his dad's simple syrup with sugar, which froze easier and gave the margarita a better consistency. That adjustment altered the taste of margaritas for Americans for decades—it's supposed to be sweet, but not saccharine. But since competitors copied Martinez, a generation of Americans enjoyed the equivalent of sugared tequila, and many of Mariano's customers returned from trips to Mexico grumbling that Mexicans didn't know how to make a correct margarita. Because of this, critics such as the

Observer trash Martinez for corrupting the cocktail, a point with which he doesn't necessarily disagree.

"Reporters ask me, 'What do you say to purists that feel like a margarita shouldn't come out of a machine?' I reply, 'Hey, I'm one of them,'" he says. "Today I'm not going to get it out of a machine—mine are fresh-squeezed lime juice, and I like the taste of Grand Marnier. That's me. And just like my tastes have evolved, so have my diners'. But without giving them that [first] taste, we would've never gotten to the point where we are today. Unfortunately, people took my machine and put the cheapest tequila you can find, and not much of it, and then sell it for ninety-nine cents. I don't know about you, but if I'm eating a burger, I'm not spending ninety-nine cents on one."

Martinez never patented the frozen margarita machine because "I wasn't interested in the machine business when I was young; I only cared about what was happening inside the four walls of Mariano's." Nor did he seek legal ownership of his other great liquor invention, prefabricated margarita mix, which he created after receiving requests on how to make his frozen margaritas from a blender at home (the reason you almost always find margarita mix in a bucket: Martinez perfected it in empty Spackle buckets while remodeling his home, finding that those buckets allowed him to pour a full bottle of tequila into a set amount of margarita mix to produce a perfect ratio for a great margarita). Martinez did try to patent the latter, but spent so much money defending it in court against bigger companies that he finally gave up. "I've learned that if something's a good idea, someone's going to copy you," he says.

But Martinez never gnashed his teeth as frozen margaritas spread across America, making billions of dollars for everything from chains to bars, mom-and-pops to county fairs. And he never winced as the Mexican alcohol industry nosed its way into his tent. Though Mexican beer brands such as Tecate had advertised in American newspapers since the 1940s, beer sales didn't compare to margaritas until the 1980s, when Mexico's major breweries discovered the doublewhammies of Cinco de Mayo and spring break. On the former front, beer companies lavished millions of dollars on advertising for the Mexican holiday, pushing it out of the Mexican-American community and into the mainstream, turning it into a mestizo St. Patrick's Day. The holiday in the United States turned from commemorating the 1862 Battle of Puebla to a nationwide encouragement for gabachos to patronize Mexican restaurants and "Drinko for Cinco." Those same companies (primarily among them Grupo Modelo, makers of Corona, the best-selling Mexican beer in the United States) also targeted college students on spring break in Mexico's tourist colonies: Baja California, Acapulco, Puerto Vallarta, and others. There, American-themed cantinas such as Señor Frog's, Papas and Beers, Cabo Wabo, and Hussong's served for many coeds as their clarion call to get *borracho* forevermore.

Mariano's continues to draw crowds, the menu only slightly changed after all these years. While the restaurant does offer higher-end tequilas, the frozen margarita remains his best seller. And while Martinez does follow Mexican food trends in this country, he's also stubbornly proud of his roots, and his intoxicating momentous contribution.

"I've seen them all over the years. They come in and do this upscale food. Mexico City style blah blah blah," he says. "Some of those places aren't there anymore. My little old place I have? Forty years later, we're still pumping the same food. Same phone number. Here I am plugging away at this little Tex-Mex peasant food that no one wanted to play with, that all the ivory tower critics made fun of. And with a drink that no one can resist."

Chapter Fourteen

What Are the Five Greatest Mexican Meals in the United States?

My favorite burrito in the United States is at Lucy's Drive-in, on Pico Boulevard and La Brea Avenue in Los Angeles, a beat-down diner where black and brown chow down on classic Cal-Mex grub. The chile relleno burrito, a hunk of milky cheese inside a slightly spicy, egg-battered pepper, next to a sweet vein of refried beans, wrapped in a tissuelike flour tortilla, and washed down with the whipped-fruit drink Orange Bang!, is edible paradise. The best tamales in the United States are at my family's house come Christmastime . . . but since you're not invited, the next best thing are those from the Mississippi Delta—specifically the ones steamed at Pasquale's Tamales, a trailer in Helena, Arkansas, run by a third-generation Sicilian-American tamalero: they are chewy, spicy temples of American multiculturalism. And oh, those lamb chicharrones at Angelina's in Española, New Mexico, fried and gnarled and succulent and so gamy you can taste the bah.

See how personal my tastes are, and how they probably don't match yours? How ultimately frustrating it is to try to compile a list of the best Mexican food in America. Is it just me, or is reading now reduced to paragraph-sized telegrams oozing authority on a certain issue by ranking and numbering? Top-five lists—who doesn't love them? I, for one—the concept is gimmicky, arbitrary, and beyond overdone. So let's do it!

There are thousands of great Mexican meals to be had in the United States, some even tastier than the plates I'll cover in this chapter. But there's a difference between the best and the greatest, and I chose the following eateries under the latter parameter because they called to me again and again during my research for this book over the past couple of years of hundreds of meals consumed, thousands of miles traveled, dozens of places searching for a sublime taco, an ideal *horchata,* a stupendous sope. Perfection doesn't exist, but a great story pared with a satisfying lunch? An eater's dream.

It's not just the food that drew me to the following list so much as what the restaurant represents. Most of these meals will never migrate past the city limits but aren't particularly difficult to replicate. But the stories behind them—their symbolism, their panoply of flavors, their customers and creators—are worthy of highlighting. If you're ever near them, make the pilgrimage. Besides, I couldn't fit any of my muses into any other chapter—with the exception of one place, they didn't create monumental shifts in how we devour Mexican. They're just *bueno.*

5. The Night Hawk Special, El Rancho Grande, Tulsa, Oklahoma

Tulsa, one of the dozen or so buckles of the Bible Belt, doesn't have the best reputation nationwide, nor is it known for anything food-wise outside of barbecue—if that. For years its most famous Mexican restaurant was Casa Bonita, a compound of Mexican-themed rooms that was like Disneyland drowned in nacho cheese. There were jungle rooms, tables and chairs made to look as if they were transplanted from a splendorous hacienda, strolling mariachis—but no thirty-foot waterfall featuring cliff divers jumping to the applause of appreciative diners, as that was the domain of its Denver-area sibling immortalized in a *South Park* episode. In its heyday, school buses from across Oklahoma drove to Tulsa's Casa Bonita to give students a taste of Old Mexico and bad chili con carne that they ordered from a cafeteria-style system of trays. But Tulsa's version—which called itself "Tulsa's Favorite Mexican Restaurant" and emblazoned the motto on a thousand-light marquee outside its fake-colonial facade—closed in 2011 after four decades of operation, no longer needed in a city now increasingly Latino.

Another Mexican relic now rules over Tulsa: El Rancho Grande, off historic Route 66, the oldest Mexican restaurant in Oklahoma and one of the oldest remaining restaurants in Tulsa, period. El Rancho Grande refers to a famous Mexican film from the *comedia ranchera* movie genre, a type of Mexican film where levity is found among the peons and dons on a ranch, where men resplendent in sombrero and charro costumes sang songs of love in bars and on horseback: Mexico's own fantasy heritage. At night the restaurant's sign lights up—a sombrero-wearing neon charro throwing a lasso that spells out "El," with the rest roping around "Rancho Grande." It's not exactly an authentic charro—the sash around his waist is more Spanish toreador than Mexican vaquero, and the yellow shirt looks more appropriate for the Grand Ole Opry than anything Latino. But inside, the interior was recently remodeled to better mimic the higher-end Mexican restaurants wrought by the Southwestern movement—mosaic tabletops, colorful paintings, tropical music.

The menu is a timeline of Mexican food's journey through the United States. Chile con queso serves as an appetizer, boiling and fiery, but the *queso flameado*—jack cheese baked on chorizo—tastes like the Americanized cousin of the Mexico City favorite *queso fundido*. "Classic" tacos come either fried or prepared in small flour tortillas, but the soft tacos are straight out of an East Los Angeles lonchera, just the corn tortilla, meat, cilantro, and onions. The fajitas platters sizzle through business hours, but more than a few people also order *camarones al mojo de ajo,* shrimp sautéed in potent garlic-spiked butter that penetrated America's Mexican restaurants during the 1980s. There are even fish tacos on the menu—in the land of Okies? Once heretical, nowadays commonplace.

El Rancho Grande's food is largely fine, if tried and true. But one grand, glorious exception exists: the Night Hawk special, a feat of Tex-Mex majesty. It's ostensibly two cheese enchiladas topped with processed cheese, then smothered in chili con carne on one half, and a soft cheese taco slathered in chili con queso on the other. In its presentation, the Night Hawk looks like a Pac-Man in reverse. The bright yellow cheese taco side occupies a third of the plate, as if the chili con carne gobbles up that last sliver in a culinary bid for domination. That cheese fights back; as the plate settles, some of the molten dairy product spills over to the chili con carne side, creating a color scheme as warm as that of the Arizona State Sun Devils.

The chili is an angry, dark red; flecks of beef sit around the spicy goop. It sings of San Antonio's queens—not too sweet, not far removed from the cauldrons that gave palpitations to the original easterners who clamored over it, unctuous enough to trap a small mammal. The heat of the plate and the steaming ingredients mean that the queso coagulates over the cheese taco and assumes the consistency of Play-Doh. The taco and enchiladas, while tasty, are afterthoughts in the battle for your palate. A fork is all you need to eat through the meal, and you can't eat each side on its own; mixture, miscegenation is a must. So you'll find yourself scooping some chili onto the queso, splitting the enchilada to join in the soft taco. No side dishes required—no beans and rice, no chips, no salsa. It's not a subtle meal: the double onslaught of queso and chili con carne disrupts your throat with dueling notes of spice and creaminess, an exclamation of Texas braggadocio. But the assertive dual notes settle long after red and yellow cake the corners of your lips, and you find yourself not wanting to wash off the remnants for the Proustian jolt that a simple flick of a tongue induces when no one watches.

Wading through the platter is following Tex-Mex from curio to accepted diet to artifact. A Mexican immigrant named Ruby Rodrigues opened El Rancho Grande in 1950 at a tiny eatery across the street from the city's Holy Family Cathedral. Rodrigues (born Guadalupe Almendares) had lived in Tulsa since the 1920s, and her husband was a tamale man. Oklahoma at the time had a small Mexican community, mostly transplants from Texas who went north in search of work, and migrant workers following the harvests and railroads. But business must have been great for Rodrigues and her husband, because they moved El Rancho Grande just a year after opening it to its present location. She promoted the restaurant's dishwasher, San Antonio native Larry Lara (real name Inez, but that's technically a woman's name, and what Mexican man wants a woman's name unless it's Guadalupe?), to head cook upon moving to the new location. The two of them perfected the menu so it became a repository of Tex-Mex classics, a place for Lone Star transplants to visit for a taste of the motherland, and ran the restaurant mostly by themselves until Rodrigues retired in the 1980s. She sold El Rancho Grande to her landlords, but Lara stayed on until 2004—nearly fifty-five years.

Lara introduced the Night Hawk special, but no one knows why Rodrigues gave it that name, although it's probably a nod to the dish's ideal audience, people looking for energy to confront the lonely night. Only one other restaurant in the United States sells the Night Hawk: Ojeda's Mexican Food in Dallas (far better are their brisket tacos, fatty and luscious; its Night Hawk is just too prim and proper, and shredded beef inside the enchiladas mucks up the meal).

Alas, the customers for El Rancho Grande, while many, dine more out of habit and loyalty and are largely Americans or assimilated Mexicans. It's a shame, because the Night Hawk is edible, intoxicating history on a plate.

4. Sonora Dog, El Güero Canelo, Tucson, Arizona

Two options exist for people who want the El Güero Canelo experience. One is to visit the original location, on Tucson's South Side barrio, a sprawling collection of benches and booths that look like the eating area at a concession stand at a drive-in movie theater. The meal everyone eats—hot dogs—adds to the surreal playground experience, especially given that the clientele ranges from children to adults, and is almost exclusively Mexican. At night, old and young, families and friends, flock to eat wieners, stand in line to the walk-up window, former kitchen trailers now bound to the ground. They order one, two, a dozen hot dogs. A cart, the original Güero Canelo, is chained near one of the order windows; nearby are multiple newspaper clippings, including a nice write-up in the *New York Times* suggesting that this restaurant is more than just a beloved hole in the wall.

Proof is about eight miles to the north, in a gleaming building as spacious as an airplane hangar. Everything gleams—the high windows that allow natural lighting to flood the inside, the new stainless-steel picnic tables (with benches painted in the Mexican tricolor), the food trays that hold dozens of condiments. The add-ons seem contradictory, even wrong for a hot dog, which also is the focus of everyone's orders. Radishes snuggle up next to petals of raw red onions next to cucumber slices next to a variety of sautéed peppers and lakes of salsa; there's even guacamole. Customers weigh down their hot dogs with the sides, take extra containers, and still make multiple trips back. It's a Fourth of July picnic at the park, open 365 days a year.

Tucson—the Old Pueblo, the city that supposedly introduced the chimichanga to American diners, the municipality that definitely introduced Sonoran cuisine, Cal-Mex's grandma—is now a hot dog town, even more so than Chicago. But it's a specific type of red hot for which *los tucsonenses* line up: bacon wrapped around a frank like the stripes on a barber pole, pork grilled on pork until the bacon binds itself to the casing, becomes inextricable without a committed chomp. The bun used is a special, fluffy kind with a tough crust used for Mexican-style sandwiches called *bolillos,* excavated split-top style instead of getting sliced, with the ends of the bolillo intact so the hot dog squeezes into the miniloaf as snug as a galosh around a foot. Inside is a smear of beans; on top go tomatoes and squirts of mayonnaise, green salsa, and mustard. It's up to eaters to further doodle with their dog in ways that make the Mission burrito seem as Byzantine as a glass of water.

Across Tucson, *hotdogueros* sell bacon-wrapped hot dogs in every imaginable setting: at roadside stands, out of vans and taco trucks, on menus of respectable Mexican restaurants, from pop-up tents on street corners, even via coolers. They're not necessarily original, of course: Americans have wrapped raw strips of bacon around hot dogs, put it on the grill so that its fat seeped into the sausage, then placed it in a bun for decades. And it's not even the first hot dog customized with Mexican flavors: chili in a bun has dominated hot dog tastes since at least the 1920s, and baseball fans have thrown in pickled jalapeños and nacho cheese on their wieners as far back as the 1970s. But it was in the desert between Tucson and Sonora where the bacon-wrapped hot dog became irretrievably Mexican and earned its proper name: the Sonora dog.

The king of Tucson's Sonora dog scene is El Güero Canelo, which gets its name from the owner: Daniel Contreras, a boulder-sized man with the flat top and imposing look of Dick Butkus, except with a perpetual smile, lighter skin, and red hair, the bases for his nickname (the Light-Skinned, Cinnamon-Haired Man, or El Güero Canelo). He had worked as a chef at another Tucson landmark, Micha's, before his wife suggested they open a food-cart business. Contreras purchased a six-foot-by-eight-foot taco cart in 1993 that he wheeled to a vacant lot in Tucson's South Side barrio.

Contreras sold various items, as he does today: burros, quesadillas, tacos, and those Sonoran dogs. (The one Tucson specialty he never sold was the cheese crisp, a flour tortilla buttered, covered with shredded cheese, then baked inside an oven like a pizza until the cheese melts into blobs and the tortilla becomes, well, crispy, then presented on a raised plate so eaters can break off slices. It seems like a creation of a poor college student stuck in his dorm during winter break, at wit's end for some food, digging into his roommate's refrigerator and finding only those ingredients, wanting pizza and not an enchilada—but it works. Good, but nothing approaching the baroque interplay in the Sonora dog. Sorry for the aside, but I had to get at least one mention of this *somewhere* in this tract. Now, back to the Sonora dog.)

But it was Sonora dogs—which Contreras remembered eating as a child in Sonora during the 1960s—that ensured his success, and Contreras moved into his first restaurant setting in the mid-1990s, taking the cart along with him as a memory. It expanded over the years, which explains the first El Güero Canelo's shabby spread. But this wasn't enough—demand was so high for El Güero Canelo that Contreras opened a second location, on the city's ritzier North Side, in 2007, a third in 2011, and has plans to expand to Phoenix soon.

Versions of the Sonora dog crossed back into Mexico, skipped over the Sea of Cortez to Tijuana, then went north to the United States again. In Tijuana, the splash of salsa turned from green to Valentina's, a mass-produced hot sauce with a vinegary finish. In Los Angeles, street vendors skipped the bolillo, returning to regular buns and adding ketchup and sliced jalapeños instead of whole roasted peppers. The Sonora name was dropped, and new names emerged for it: Border dogs. Ghetto dogs. Barrio dogs. Danger dogs. Heart attack dogs. Tijuana dogs. Americans always need a dash of illegality with their Mexican food, eh? It also doesn't help that Southern California health officials continually target bacon-wrapped hot dogs, arguing that the marriage of bacon and wieners unleashes unknown pathogens without ever offering complete proof, or that many vendors of bacon-wrapped hot dogs are unlicensed street vendors, setting up stands and coolers outside bars and concerts after they empty out in the late nights, like the city's tamale wagons of yore.

Back in Tucson, the city shrugs. How can anyone be opposed to the Sonora dog? The grilled frank, plump with a slight snap? The snake-wrapped bacon, shattering upon contact? A soft, slightly toasted bun, one that keeps its structural integrity despite all the toppings one may put on, soaking the various condiments? Customizable—isn't that the American way?

Is this hot dog truly Mexican? Who cares? In Tucson, the birthplace of Linda Ronstadt, Americans became Mexicans long ago; it's now the rest of the country that's finally wising up.

3. Taco Acorazado, Alebrije's Grill, Santa Ana, California

Pink. Cadillac pink. The original owner of Alebrije's Grill in Santa Ana, California, picked that color because he knew it'd stand out in a sea of white taco trucks; the current owner of the Alebrije's on the corner of Main and Cubbon Streets in Santa Ana, Albert Hernández, kept the shade for the same reason. Even when he participates in clustertrucks,[1] parking next to luxe loncheras with outlandish designs and murals and coloring, the soft, welcoming pink of Alebrije's captures eyes, entices the curious—and they usually haven't even heard of the masa marvel that Hernández will recommend: the *taco acorazado,* which translates as the battleship taco.

Okay, so deeming an Orange County taco truck as harboring the third-greatest Mexican dish in America is *totally* provincial, but hear out my reasoning. I wanted to include a street vendor, because the informal economy is what has long pushed and innovated Mexican food. California had to make the list, or I'd face exile from the Golden State to Texas. It wouldn't be a proper list without, you know, a taco, given the title of this book. Finally, although the Sonora dog is a glorious immigrant worthy of adulation, I needed to include at least one more shout-out to the current wave of regional Mexican food that, if it hasn't yet reached your city, will get there within a decade, if not sooner.

All of this aside, Alebrije's taco acorazado doesn't even need a backstory. Hernández and his crew of aunts and female cousins grab a ball of fresh masa, give it a couple of rolls, then smash it down with a press so it flattens into something as wide and thick as a pamphlet. The masa sheet gets tossed onto the grill—it'll turn into a tortilla, stretched to the point where corn tortillas can stretch until they collapse under their own weight and begin splitting. This tortilla packs unadulterated corn flavor—no preservatives, no additives, no extra salt or sugar, but the straightforward taste that immediately entranced the Spaniards.

Alebrije's tortilla alone beats three quarters of any Mexican meal you might buy in your life, but it's a mere vessel for the mountain to come. As the cooks tend to the tortilla, flipping it every minute so it thoroughly cooks and turns a tanned yellow while adding specks of char, another chef takes slices of beef, dunks them in egg batter, rubs the slices with bread crumbs, and grills them on the stove. They've just started cooking the *milanesa,* the breaded beef cutlet that came to Mexico with—take your legend—Italian immigrants by way of Argentina who were familiar with Milanese cooking styles (hence the name, which in Spanish refers to "Milanese style"), or the German and Czech immigrants who brought along their German/Austro-Hungarian Wiener schnitzel. Alebrije's milanesa is thin, buttery, with expertly grilled meat inside the crunchy blanket that the bread crumbs have become. The milanesa alone makes a filling meal, but that's going on the taco—but wait, there's more!

Once the tortilla and milanesa are ready, Alebrije's puts the tortilla on a flat plate, then covers the tortilla with a bed of fluffy Mexican rice. Then go the slices of milanesa; their gnarled, imposing appearance can look, in a pinch, like the steel plates of a battleship—at least that's what the people of Cuernavaca in the Mexican state of Morelos thought when the dish first appeared in the Mexican city during the 1940s. This is the taco acorazado, but Hernández modifies it further—on the side of the taco he places sautéed jalapeños, onions, and a grilled cactus paddle, free of any slime. On top of the milanesa go avocado slices, pickled carrots, and a dusting of salty *queso cotija.* It's up to you to decide which of the three salsas (piquant green, smoky red, or sweat-inducing orange) you'll squeeze from the bottles on hand, or how much of the purple pickled onions packed with slivers of habanero that sit in brine, nearly pulsating with their decadent hell, you'll toss as the final dressing before the coming deluge.

You don't eat a taco acorazado so much as deconstruct it. Start by alternating bites among the cactus, the milanesa, the onions, the jalapeños, and a scoop of rice to add that last dash of unami. Spice, sweet, vegetal, sour, crunchy, smooth, even dairy: the acorazado represents nearly every flavor imaginable, all accentuated by whatever salsa you may have drizzled. You whittle away at those toppings, forkful after forkful after forkful, until a few stray milanesa slices are left, until the mound of rice is reduced into a knoll, until the cactus paddle, smoky and chewy, is gone. You're already stuffed—but now, before you, is a proper taco.

While you were slicing through the acorazado, the flavors of all the ingredients seeped into the tortilla on the bottom. Its thickness means that the tortilla won't disintegrate when you finally fold it in half to complete your meal, nor will it wobble like an inferior product. It's now moist, absorbent to all the ingredients it held, Atlas-like, above itself. The taco acorazado isn't a taco so much as bliss by a thousand bites.

Hernández is a native of the Mexican state of Guanajuato, and Alebrije's actually specializes in Mexico City–style food, which is really just a hundred different ways around masa: *huaraches* (a sope extended until it's the shape of a sandal), *tlacoyos* (an elongated gordita stuffed with fava beans), *alambres* ("wires" in Spanish, and named as such because six double-folded corn tortillas are the base for a jumble of carne asada, ham, bacon, bell peppers, and thick cheese melted on top of the mess), and the region's take on quesadillas, folded in half, looking like a crepe, and stuffed with a buttery cheese à la Brie. But early on, Hernández latched on to the acorazado as his ticket to success. "No one else was making it," says Hernández, who learned of the dish in the United States. "It is such a big meal that I knew if anyone tried it even once, they would tell anyone who ate it what a huge taco this was."

Soon the Orange County buzz for the taco acorazado was such that other loncheras ripped off the meal, as well as their Los Angeles counterparts. It even made a cameo on *Last Call with Carson Daly* when they profiled me, because I insisted on the setting. Will the dish go nationwide? Not too many people from Cuernavaca live in the United States outside of Southern California—but then again, it didn't take Mexicans living across this country to popularize chili in the late nineteenth century, did it?

2. Rolled Tacos, Chico's Tacos, El Paso, Texas

At night, a light looms over El Paso, the hardscrabble town on the U.S.-Mexico border just a couple of border guards away from one of the world's murder capitals, Ciudad Juárez. It's the largest man-made illuminated star in the world, 459 feet tall and 278 feet wide, shining with 459 150-watt bulbs strung across Franklin Mountain to let the world know you're entering Texas. Visitors to the city can see it from 100 miles up as planes descend onto El Paso International Airport, and drivers can view its icicle-white lights, shaped into the Lone Star, from 30 miles away.

Chico's Tacos, El Paso, Texas, where the hot dogs come in hamburger buns and the tacos bob in a sea of tomato salsa. *(Photo by Melody Parra,* What's Up Weekly*)*

Across the city, not far from the airport, stands another bright monument, a humbler one: a small, smiling boy in serape and sombrero, holding a carton tray of taquitos drowning in a sauce in his left hand while the other makes the A-OK sign. This is Chico's Tacos, a small El Paso chain started in 1953 by Joe Mora and two friends but now wholly owned by Mora's children. The restaurant is perpetually full—immigrants probably hours removed from crossing *la frontera*, youth sports leagues coming for a celebratory (or consolatory) postgame meal, everyone getting their orders within minutes. Street vendors waving candies and other snacks enter the restaurant, but the owners don't drive them away. Security stands by, but spend most of their shift flirting with the girls behind the counter instead of monitoring for roughhousing. The *chicas* yell out order numbers in English and Spanish, even though everyone understands either language. It's the kind of restaurant where the high-pitched laments of *conjunto norteño* (the Mexican music with the accordion in it that sounds like polka because it basically is) icon Ramón Ayala spin on the jukebox just after a No Doubt paean to suburban angst, and not only does no one blink, but also most sing along flawlessly to the two.

All tables possess at least one order of Chico's tacos—thin, tightly rolled taquitos stuffed with ground beef that tastes more like burned nubs than anything bovine, placed in a nacho carton filled to the brim with a weak, watery salsa more tomato than chile and more soup than salsa; the actual heat is a green condiment offered in a small thimble on the side. The taquitos are stacked so some are fully submerged in that soup; others stay dry save for their shiny shell. A flurry of processed American cheese covers the stack, some of which stays above the soup and melts only slightly upon resting on the taquitos; the strands that slip into the broth turn it into Texas-style queso.

It's a bizarre dish, about as Mexican as Chico's hot dogs—two crimson wieners spliced and placed in a bun on top of pinto beans, pickles, mustard, and green chile. But no one cares. A single order of Chico's tacos is three tacos; the double is six. Most people ask for two doubles. They're crunchy, if a bit stale-looking, and the best way to eat them is to order extra melted cheese, keeping as much of that tomato soup as possible, using each taquito as a straw to stir the cheese into the liquid, then scooping up the liquefied cheese and taking a bite. The soup still remains at the end: slurp it up by tipping the carton, craning your neck so you don't spill too much on your shirt. Anyone looking for a prim sit-down feast is better off at another place, but a warning: most residents of Chuco (the nickname the city's Mexicans gave it long ago) will end every proper meal with a midnight run.

El Paso loves Chico's, but the restaurant has met controversy in the past. In 2009, two gay men were kicked out for what they claimed was kissing in public, and they also alleged that police officers threatened to jail them under an obsolete antigay statute that the U.S. Supreme Court ruled unconstitutional in 2003; a lawsuit is pending. Chico's also is where the Great Taco Riot of 2008 occurred. At about two in the morning one February, a fire broke out in the attic of one location, forcing the evacuation of Chico's and costing the restaurant more than $45,000 in damages.

Many in the late-night crowd were drunk, which explains what happened next: when the firefighters evacuated the restaurant, and the owners announced that Chico's was closed and they couldn't get refunds or reclaim the tacos left behind, people started yelling and throwing cans. It got so bad that firefighters called for police backup; thankfully, no arrests were made. It was a local embarrassment, but ask El Paso residents about the Great Taco Riot and you'll find more than a few sympathetic ears. "We understand the sacrifice they had to make leaving possibly a double order of Chico's Tacos with extra cheese behind, but when an emergency response agency asks you to evacuate, including firefighters and police officers, it's usually because it's an emergency," a bemused spokesman for the Fire Department told the *El Paso Times*.[2]

All this, over taquitos? Damn straight. This is El Paso, the type of town where an Irish-American gets elected to head the Mexican-American Bar Association, and no one has a problem with it. El Paso is the Mexican future of this country—not always hunky-dory, of course, and with problems, but ultimately no different from any other metro area, if not a bit better. And with a double order at Chico's tacos, fried and slightly spicy and sweet and crunchy as a communal meal, El Paso is as good a harbinger as any that not only will everything be all right, it'll also come with a hell of a lot of cheese.

1. Mexican Hamburger, Grandma's The Original Chubby's, Denver, Colorado

Stella Cordova lived to be a hundred years old, a century well lived that took her from the farming town of Walsenburg, in the heart of Colorado's Hispano country, to Denver, where she became a beloved Denver icon on a par with John Elway. At age fifty-nine, after having raised ten biological children and two adopted ones, she reentered the workforce as a cook in a restaurant called Chubby Burger Drive-in, in the city's Italian neighborhood, which over the years became Latino. Chubby was failing, but Cordova bought the place and saved it by introducing burritos, tacos, and tostadas, all topped with her fabulous green chile. An institution was born, gradually changing its name to just Chubby's.

At five foot nothing and just a bit over a hundred pounds, Cordova was the quintessential Mexican *abuelita,* frequently giving away free meals and always quick to flash a smile. But the diminutive build belied a tough-as-nails *mujer* who worked the fields as a child harvesting corn and melons. At Chubby's she commanded everyone's attention, whether riffraff during the day or rowdy bar crowds that begged her to stay open past the 3:00 A.M. last call, people who couldn't wait the three hours until Chubby's reopened at six in the morning. And then there was the Frightened Thief.

As she told the Denver paper *Westword*, Cordova was washing the pots one night from another long shift when she realized that a customer who had been loitering inside had vanished. Just as soon as Cordova noticed, the customer reappeared, now at the back door of the restaurant and masked with a plastic bag.

"This is a stickup!" he yelled at the kitchen. Cordova didn't flinch.

"Okay," she replied. "Go right ahead."

"This is a fucking stickup!" the would-be robber screamed again, adding an expletive for good measure.

Cordova stopped washing the pots.

"I want the money!" the robber spat out, his hand in a pocket trying to form a bulge that might look like a gun.

"You wait a minute!" Stella snapped back. "Let me finish my pot." And she did, while the criminal stood outside the kitchen, shocked.

It took a couple of minutes, which included Cordova drying her hands, but she finally found time to get robbed. The gunman entered the back door of Chubby's when he saw Cordova approaching the register, but Cordova stopped him.

"No. You go around the other way," she ordered, to which the robber dutifully complied.

As the gunman walked around the building, Cordova hid a stack of twenty-dollar bills in her pocket, grabbed a bag and filled it with fives and ones, and handed it to the thief. He grabbed it and ran, not even bothering to pick up the money that dropped to the floor.

You never interrupted Stella Cordova while she was at work. And you never left Chubby's without a meal: as the thief took off into the night, the counterman—who had witnessed this entire episode without once leaving his post—realized that there was a problem. "Hey!" he yelled fruitlessly. "You want a burrito?"[3]

Chubby's is not even a restaurant per se: just a cinder-block building with a tiny waiting area, a kitchen, and a sign. All orders are to go, and the counters inside, while accompanied by stools, are really for people to relax on while waiting for their grub. Outside are a couple of scratched lunch tables. For years they've had plans to expand, but the soul of Chubby's will forever be that front counter, which affords everyone a view of the small kitchen where Cordova greeted generations of Denverites with a fix for Mexican hamburgers.

Denver's addition to the burrito family is the Mexican hamburger, a bean-and-chicharrones burrito stuffed with a hamburger patty inside, then smothered in chile. Nearly every Mexican restaurant in the Mile-High City—and more than a few non-Mexican places—offer this blend of American and Mexican tastes, from high end to taquerías, places run by Mexican immigrants and those from Cordova's generation. Cordova never claimed to have created the Mexican hamburger, although she told reporters that her inspiration for selling it at Chubby's came one day when she was cooking a hamburger, sliced the patty in half, then stuffed it into a burrito. Denver consensus states that the first Mexican hamburger was sold at Joe's Buffet, a now-gone eatery in one of Denver's Chicano neighborhoods, beginning as a blackboard special in the late 1960s and advertised as "Linda's Mexican Hamburger," after a waitress. The Mexican hamburger spread across Denver—but only Denver, much to the surprise of Mile-High City denizens, who always assumed that their dish, like the local NFL squad, had a national reach. Perhaps because it's so straightforward—putting a hamburger patty inside a burrito? How truly revolutionary is that? Yet that's what makes the Mexican hamburger so brilliant—its simplicity, its utterly unremarkable nature, the effortless mixing between two peoples. And at Chubby's, the Mexican hamburger reaches every overblown food cliché one can imagine.

Chubby's is most famous for their chile, a gravy which comes smothered on everything—inside actual cheeseburgers and on top of them. On burritos and over fries, a hearty condiment for a hardy city where you need all the comfort you can get. It works best, though, smothered on the Mexican hamburger, the greatest Mexican dish in the United

States. Brace yourselves, folks: underneath that Broncos-hued chile lies the structure of a burrito—a flour tortilla containing refried beans, your choice of meat, and a grilled hamburger patty, almost extant in shape. On top of this is the chile: smothered completely over the burrito until it's little more than a beached whale over a viscous, spicy sea. The flour tortilla itself is cooked well until it becomes firm, almost crispy, so you can slice off a chunk of Mexican hamburger and it won't flop around on your fork as it enters your mouth. The patty sits in the center, well done, its beefiness absorbing the lard of the chicharrones and of the refried beans. When you order one, the Chubby's staff serves it on a cardboard plate, then puts another plate on top and staples them together, to ensure that not a drop of the ambrosia spills and wastes.

I've had puffy tacos in San Antonio that produced visions of grandeur, glorious bowls of the green in Hatch, fabulous taco pizzas in Minnesota, and python-esque Mission burritos in San Francisco, but the Mexican hamburger is the dish that best personifies the Mexican-American experience, a monument to *mestizaje*. The tortilla is wholly indigenous; its flour version, the legacy of Spain. The focus on green chile places the Mexican hamburger firmly in the Southwest; its gravy, the legacy of Tex-Mex. The hamburger patty, of course, is wholly American—but even that has a German past. This fugue is pure *rascuache*, the Mexican concept of creating beauty from seeming junk. And the taste? Heavy, thick, yet Chubby's Mexican hamburger at its best retains all the flavors of its distinct parts. No added salsa is necessary—amazingly, underneath all that heartiness, the chile comes through and zaps every cell of your body to attention.

Let the Baylessistas scream—this is a dish as Mexican as the Templo Mayor, as American as the Washington Monument, as Chicano as George Lopez. But like so many other tales of Mexican empires, Chubby's Mexican hamburger is also emblematic of the messy, sometimes acrimonious saga of how Mexican food has evolved in this country.

Cordova allowed some children to operate other Chubby's using the same name. But soon other imitators—a few with no connection to the family, but most Stella's squabbling progeny—opened their own Chubby's knockoffs, some as far away as Hawaii. The king of these familial franchisers is Stella's grandson Leonard Cordova, whose Bubba Chinos has ten locations and is expanding. He's an affable, large man who bought a fleet of tricked-out Hummers done up in street art advertising Bubba Chinos and sells jars of the chile Cordova used to offer—and for that, many of the other Cordovas despise him. In fact, his restaurant used to be called Chubby's Bubba Chino until a cousin sued to stop Leonard from using the Chubby's name. "I'll tell you, if our family would have acted like a family, then Chubby's would have been way up there, like Chipotle," the litigating cousin, Julian Cordova, told *Westword*. "We would have been all over the world."[4]

Stella's Chubby's—now known by the cumbersome title Grandma's The Original Chubby's—still stands, on the corner of 38th and Lipan Avenues, run by Stella's grandson Danny Cordova, whom she raised like a son and who took care of her in the last decades of her regency. Danny hasn't changed much in the three years since her passing—the calendars, for one, now have a portrait of Stella and her husband, Alex, a former oil worker to whom she was married for nearly seventy years, creating a family forest of hundreds of grandchildren, great-grandchildren, and even more generations. Danny is rightfully protective: all the takeout menus, the ones with the angelic portrait of Stella and Alex, blare at the bottom "NOT AFFILIATED WITH ANY OTHER CHUBBY'S," and above the entrance is a sign listing the many imitators they disavow—principal among them Bubba Chinos.

There you go, folks: America's five greatest Mexican dishes. Send me angry letters—isn't that the point of lists? You can disagree with my choices, but you cannot understand the allure of Mexican food without trying these places. Americans: unite under Mexican food, just like your ancestors, just like your descendants! It doesn't matter your dish choice: it'll be sometimes derided, sometimes mysterious, oftentimes scorching, and not always good, but always, always eaten. A *lot*.

Conclusion

What Happens After the Burrito Has Gone Cosmic?

S O . . . what. Does. It. All Mean.

Don't worry, folks: I won't pontificate here *too* much. The purpose of this book is not just to cover a cuisine whose history barely registers in the official American story, but to make *ustedes* hungry. I want not only to make you desire Mexican food, but also to understand it, to appreciate it further. To make you realize that whether you're inhaling a burrito, crunching through a hard taco, getting *borracho* on mescal, or prepping to make a mole that'll impress your friends, every Mexican foodstuff has a story and didn't just drop into our scene deus ex machina . . . save Jesus on a tortilla.

Most important, however, what I hope everyone gets by reading this book is a sense of awe—not just at the great flavors of Mexican cuisine, but also at its chameleonic qualities that ensure Americans will never tire of the tradition. That's how I got here in the first place: I began thinking about this book in the beginning of 2007—long before I even had a discussion with my editor about the possibility of trying to attempt the feat. It wasn't my lifelong relationship with Mexico that triggered the thought, or even the excitement of digging up long-buried anecdotes, but rather Korean tacos.

In early 2007, a photographer named Dylan Ho, who blogs at Eat Drink + Be Merry, reminisced on his site about a barbecue five years earlier while he attended school at the University of California, Irvine where he and friends grilled carne asada for tacos and *kalbi* (Korean-style ribs) for noshing. After hours of eating and drinking, the carne asada was gone, but kalbi remained, as well as tortillas. A drunken Ho suggested the party put the kalbi in the tortillas and use Sriracha and the spicy Korean side dish kimchi for heat, since partygoers had tapped out the salsa as well. Ho threw in cilantro, green onions, and guacamole. "Honestly it was good . . . for being drunk," he wrote.

In the present day, a sober Ho tried to re-create those Korean tacos in his kitchen, adding sesame seeds to accentuate its Korean nature. He offered them to another blogger, who thought they were okay.

"Would these do well in the L.A./Koreatown area? Probably not," Dylan admitted on his blog. "Hey! Guys like weird food. We like Yoshinoya—girls don't! But, one day, if you happen to see a shoddy taco truck running on one spare tire, spitting out black exhaust with Korean & Spanish written on it . . . it's probably yours truly." In addition to publishing pictures of his kalbi taco, Dylan photoshopped a lonchera with Hangul script that read, "Kim's Taco."[1]

Such a cross-cultural offering was genius, and simultaneously revolutionary and revelatory to me. How did Korean college kids know about the cuisine of my life, let alone enjoy that *comida* and shape it toward their culture? Oh, I knew about the Oki dog, and had enjoyed pastrami burritos for years, so the idea of cross-pollination wasn't exactly foreign to my belly. In my days as a cub reporter, I even did a series of stories showing the similarities between Vietnamese and Mexican food. But to combine them, and celebrate the commingling of Mexican and something else as awesome? An earlier me would have dismissed the idea as heresy; the mature me wanted to eat them. And fast.

Ho's post set off a commenting frenzy. "Well done, my friend," one wrote. "I think you've stumbled upon culinary serendipity." Ho didn't know how prescient those words were, as they fundamentally changed the course of Mexican food in the United States for like the thirtieth time ever.

One of Ho's readers was Alice Shin, whose brother-in-law, Mark Manguera, already had an idea for a Korean taco truck after eating tacos to cap a late night of bar-hopping but hadn't yet embarked on the concept. Together the two of them settled upon turning Ho's joke into reality by renting a truck—but they needed a chef. They contacted Roy Choi, the son of Korean immigrants who had grown up in Orange County, graduated from the Culinary Institute of America, and had cooked at Le Bernadin but grew tired of the restaurant industry. Choi took charge of the cuisine; Manguera handled the numbers; and Shin became the social media maven, creating a strategy in which they eschewed press releases and mainstream reporters in favor of social media. And Shin's mother provided the *bulgogi* recipe. The Kogi BBQ Truck was born.

It was only upon researching for this book that I discovered that Korean-Mexican hybrids had actually popped up in Los Angeles restaurants during the mid-1990s, most notably at José Bernstein, a dive near the University of California at Los Angeles, where they sold burritos stuffed with kimchi and bulgogi. But for the Kogi crew to sell the fusion as hipness instead of mere belly stuffers for undergrads, in an era where social media took the most mundane topics and turned them into buzz, was genius—and then, the deluge.

In October 2008, Shin sent out invites to select, influential Southern California food bloggers for a free November tasting, in the hopes that they might offer feedback on their Kogi idea. "YES. K-town Tacos. Drippy, meaty bulgogi, dak kalbi (chicken kalbi), and spicy pork tacos. (NOT carnitas, though they are just as delicious)," she wrote in one e-mail. "I am NOT asking you to do a blog entry about it *(though if you wanted to, you could feel totally free to do so). Thanks so much for taking the time to read my email and I do hope you all get to come join us and help us bring the most bomb arse K-town tacos to the peoples."[2]

Kogi BBQ Truck debuted in late December, to almost instantaneous praise. The initial menu focused on tacos and burritos—the meat was Korean, the tortilla Mexican, the shredded cheese American, and the seamless ingenuity pure Southern California. "We're Korean, but we're American and we grew up in L.A.," said Choi shortly after Kogi's unveiling. "It's not a stigma food, it's a representation of who we are . . . everything you get in that taco is what we live in L.A. . . . That was our goal. To take everything about L.A. and put it into one bite—it's Mexican, it's Korean, it's organic, it's California, it's farmer's market, it's drunk people after midnight."[3]

Within weeks, Kogi inspired hundreds-long lines across Southern California; within a couple of months, the national media swooped in; by the end of that first year, they'd made about $2 million in sales. Almost immediately, hipsters who had long patronized loncheras began creating their own spins, all copying the Kogi model of manufactured excitement. Kogi spawned a bona fide movement that transcended even Mexican food. Soon food trucks followed Kogi like remoras; then those competitors set up in parking lots—first a couple, then a dozen, the happenings growing larger and larger, attracting bigger crowds each time until they numbered into the tens of thousands. Choi was named best new chef by *Food & Wine* in 2010, the first time a food truck purveyor had won the honor, an almost-impossible-to-imagine achievement just four years earlier.

Across the country, other young cooks abandoned restaurant careers for the allure of the food truck. Most navigated through antiquated laws that prohibited or severely curtailed the selling of food from trucks—some written back in the days of the original tamale men, others crafted to meet the pioneer loncheras in the 1980s and 1990s—and enlisted help to chip away at them; cities, desperate for new tax streams, complied even though many had opposed traditional loncheras when they attempted the same just years before. And a movement swept across the land, with these luxe loncheras making cool and acceptable what Mexicans have been doing for nigh onto eighty years. Their light has dimmed a bit as of this writing in the winter of 2011, but it will be a phenomenon with long-standing repercussions—and it was a taco that started it all.

I would have loved to speak to Choi. But in the summer of 2010, when I contacted Kogi to request an interview, Shin said he had just embarked on a six-month sabbatical in which media interviews were forbidden, promising that he'd be available the following year. When 2011 came around, I e-mailed Shin again; this time she had "a few questions prior to considering involvement with your book project," wanting to know if this book was "confirmed to be published" and "when and with which publishing house? Or is this an independent work-in-progress project?"

It is absolutely a work in progress, Alice. For while this book is nearing its end, the love affair between the United States and Mexican food continues its eternal dance, like the sun chasing the moon across the sky.

Mexican curio, regional American treat, nationwide fad, complete assimilation: this is the course of Mexican food in the United States. It happened to tamales and chili con carne, to the hard shell and soft taco, to burritos and tequila, salsa and tortilla chips, chocolate and Southwestern chicken salad, canned food and loncheras. From barrios to restaurants to supermarkets to school cafeterias. Consumers forget the pioneers, but the legacies of William Gebhardt's Mexican dinner packages, Larry Cano's sit-down Mexican eateries, Elmer Doolin's Fritos, Mariano Martinez's frozen margarita machine, Bertha Haffner-Ginger's Mexican cooking classes, and so many others reverberate decades after their innovations—and more are to come.

So if Mexican food has graced the heavens, has spread to dozens of countries around the world—if every possible manifestation has been subsumed in the United States over the span of 130 years, and reloads seemingly each decade, then what's the future of Mexican food in this country?

Hey, if I knew, I wouldn't be a writer. I'd open the next Chipotle, the next California Chicken Tamale Company, import a tequila no one has yet heard of. But I *can* divine one thing: in Mexican food's rumble through this country, in the trail behind and the road ahead, I see us—always evolving, never stagnant, continually striving for something better, consistently delicious. The American spirit manifested as a combo plate, heavy on the salsa.

Now excuse me while I finish off some Korean tacos washed down with a bottle of Mexican Coke.

Postscript

Special "¡Ask a Mexican!" Question: How and why did the image of a sleeping Mexican under a saguaro cactus become such a popular mascot for Mexican restaurants?

What, you think I'm not going to take an opportunity to plug my syndicated column (and book) in some way, shape, or form? But at least this shameless inclusion is relevant to this tome.

One of the big questions I had in doing research for this book was discovering the origins of an image that exists in Mexican restaurants from San Diego to Baltimore to Bangkok and all around the world: the sleeping Mexican in sombrero and serape, sleeping under a saguaro cactus. How did the image become ubiquitous, especially since the saguaro grows only in the Sonoran desert and is hardly the most popular cactus in Mexico? But instead of offering my own explanation, I turn the page over to Maribel Alvarez, a professor at the University of Arizona and one of the founders of Sabores sin Fronteras/Flavors without Borders, which seeks to preserve and celebrate the unique foodways of the Arizona-Sonora border: the land of wheat tortillas as large as basketball hoops, Sonoran hot dogs, shredded beef cured under the sun, and other traditions I didn't focus enough on in this book. She's the world's leading expert on the history of the sleeping Mexican, and she graciously summarized her forthcoming book on the subject into the following mini-essay:

The short answer is that the sleeping Mexican became popular because, despite a boatload of inglorious uses of the image as stereotype, the image is also ambiguous, functioning in the iconic world of advertisement for many working-class Mexicans and Mexican-American restaurants as an emotional and residual reference to Mexico's indigenous, rural, hardworking, thrifty, and resourceful populations ("*la gente humilde*") and a folk culture that places value on balance, rest, nourishment, and relaxation in order to carry on. Jill Janis of Tucson has collected dozens of Yellow Pages from all over the United States as well as Europe with the image associated to Mexican restaurants and motels (presumably, invitations for the weary traveler); her extensive collection includes more than two thousand pieces, from matchboxes to lamps, clothing, and antique furniture, that depict the image.

The earliest known representations of the image were not visual and did not include the saguaro; the large cactus indigenous to the U.S. Southwest desertlands was most likely added as a redundant reference to vacationing (resting) in the American Southwest in the post–World War II era, when widespread automobile ownership facilitated travel to border towns for middle-class Anglo families. Generally known as the Sleeping Mexican, but also frequently described simply as "Pancho" (some people think as a reference to Pancho Villa being a champion of the working poor against oligarchy) or as the Siesta Motif, the earliest references were written descriptions of travelers to Mexico between 1880 and 1920 who observed the common practice of Mexican Indians wrapping themselves in blankets to catch some rest while leaning against a wall. The image was considered by Anglo visitors to Mexico "picturesque" and started to gain popularity in the United States.

Not everyone at first imputed negative meanings to the supine, huddled, or squatting position of the peasant depicted; Diego Rivera included it in an early drawing circa 1920 as a straightforward representation of the farmhands who enriched the large landowners. In the context of late-nineteenth-century U.S. expanding economic interests in Mexico, however, in railroad, mining, agricultural holdings, and oil industries, the image became associated with the despised (yet necessary) labor force of the Mexican peon, and derogatory associations to laziness, lack of initiative, and the "mañana syndrome" stuck to the image. Anglos were not the sole creators of this prevalent view: Mexican elites working with the regime of dictator Porfirio Díaz advanced these same beliefs about peasants and Indians. For this reason, the image's interpretation varies considerably across class lines, with working-class *mexicanos* often identifying with the image as symbol of hard work and endurance and calling any negative association of the image to laziness an absurd, illogical distortion that only a racist would fathom. For Chicanos or Mexican Americans who fight for civil rights issues it is nearly impossible to overlook the negative implications of the image (for example, depicted as a neighbor's offensive lawn ornament in an episode in the George Lopez show in 2007 titled "George Can't Let Sleeping Mexicans Lie"). Many Chicano/a artists, however, have taken a different route to the stereotype, refashioning it into parody, calling out its original references to the working masses, and attributing to its huddled position imaginary scenarios of quietly "spying" on the powerful, or pretending to be quiet only to "wake up" and take his/her place, or simply as a Mexican in America dreaming up a more just society.

Notes

Introduction: What's So Cosmic About a Burrito?

1   Sandra Magnus's Journal, "Food and Cooking in Space." Online at nasa
    .gov/mission_pages/station/expeditions/expedition18/journal_sandra
    _magnus_6_prt.htm.

Chapter One: You Mean Mexico Gave the World More Than Just Tacos?

1   Bartolomé de las Casas, *Historia de las Indias* (1561).

2   Bernal Díaz de Castillo, *Historia Verdadera de la Conquista de la Nueva
    España* (1575).

3   Manuel Orozco y Berra, *Historia Antigua y de la Conquista de Mexico,
    Cuarta Parte: La Conquista* (1880).

4   Castillo, *Historia Verdadera.*

5   Ibid.

6   Miguel León-Portilla, ed., *The Broken Spears: The Aztec Account of the
    Conquest of Mexico* (1960).

7   As documented in Pilcher, Jeffrey, M., *¡Que vivan los tamales!: Food and
    the Making of Mexican Identity* (Albuquerque: University of New Mexico
    Press, 1998).

8   *About Vanilla* (Boston: Joseph Burnett Company, 1900).

9   International Cocoa Organization figures (2011).

Notes

Chapter Two: Whatever Happened to the Chili Queens and Tamale Kings?

1 Edward King, "Glimpses of Texas," *Scribner's Monthly* (1874).

2 Stephen Gould, *Alamo City Guide* (1882).

3 Lee C. Harby, "Texas: Types and Contrasts," *Harper's New Monthly Magazine* (June–November 1890).

4 *Favorite dishes: A Columbian autograph souvenir cookery book. Over three hundred autograph recipes, and twenty-three portraits, contributed by the Board of lady managers of the World's Columbian exposition* (1893).

5 Frank H. Bushick, "The Chile Queens of San Antonio," *Frontier Times* (July 1927).

6 See *Washington Post* (December 21, 1881).

7 "Detailed List of the Exhibits from the United States," *Universal Exposition Paris,* vol. 5 (1889).

8 Mary E. Green, M.D., *Food Products of the World* (1895).

9 Charles Ramsdell, *San Antonio: A Historical and Pictorial Guide* (Austin: University of Texas Press, 1959).

10 As quoted in Benjamin Botkin, ed., *Sidewalks of America: Folklore, Legends, Sagas, Traditions, Customs, Songs, Stories, and Sayings of City Folk* (Indianapolis: Bobs Merrill, 1954).

11 Sigmund Krausz, *Street Types of Chicago* (1891).

12 Sigmund Krausz, *Street Types of Great American Cities* (1896).

13 See *Sunday World-Herald Omaha* (May 12, 1895); *Atlantic Monthly* (1898).

14 "A Tamale Tragedy," *Boston Journal* (May 31, 1895). The story actually deals with someone who ate too many tamales too fast.

15 *Epicure* (September 1901).

16 *Brooklyn Eagle* (September 4, 1894).

17 Mary E. Blain, *Games for All Occasions* (1909).

18 *St. Louis Republic* (March 9, 1900).

19 *Brooklyn Eagle* (February 18, 1913).

20 "Wienerwurst Man Has Regular Customers," *Syracuse Journal* (October 6, 1904).

21 See "A Contribution Towards a Vocabulary of Spanish and Mexican Words Used in Texas," *Dialect Notes* (American Dialect Society, 1896).

22 "The Lakeside City," *San Francisco Chronicle* (February 14, 1892).

23 Ibid.

24 "By the Lakeside," *San Francisco Chronicle* (April 3, 1892).

25 "By the Lakeside," *San Francisco Chronicle* (July 24, 1892).

26 *New York Herald* (November 5, 1893).

27 As quoted in the *Ventura Democrat* in the *Los Angeles Times* (December 14, 1895).

28 "Under the Dome," *San Francisco Chronicle* (October 27, 1893).

29 "Swinging into Line," *San Francisco Chronicle* (October 27, 1893).

30 Ninetta Eames, "The Wild and Wooly at the Fair," *Overland Monthly* (April 1894).

31 "Market Curiosities," *Good Housekeeping* (January 1894).

32 "Hot Tamales Return with the Corn," *Chicago Daily Tribune* (August 31, 1896).

33 "Report of the Immigration Commission: Immigrants in Industries (in Twenty-five Parts), Part 25: Japanese and Other Immigrant Races in the Pacific Coast and Rocky Mountain States." United States Immigration Commission, 1911.

34 "Hot Tamales Street Sale Is Barred by Police," *San Francisco Examiner* (July 21, 1917).

35 "Rediscovering San Francisco," *San Francisco Examiner* (February 28, 1925).

36 "Evolution of the Chicken Tamale," *San Francisco Examiner* (July 14, 1895).

37 E. W. Cahill, "Builders of Business," *Magazine of Business* (January 1920).

38 See *Honolulu Independent* (June 7, 1899).

39 *Catalogue of exhibitors in the United States sections of the International Universal Exposition, Paris, 1900.*

40 "A California Industry Honored at Paris," *San Francisco Call* (September 23, 1900).

41 *Canning Age* (June 1922).

42 "Label Collecting Work Is Growing," *Daily Call* (April 21, 1913).

43 Cahill, "Builders of Business."

44 Frank Morton Todd, *The Story of the Exposition; Being the Official History of the International Celebration Held at San Francisco in 1915 to Com-*

memorate the Discovery of the Pacific Ocean and the Construction of the Panama Canal (1921).

45 "Demonstration of Table Delicacies at Anthony Horderns," *Sydney Morning Herald* (April 30, 1918).

46 "What Has Become of the 'Tamale Man'?" *Official Year Book and State Labor Manual of the California State Federation of Labor* (1916).

Chapter Three: How Did the Taco Become Popular Before Mexicans Flooded the United States?

1 The earliest recipe for tacos I could find was in *Recetas Practicas para la Señora de Casa (Practical Recipes for the Woman of the House)*, an 1893 collection of recipes drawn from women who were raising funds for a hospital in the city of Guadalajara—but they used the term *taquitos* to describe how to shape a dessert.

2 Olive Percival, "An Idler's Note-Book," *Los Angeles Times* (1899).

3 *Los Angeles Herald* (August 28, 1880).

4 "Peripatetic Restaurants," *Los Angeles Times* (December 30, 1901).

5 "Hot Tamale Men," *Los Angeles Times* (December 20, 1901).

6 "Tamale Politicians to Petition Council," *Los Angeles Times* (February 9, 1903).

7 "Lunch Wagons Go," *Los Angeles Times* (February 25, 1924).

8 Raul Rodriguez, "Do You Know That . . . ," *Los Angeles Times* (May 17, 1931).

9 "News of Food," *New York Times* (May 3, 1952).

10 This and all subsequent Bell quotes are taken from Debra Lee Baldwin, *Taco Titan: The Glen Bell Story* (Sarasota, Fla.: Bookworld Services, 1999).

11 Justin Gooderl Longenecker and Maria Estela Tena Loeza, *Small Business Management* (2010).

Chapter Four: Who Were the Enchilada Millionaires, and How Did They Change Mexican Food?

1 "Spanish Dinner," *Los Angeles Times* (January 27, 1887).

2 "The Social World," *Los Angeles Times* (May 12, 1889).

3 "An Appetite for Success: Ramon Gallardo Shows Off His Restaurant Savvy with Ramón's Jalapeño," *St. Louis Commerce* (September 1993).

4 Ibid.

5 John Greenwald, Sheila Gribben, and Janice C. Simpson, "The Enchilada Millionaires," *Time* (November 29, 1982).

Chapter Five: How Did Americans Become Experts at Writing Cookbooks on Mexican Food?

1 Jonathan Gold, "What Is a Burrito? A Primer," *LA Weekly* (October 22, 2009).

2 "Letter to the *Chillicothe Leader*, Nov. 25, 1884" (reprinted in Charles Fletcher Lummis, *Letters from the Southwest*, James W. Byrkit, ed.) (Tucson: University of Arizona Press, 1989).

3 Ibid.

4 Charles Fletcher Lummis, ed., *The Landmarks Club Cook Book* (1903).

5 Corinne King, "Spanish Dainties," *Los Angeles Times* (1898).

6 "Seventy Recipes for the Spanish Dishes," *Los Angeles Times* (May 22, 1902).

7 "Progress at the *Times* School of Domestic Science," *Los Angeles Times* (April 22, 1913).

8 Bertha Haffner-Ginger, *California Mexican-Spanish Cook Book* (1914).

9 "New Cooking Classes to Open Today," *Los Angeles Times* (September 7, 1932).

10 Elena Zelayeta, *Elena* (Englewood Cliffs, N.J.: Prentice-Hall, 1960).

11 Elena Zelayeta, *Elena's Favorite Foods, California Style* (Englewood Cliffs, N.J.: Prentice-Hall, 1967).

12 Norman Vincent Peale, *The Amazing Results of Positive Thinking* (1959).

13 Craig Claiborne, *A Feast Made for Laughter: A Memoir with Recipes* (New York: Holt, 1983).

14 Craig Claiborne, "Cooking Classes Should Please Armchair Travelers," *New York Times* (September 8, 1970).

15 Diana Kennedy, *The Cuisines of Mexico* (New York: Harper & Row, 1972).

16 Alison Cook, "La Reina Diana," *Texas Monthly* (June 1985).

17 JeanMarie Brownson, "Mexican-Food Enthusiasts Put the Accent on Authenticity," *Chicago Tribune* (April 2, 1987).

18 Ruth Reichl, "First Impressions," *Los Angeles Times* (April 5, 1985).

Chapter Six: Whatever Happened to Southwestern Cuisine?

1 Marc Simmons, *New Mexico: An Interpretive History* (Santa Fe: University of New Mexico Press, 1988).

2 George Peter Hammond and Agapito Rey, *Narratives of the Coronado Expedition, 1540–1542*, vol. 2 (Albuquerque: University of New Mexico Press, 1940).

3 James Harvey Simpson, *Journal of a Military Reconnaissance from Santa Fe, New Mexico, to the Navajo Country* (Philadelphia: Lippincott, Grambo, & Company, 1852).

4 Charles Fletcher Lummis, *The Land of Poco Tiempo* (New York: Charles Scribner's Sons, 1897).

5 Pearl Cherry Miller, *Mexican Cookery: A Thesis* (Las Cruces: New Mexico State University Press, 1904).

6 Chris Wilson, *The Myth of Santa Fe: Creating a Modern Regional Tradition* (Albuquerque: University of New Mexico Press, 1997).

7 Ibid.

8 Antonio Goubaud Carrera, "Food Patterns and Nutrition in Two Spanish-American Communities" (1943).

9 George I. Sanchez, *The Forgotten People: A Study of New Mexicans* (Albuquerque: University of New Mexico Press, 1996).

10 Cleofas Martinez Jaramillo, *Romance of a Little Village Girl* (San Antonio, Tex.: Naylor, 1955).

11 Fabiola Cabeza de Baca Gilbert, *Historic Cookery* (Layton, Utah: Gibbs Smith, 1997).

12 Ibid.

13 Fabiola Cabeza de Baca Gilbert, *We Fed Them Cactus* (Albuquerque: University of New Mexico Press, 1954).

14 See Victoria E. Dye, *All Aboard for Santa Fe: Railway Promotion of the Southwest, 1890s to 1930s* (Santa Fe: University of New Mexico Press, 2005).

15 Barbara Hansen, "Timeless and Trendy," *Los Angeles Times* (December 1, 1983).

16 Ibid.

17 Craig Claiborne, "French Style Enlivening Native Foods of Southwest," *New York Times* (January 9, 1985).

18 Barbara Hansen, "'. . . But We All Agree It Tastes Good,'" *Los Angeles Times* (April 18, 1985).

Chapter Seven: Is Tex-Mex Food Doomed?

1 From David J. Weber, ed., *Personal Memoirs of John N. Seguín, From the Year 1834 to the Retreat of General Wall from the City of San Antonio*, as published in *Foreigners in Their Native Land: Historical Roots of the Mexican Americans* (Albuquerque: University of New Mexico Press, 1973).

2 Diana Kennedy, *The Cuisines of Mexico* (New York: Harper & Row, 1972).

3 Patricia Sharpe, "Let's Have Mex-Tex," *Texas Monthly* (December 2010).

4 *New York Daily Tribune* (December 13, 1886).

5 "At a Mexican Breakfast," *New York Sun* (December 19, 1886).

6 Ibid.

7 John G. Bourke, "The Folk-Foods of the Rio Grande Valley and of Northern Mexico," *Journal of American Folklore* (July–September 1894).

8 Ibid.

9 *Brenham Weekly Banner* (November 22, 1878).

10 *Shiner Gazette* (November 21, 1907).

11 *Rotarian* (June 1922).

12 "Mexican Fajitas Spicing Up Menus Across the Country," *Nation's Restaurant News* (March 25, 1985).

13 Anne Linsey Greer and Michael Bauer, "With Tex-Mex, Try a Pouilly Fumé," *Philadelphia Inquirer* (October 30, 1985).

14 "Roast of the Town," *Texas Monthly* (July 1980).

Chapter Eight: What Took the Burrito So Long to Become Popular?

1 I wish that I coined this phrase, but it's taken from John Rohmer, "Cylindrical God," *SF Weekly* (1993).

2   I can't find the article, but I swear I read it when I spoke at Missouri State in the fall of 2010.

3   Feliz Ramos I. Duarte, *Diccionario de Mejicanismos* (1895).

4   "An Oral History with Cecil Marks," OH 1858, Center for Oral and Public History, California State University at Fullerton.

5   Robert S. Saito, *My Life in Camps During the Wars* (2006).

6   Anais Acosta, "Jesus Silva," in Bracero History Archive, item 143, braceroarchive.org/items/show/143 (accessed April 25, 2011).

7   Interview with Fernando Rodríguez by Fernanda Carrillo (March 5, 2003), interview 51, Institute of Oral History, University of Texas at El Paso.

8   See Francisco Arturo Rosales, *Chicano! The History of the Mexican American Civil Rights Movement.*

9   "Burritos Gaining a Foothold in U.S.," *Los Angeles Times* (May 7, 1964); "Burritos Anyone Can Make at Home," ibid. (November 4, 1965).

10 *El Bohemio* (August 1981).

11 Peter Fox, "Burritos—a Search for Beginnings," *Washington Post* (November 4, 1998).

12 John Roehmer, "Cylindrical God."

13 Marie Bianco, "Burritos. They're poised to take Manhattan. In pure California style, they arrive wrapped, a foot long," *Newsday* (October 18, 1989).

Chapter Nine: When Did Mexicans Start Making Food for Mexicans?

1   *New York Sun* (June 2, 1905).

2   Francisco J. Santamaria, ed., *Diccionario general de americanismos* (1959).

3   "Katy Jurado Wants Us to Take Up the Taco," *Chicago Daily Tribune* (May 23, 1958).

4   Robb Walsh, as quoted in "Mexico City Tex-Mex," *Houston Press* (September 4, 2003).

5   Robb Walsh, *The Tex-Mex Cookbook: A History in Recipes and Photos* (New York: Broadway, 2004).

6 See Robb Walsh, *The Tex-Mex Grill and Backyard Barbacoa Cookbook* (New York: Broadway, 2010), p. 158. The company he mentions is B. Martinez Sons, which we'll discuss in the next chapter.

7 Luis Felipe Recinos, "Vendimas por la calles," in the Manuel Gamio Papers, Bancroft Library, University of California at Berkeley.

8 Craig Claiborne, "From a Taste of Taco, a New Shop," *New York Times* (November 21, 1966).

9 Jesus Sanchez, "Taco Trucks Put Aspiring Immigrants on Wheels," *Los Angeles Times* (November 16, 1987).

10 Craig Claiborne, "Memorable Dishes from a Master Mexican Chef," *New York Times* (July 21, 1982).

11 Craig Claiborne, "All-American Menus for the Economic Summit," *New York Times* (May 18, 1983).

12 Nancy Harmon Jenkins, "It's Called Mexican, but Is It Genuine?," *New York Times* (April 23, 1986).

Chapter Ten: How Did Mexican Food Get into Our Supermarkets?

1 "San Antonio Siftings," *Galveston Daily News* (May 9, 1879).

2 "Chili-con-Carne," *San Antonio Evening Light* (May 27, 1882).

3 *San Antonio Daily Express* (December 26, 1885).

4 Gebhardt Chili Powder Co., *Mexican Cooking* (San Antonio, 1911).

5 "Visitors Will Get Mexican Dinner," *Light* (August 3, 1924).

6 *Rotarian* (November 1923).

7 Randall Benham, "A Lot Like It Hot," *Texas Parade* (February 1976).

8 "Ventura Brevities," *Los Angeles Times* (May 26, 1900).

9 Frank J. Mangan, *Bordertown* (El Paso: C. Hertzog, 1964).

10 See Patricia Bowman, "History of Ashley's Incorporated and a Sketch of Its Founder, George N. Ashley, Sr." (May 1955). Available at the University of Texas, El Paso, special collections.

11 *El Paso Herald-Post* (April 21, 1934).

12 "Mammoth Café Business Told," *El Paso Herald-Post* (October 14, 1936).

13 Ibid.

14 Ibid.

15 "E. P. Tortillas, *Herald-Post* Go to Persian Gulf," *El Paso Herald-Post* (October 10, 1938).

16 Susan Guerrero, "The Real Rosarita," *Saveur* (February 2008).

17 Dean Smith, *La Gloria Escondida: The Guerrero Story* (Phoenix: Sims, 1967).

Chapter Eleven: Is the Tortilla God's Favored Method of Communication?

1 Nicholas C. Chriss, "Thousands View 'Jesus on a Tortilla,'" *Los Angeles Times* (July 23, 1978).

2 Ibid.

3 "Annual Survey of Manufactures: General Statistics: Statistics for Industry Groups and Industries: 2009 and 2008," 2009. NAICS; 2002 NAICS 311830.

4 Francisco Bulmes, *El porvenir de las naciones Hispano-Americanas ante las conquistas recientes de Europa y los Estados Unidos* (Mexico City: Imprenta de Mariano Nava, 1899).

5 See Jeffrey M. Pilcher, *¡Que Vivan los Tamales! Food and the Making of Mexican Identity* (Albuquerque: University of New Mexico Press, 1998).

6 "Seventy Recipes for the Spanish Dishes," *Los Angeles Times* (May 22, 1902).

7 Jessup Whitehead, *The American Pastry Cook*, 7th ed. (Chicago: Whitehead, 1894).

8 May E. Southworth. *One Hundred & One Mexican Dishes* (San Francisco: Elder, 1906).

9 "Family Tradition," http://www.angelfire.com/tx2/martinez/chip.html.

10 Filed July 18, 1932.

11 "Maury Mavericks Round Up S.A. Friends," *San Antonio Light* (April 18, 1937).

12 Letter from Roy G. Martinez to Vanessa Fonseca (November 10, 2003).

13 "El Nacimiento de Un Coloso," http://www.gruma.com/noticias/seccion_3/articulo_47/Pagina_140.asp.

14 *San Antonio Express* (July 10, 1932).

15 "The Birth of the Frito," *Morning Edition*, National Public Radio (October 18, 2007).

16 *Life* (October 3, 1949).

17 In the Southern California baseball fields of my youth, we knew them as Chili Billies, but they were sold only during Little League season.

18 "Charles E. Doolin, Founded Frito Co.," *New York Times* (July 24, 1959).

19 William Dampier, *A New Voyage Round the World* (1717).

20 See Jeffrey Charles, "Searching for Gold in Guacamole: California Growers Market the Avocado, 1910–1994," in *Food Nations: Selling Taste in Consumer Societies* (London: Routledge, 2001).

21 Stacy Feducia, "Nacho, Nacho Men: Ballpark Staple Got Start in Arlington," *Fort Worth Star-Telegram* (September 20, 1997).

22 Chris Petersen, "The Big Cheese: Ricos Products Created Stadium Nachos and Builds on Their Success," *Food and Drink* (March 22, 2011).

Chapter Twelve: How Did Salsa Become America's Top-Selling Condiment?

1 "Ketchup vs. Salsa: By the Numbers," *Wall Street Journal* (September 20, 2007).

2 "Salsa Outsells Ketchup in U.S. Stores," *Weekend Edition*, National Public Radio (April 11, 1992).

3 Marian Burros, "Vegetable Power: Doing the Tecate Tone-Up," *Washington Post* (June 23, 1977).

4 Molly O'Neill, "New Mainstream: Hot Dogs, Apple Pie, and Salsa," *Los Angeles Times* (March 11, 1992).

5 "Texans Add New Spice to Hot Salsa Market: Lawsuits," *Los Angeles Times* (May 23, 1983).

6 See ad in *Texas Monthly* (October 1985), p. 195.

7 "Family-Held Company Tops Mexican Hot Sauce Market," *San Antonio Executive* (August 11, 1986).

8 Florence Fabricant, "Riding Salsa's Coast-to-Coast Wave of Popularity," *New York Times* (June 2, 1993).

9 O'Neill, "New Mainstream."

10 Ibid.

11 "Pace Mexican Sauces Stampede into . . . New York City?! 'Get a Rope!,'" PR Newswire (July 19, 1995).

Chapter Thirteen: Tequila? Tequila!

1 "México tiene liderato en exportación cervecera," *El Economista* (July 5, 2011).

2 "U.S. Tequila Market at a Glance," Distilled Spirits Council of the United States (February 2011); "Tequila Gaining U.S. Favor; Sales Up 6-Fold Since '70," *New York Times* (April 7, 1975).

3 *Los Angeles Daily Herald* (April 25, 1882).

4 "At a Mexican Breakfast," *New York Sun* (December 19, 1886).

5 "Will Build San Rafael Plant to Make Tequila," *San Francisco Chronicle* (November 11, 1907).

6 "Drys Raid Tequila Plant," *Los Angeles Times* (August 16, 1926).

7 "Tequila Drinking," *Los Angeles Times* (June 21, 1924).

8 Joanne Herschfield, "Race and Class in the Classical Cinema," in *Mexico's Cinema: A Century of Film and Filmmakers,* ed. Joanne Herschfield and David R. Maciel (Lanham, Md.: Rowman & Littlefield, 1999).

9 Robert Berrellez, "Mexicans Seeking Prestige for Tequila," *Los Angeles Times* (October 11, 1964).

10 Craig Claiborne, "Margarita Is Now Competing with Bloody Mary at Cocktail Hour," *New York Times* (February 9, 1966).

11 "National Museum of American History Acquires Frozen Margarita Machine," National Museum of American History (September 28, 2005).

Chapter Fourteen: What Are the Five Greatest Mexican Meals in the United States?

1 A term created elsewhere but pushed by myself and fellow bloggers at the *OC Weekly*'s food blog, Stick a Fork in It, as the descriptive noun for a gathering of food trucks. If you can think of a better term, please let me know—but isn't it perfect?

Notes

2 "Fire at Chico's Tacos Leads to Angry Customers," *El Paso Times* (February 16, 2008).

3 Harrison Fletcher, "The Heat Is On: For the Cordova Family, the Forecast Is Always Chile," *Westword* (August 3, 2000).

4 Adam Cayton-Holland, "Smothered: The Saga of the Chubby's Empire," *Westword* (November 29, 2007).

Conclusion: What Happens After the Burrito Has Gone Cosmic?

1 Dylan Ho, "Korean-Mexican Fusion: Korean BBQ Kalbi Tacos?" eatdrinknbemerry.blogspot.com (January 29, 2007).

2 E-mail correspondence (October 14, 2008).

3 Zach Behrens, "Eat This: Korean BBQ with the Edge of a Street Taco," laist.com (December 4, 2008).

ACKNOWLEDGMENTS

Where to begin? I know! This book would've been impossible without the women of my childhood: my mom, aunts, sisters, grandmas, *comadres,* cousins, and the moms, aunts, sisters, grandmas, *comadres,* and cousins of my friends who instilled in me from a young age a love for Mexican food. I got lucky: all of those *mujeres* were amazing cooks who ensured I was always fed, from when I was a small boy until today.

This book also would've been impossible without the wonderful people at Scribner, who long ago put their faith and publishing power in me to the tune of three books. Brant, Anna, Cody, Susan, Nan, and the rest of the gang: *gracias* for believing in me, and sorry it took so long to finish this book—but I do believe it was all worth it.

And it would've been especially impossible without the *chingones* over at Kuhn Projects, which started as a two-man operation and is growing and growing. David and Billy are my main guys there, but to the rest of the crew: *gracias.*

Those are the professional, sincere thanks. Now, on to the personal:

To my *mujer,* Delilah, whom I love so much. Your fish tacos are the best around. Now, time to teach you how to make *asado de boda.*

To Marge, the cutest face in the world!

To my nuclear and extended family, for your support, love, and many *carne asada* Sundays.

To my employers, Village Voice Media, specifically my perpetually drunk mick overlords, Mike Lacey and Jim Larkin, and my always supportive boss, Andy Vandevoorde: *gracias* for being so supportive of my extracurricular activities.

To my inglorious basterds over at the *OC Weekly*—each one of you deserves your own book. Get to it!

To my forkers over at *Stick a Fork in It*: You, too!

To my friends who joined me on multiple eating expeditions over the years for this: Art, Theresa, Lea, Monet and Andrew, Plas, Vic, Randy, Frank, Danny, Dave and Linnea, Jackie and Rudy, Gabriel San Blogman, the Centro crew, William Nericcio, and all the friends I have on Facebook whom space does not allow me to list.

To all the wonderful food people in Southern California who kept me drunk and filled for this: Memphis at the Santora, the Crosby, Break of Dawn, Javier Cabral, Bill Esparza, Russ Parsons, and so many more.

To all the librarians who helped me along the way, from San Francisco to San Antonio to most of Orange County, but especially the crew at the Fullerton Public Library. If this book becomes a best seller, new microfilm machines!

To the amazing people over at the Chicana and Chicano Studies Department at Cal State Fullerton: Professor Jefe Alexandro José Gradilla, the CASA kids, and all the students who have ever taken my classes. Be nice to Sonia or she'll get *gangsta*!

To everyone who sat down with me for this book, whether the interview went in or not: your insights were invaluable.

To Lee Healy, for making me realize that corporations aren't always *that* bad. . . .

To Evan Kleiman, *la mera mera*. *Gracias* for not only being my partner in crime, but for being my genuine *amiga*.

To everyone whom I forgot and will get hell for the oversight: you know I love you; you know I'm scatterbrained. I owe you *tepache*.

And finally, and definitely not leastly—actually, most important: to all my readers, whether you like or loathe me. Without *ustedes*, I would've never gotten any book deal, let alone all the tips that made this book sing. Onward to the fourth book—or hologram, the way technology is going. . . .

INDEX

291

INDEX

INDEX

INDEX